A
Great Task
of Happiness

A
Great Task
of Happiness

THE LIFE OF KATHLEEN SCOTT

◆

Louisa Young

MACMILLAN

First published 1995 by Macmillan

an imprint of Macmillan General Books
Cavaye Place London SW10 9PG
and Basingstoke

Associated companies throughout the world

ISBN 0 333 57838 4

1 3 5 7 9 8 6 4 2

A CIP catalogue record for this book is available from
the British Library

Typeset by Intype, London
Printed by Mackays of Chatham PLC, Kent

For her descendants:
Wayland and Peter; Easter, Emily, Mopsa, Thoby and Zoe;
Nicola, Falcon and Dafila; Alice, Louis and Theo; Arthur; Joe, Lily
and Tom; Maud and Archie; Emily, Dan, Lucy-Kate and Ben;
Freddie and Helena; Lucy; Peter and Amber; and my Isabel.

If I have faltered more or less
In my great task of happiness . . .

from 'The Celestial Surgeon'
by Robert Louis Stevenson

Contents

Acknowledgements

My thanks to Lord and Lady Kennet, Lady Scott, Geoffrey Dearmer, James Lees-Milne, Elizabeth Jane Howard, Verily Anderson, Alex Walker, Jane Hampton, Elspeth Huxley and Claus von Bulow. To Robert Headland and staff at the Scott Polar Research Institute, Patrick Zutshi and staff at the Cambridge University Library, Helen Langley at the Bodleian, the staff of the London Library, Mrs Rees at the Artists' General Benevolent Institution. To Felicity Rubinstein, Roland Philipps, Tanya Stobbs, Jane Wood, Imogen Parker, Derek Johns, Susan Swift and Zoe Young. Also to the Society of Authors for £1000, and to Terese O'Connell, Louis Adomakoh and Clare Brennan for time, sine qua non.

List of Illustrations

All pictures not credited otherwise are reproduced courtesy of Lord Kennet.

Introduction

In the course of my parents' fortieth wedding anniversary party in
1988 I was sitting on the old green velvet sofa at their house in Bayswater with my ancient cousin Verily, who was hooting with laughter.
She told me that a good sixty years ago she'd been sitting on that
same sofa in that same room with my grandmother Kathleen, her
aunt, and that I was saying exactly the same thing that Kathleen had
been saying. I think it was something about how I work best if
I've been out dancing the night before, or how lovely it is to sleep
out of doors. Kathleen always slept out of doors, given half the chance.
In Bayswater she slept on the balcony.

Kathleen was my father's mother. She was born in 1878 and died
in 1947 so I never knew her, but statues she had made were all over
the house and garden, and sometimes my father would point one out
in a public place: Adam Lindsay Gordon in Westminster Abbey;
Lloyd George in the Imperial War Museum, and The Man Who
Wasn't My Grandfather on Waterloo Place. I knew he wasn't my
grandfather because my grandfather had only one arm and wasn't all
bundled up. Gradually I realized who he was: Con, Captain Robert
Falcon Scott, her first husband; and that he was heroic and tragic and
had died of cold and hunger in a tent in a blizzard in the Antarctic,
having got to the South Pole too late. I knew this was unspeakably
sad but I was worried too because if he (and Oates and Evans and
Bowers and Wilson) had come back, Kathleen would never have
married my grandfather, and my father and I and my five siblings
would never have been born. I wondered if Uncle Pete, who was nine
months old when he last saw his father, minded about us. I realized

quite soon that he probably didn't, as he had named a family of swans after us.

Kathleen had written a short autobiography, largely for her own pleasure, in 1932; it was published along with a tiny selection from her thirty-six years' worth of diaries after her death. I read it when I was sixteen, and was delighted to find that a grandmother could have lived like a vagabond on a Greek island, could have had friends who got pregnant out of wedlock, could have been annoyed by the hounding of the press, could have worried about what to wear, could have fallen in love and ridden with cowboys, could have run away to Paris to be an artist, and to Macedonia to tend to refugees, could have been financially independent and brought up a son alone. Equally I was shocked to find that a grandmother – *my* grandmother – could have not supported female suffrage, could have visited South Africa and not exploded at the injustices there, could have moved happily in circles where people referred to 'little Jews', could have lived so comfortably with being looked after by servants. I had to accept that I could not in justice expect one woman within her generation to be in every way ahead of that generation in matters of humanity and justice. Things unacceptable to me now *were* generally accepted then; some of them (not all) Kathleen accepted.

But then the humanity in her friendships, with passing strangers or with famous people – George Bernard Shaw, Isadora Duncan, Asquith, Sir James Barrie, Lawrence of Arabia, Max Beerbohm, Austen Chamberlain, Rodin, Colonel House – delighted me. The details of how a woman was, and how women could be, in those days, were fascinating. She was funny and adventurous and innocent and proud. She travelled all over the world. I was pleased to be descended from her.

I was thirty before I realized that I could read all her diaries, written almost every day for thirty-six years. She started them for Con when he went south; they were to be a record for him of their son and of her day-to-day activities. After she learnt that Con was not coming back she kept them up. No one knew she did. Her handwriting races along, illegible unless you really practise reading it, recording adventures, anecdotes and observations, interspersed with photographs and little sketches, from 1910 to 1946. They cover politics and exploration, art and sex, literature and travel, Mexican trains and plastic surgery, love and death, folly and creativity, childbirth and flying, iguanas and vicars and eating chicken sandwiches out of her coronet at the coronation of George VI. They notably lack self-absorption, self-pity and self-indulgence. I realized that the story sitting in her papers – she kept many letters too – at the University Library in Cambridge was begging to be searched out.

My father wanted me to do it, and if I mentioned her, people would say, 'Oh, now I know something about her, wasn't she the one who . . . /Didn't she . . . /I remember in so-and-so's biography she . . . / My mother told me about her . . . /Oh yes, she was extraordinary, wasn't she?'

The reason I got round to it was because I heard Beryl Bainbridge say on the radio one morning that really someone should write Kathleen Scott's biography, and I was seized with fear that someone else might. So I did. It is not a history of the first half of the twentieth century, a discourse on feminism and the Empire, or another contribution to the well-documented and much-discussed arguments over the comparative merits of dogs/ponies/skis/motorsledges in pre-First World War Antarctica, or what really happened to the oil supply at the Southern Barrier depot. It is the story of a woman's life. There is no special reason why it should be extraordinary, but it is.

Louisa Young
The Lacket, 1994

ONE

✦

Motherless Daughter, Victorian Child

✦

1878–1898

KATHLEEN BRUCE wanted written on her gravestone: 'No happier woman ever lived'. The first thing to happen to her, however, was that her brother – her favourite brother – slapped her face, complaining that her eyes were too red. Then her mother went blind and died. Then her father died, then her great-uncle who had been looking after her. Then she was packed off to school, then she ran away to Paris to study with Rodin, then to Macedonia to sit in freezing mud and give blankets to the dying. She nearly died there in an epidemic of typhoid fever, and again later during surgery. She helped to deliver Isadora Duncan's illegitimate child. At twenty-nine she found love with a man named Robert Falcon Scott, married him and had a son. A year later her husband died, frozen and starving on his journey back from the South Pole. By the time she found out, he had been dead a year. After that things looked up a bit.

Kathleen was descended from the brother of the fourteenth-century king of Scotland, Robert the Bruce, of cave and spider fame. On her grandmother's side she was descended from Nicolae Soutzo, who was in turn Grand Drogman of the Sublime Porte, Grand Logothete, Grand Postlenik of Wallachia and Grand Cepoukehaya, and decapitated in 1769. This side of the family was Phanariot; Greek from Constantinople. The glorious titles denoted positions in the Turkish imperial rule of central Europe. An early ancestor was Michael Rangabe, Michael I, who was Emperor of Constantinople for a very short time in the year 800. His son married an illegitimate daughter of the rather more successful Emperor Charlemagne, who brought as part of her dowry a little fishing village now known as Venice.

One thousand and thirty-two years later their descendant Rhalou

Rizo-Rangabe, aged sixteen, was frightened by a mastiff in a street in Athens: so frightened, she said, that she rushed into a nearby house and jumped on the table. The dog's master, a twenty-one-year-old soldier from Edinburgh named James Henry Skene, over from Malta to shoot duck, followed her in, lifted her off the table and fell in love. They were Kathleen's grandparents. Rhalou was the daughter of Jacovaki Rizo-Rangabe, the last Grand Postlenik of Wallachia, and Princess Zoe Lapidi; James was the son of Sir Walter Scott's best friend, James Skene of Rubislaw, a brilliant watercolourist whom Scott described (in the preface to *Ivanhoe*) as 'the best draughtsman in Scotland', and who is the only non-Greek to have a room devoted to his work in the National Gallery in Athens. James junior's mother was Jane Forbes, whose great-uncle, Lord Pitsligo of Monymusk, had dashingly served the Young Pretender, disguised as a beggar, at the age of seventy.

James and Rhalou were married in 1833. Later James's sister Carrie married Rhalou's brother Alexander Rangabe. James sold his commission in the King's 73rd (later the 2nd Black Watch) to become a writer and diplomat, and they moved in with his parents, who, following their children's example, had moved to Athens. James and Rhalou had seven children, including a daughter named Janie after James's mother: she was to be Kathleen's mother. The children's aunt, Fifi Skene, would take them on walks to the Acropolis and tell them how the caryatids wept each night for their sister, kidnapped by wicked Lord Elgin (who was another cousin) and imprisoned in the British Museum; and their Greek nurses told them tales of Turkish cruelty. The family travelled a great deal: James Skene lived 'as a sheik' in Syria, and Fifi took the children to Paris, introduced them to a pasha's wife in Bulgaria and, when the opportunity arose, showed them slaves being sold in the market and the head of a decapitated bandit.

When Janie was seven the Skene grandparents returned to Britain, and Janie and her sister Zoe, aged eight, went too. They lived a while in Oxford, where the sisters took lessons with dons and attended lectures. At seventeen Zoe married Dr William Thompson, a cleric who was promoted every time Zoe had a child: when he became Archbishop of York, Bishop Wilberforce commented that Mrs Thomp-

son had better be careful, because 'there are only Canterbury and
Heaven before him'. (Their son Basil became prime minister of Tonga.)
Janie was twenty-seven when she found a priest of her own, the Rev.
Lloyd Bruce, whom Zoe described as 'dull, shabbily dressed and too
old' (he was thirty-four). Janie felt otherwise: 'Oh, dear Zoe,' she
wrote, 'I wish you could see him a little more with my eyes!' In 1863
they were married at St Michael's, Oxford.

Janie was energetic and charming and something of a beauty:
Rossetti asked her to pose for him. However, her health was intermittently bad. Having six children (including two sets of twins) in three-
and-a-half years did not improve it, though she said it was the raising
not the bearing that wore her out. In 1868 she had a complete
collapse and had to be fed at half-hourly intervals:

9am	Beef tea
9.30	Champagne
10	Chicken broth
10.30	Arrowroot with milk
11	Turtle soup or beef tea
11.30	Medicine
11.45	Champagne
12	Custard pudding
12.30	Beef tea
1pm	A sandwich of chicken or mutton with a little brandy and water
2	Medicine
2.30	Chicken broth
3	Champagne
3.30	A cup of milk
4	Brandy and water
5	A cup of cocoa
5.30	Turtle soup
6	A cup of tea with two teaspoonsful of brandy with a little heated butter
7	Medicine
7.30	Beef tea
8	Cocoa with a rusk
9	Chicken broth followed by champagne
10	Arrowroot with milk

11	Cup of tea with brandy
12	Chicken broth and champagne
1	Cocoa
2	Cup of tea. Brandy
3	Beef tea and a glass of champagne
4	Arrowroot and medicine
5	Cocoa
6	Beef tea and champagne
7	Tea and toast
8	Arrowroot with brandy and medicine

Janie largely recovered from this illness (hysteria, said a London specialist, and who could blame her on that diet?) and on the advice of her doctor had more babies. Betweentimes she took to illustrating photo albums with beautiful pictures of flowers, to raise extra money for the family (the pre-Raphaelite William Riviere had taught her to draw in Oxford). Zoe would sell them for three guineas each. The Bruces were not as well off as Zoe's constantly elevated family, and Zoe continually (and in the face of Janie's well-bred protests and deeply felt gratitude) plied them with petticoats and soldier outfits and whatever was needed. 'You really are a witch to find out our wants as you do,' Janie wrote.

In 1878 the Bruces were living in the Jacobean rectory at Carlton-in-Lindrick, near Worksop. It was a grand place, with stables and a lake, a millpond, pillars in the drawing room and Italian mosaic floors upstairs, and a garden large enough to hold the village fête in. Archbishop Thompson was to thank for putting this suitable living the way of his impoverished but fecund brother-in-law. Here Janie gave birth to her eleventh child, which made it another five in seven years. This last, born on 27 March 1878, was Kathleen.

Kathleen weighed eleven pounds when she was born, and her hands were nearly as big at birth as those of her two-year-old sister Jane. Jane, known as Podge, and the littlest brother, Wilfrid, were taken in to see the new baby: Wilfrid stared at her, slapped her face and ran away. Podge remembered Kathleen as a baby 'scrambling over poor unfortunate mother'. Not surprisingly, Janie was ill again. She wrote to her sister Zoe, telling her everything the doctor had said: 'I am using my spectacles . . . they do not help me as yet as much as

I had hoped . . . failure of sight . . . disease of the kidneys . . . paralysis of the optic nerve . . . my heart etc. is weak . . . I might have burst a little vessel in the brain.' She finished up admitting that 'I have given you a horrible history of my proceedings.' But the proceedings were horrible. She went to the seaside for a couple of days to rest, and wrote again to her sister, in pencil: 'I have been very badly since Thursday, two days in bed and two days creeping around wrapped in a shawl . . .' She had slept in a damp bed, but didn't want to make a fuss and get the servants into trouble. On 1 October 1880 she died of pneumonia, aggravated by what was known then as Bright's Disease – inflammation of the kidneys. She was forty-two, and her youngest daughter was one.

Kathleen, writing in 1932, recalls her mother thus: 'This long-suffering lady went blind when I was born, and for the brief time that she lived afterwards she lay gently feeling her last lusty baby's face, tracing the small features. Even a dozen had not taken completely from her the sense of the miraculous. How would it have been had she been able to hear, twenty, thirty, forty years later, this same me stretching out my arms to love, or the sun, with a "Thank God my mother had eleven children; just suppose she'd stopped short at ten!"'

The day Janie died Kathleen was propped in the window-sill of the day nursery. She would have seen the servants passing through from the back stairs to the front stairs, and then back again, weeping and covering their faces with their aprons. Then Aunt Zoe Thompson took Kathleen, Podge and Wilfrid into the spare bedroom and told them, crying, that their mother was dead. Podge claimed it meant 'nothing, absolutely nothing'. She was speaking for herself – some years later she and Kathleen saw the corpse of a man who had fallen from scaffolding and been killed: Kathleen was haunted by the sight of his boots sticking out from under the blanket on the stretcher, they filled her 'with every form of creepiness', but Podge 'had no such feelings. Death and dead bodies never affected me.' The same cannot be assumed of Kathleen.

The Bruces were very much a Victorian family: huge, resilient, religious, stiff-upper-lipped, and with a streak of eccentricity. They were brought up on Robinson's Patent Barley and Groats, with nursery maids, schoolrooms and white pinafores. Lloyd Bruce was by this time a canon of York and used to pay his little daughters a halfpenny a time to collect wheelbarrowsful of weeds, and tell them not to spend their earnings all at once. Though he had adored Janie and was griefstricken at her death, nine months to the day later he married a well-to-do widow from Sheffield named Mrs Parker, who he hoped and believed would help with the children. She had a bonnet with both roses *and* feathers on it, and the elder children were not at all sure about her, even though she had been a friend of their mother. Douglas, the eldest boy, suggested that they call her mother in gratitude for her coming to look after them, but Rosslyn, the seventh child, said he would only ever call her Mrs Parker. The only benefit he saw was the fact that Mrs Parker's sister was married to Sir Luke Mappin, who had built the bear and goat terraces at London Zoo. Even that didn't help much. Rosslyn had a performing flea, and when Lady Mappin came to stay there was an uproar because it was discovered on her ladyship's pillow. 'Sorry,' said Rosslyn, 'that's not mine. Mine is a cock flea. That's one of her own.'

Podge recalls nothing between her mother's funeral and being instructed to put on a clean pinafore to go and meet her 'new Mamma'. The Canon married for the children's sake, and Mrs Parker herself was not entirely happy with the situation. Although eventually all the children came to call her Mamma, she felt that she was 'only Mrs Bruce'. She did try to enter into the spirit, but even Elma, the eldest sister and the 'sensible one', said that whereas her mother had been 'all gentleness and humility, this one was all pomposity and boss'. Mamma took a great fancy to the toddler Kathleen, and used to read picturebooks with her after lunch. A favourite was called *Wee Babies*; Kathleen specially liked the part about the twins Horace and Maurice, who were so alike their nurse couldn't tell them apart – this is the first appearance of a life-long inclination towards males, babies, and in particular male babies. But Mamma did not work out. On one occasion she slapped her husband's face during a dispute about the fish for dinner; after that she took to spending long spells abroad. No one else took much notice of Kathleen.

Podge's first memory of Kathleen was of her in 'a white woolly pelisse and cape, the latter ornamental round the edge with little woolly blobs which you invariably sucked and pulled off. I remember

Rachel the nursemaid's grief to find another blobble gone, as usual.'
Rachel was popular, and Mamma's sacking her (because she was rather
vulgar and could not sew) did not endear her to her new family. The
new nurse was called Emma; she had been Janie's maid and Kathleen
used to get into her bed every morning and learn German words and
prayers. Podge would amuse herself at night by making ogre faces at
her baby sister over the edge of her cot to make her cry, until the
nursemaids in the room below banged on the ceiling with a broom-
handle to make them stop. Podge never knew where the banging was
coming from, but she knew what it meant.

The Canon was not well, Mamma was largely absent, and Elma
was taking over as the organizer of the brood – their great-uncle Sir
Hervey Bruce even referred to her by mistake as 'your Aunt Elma'
rather than 'your sister'. Several of the children, including Podge,
were dispatched to Edinburgh to stay with their great-uncle William
Skene, Janie's uncle, the brother of James and Fifi Skene, to lighten
the load. He was perfectly accustomed to this: for the past fifty years
his house in Inverleith Row had rarely been without nephews and
nieces and great-nephews and great-nieces staying. In between being
Historiographer Royal for Scotland, a writer and scholar of Celtic and
Gaelic history and a family lawyer, he liked to take them swimming
(even in his old age) and tell them tales of Highland history.

Kathleen said later that Mamma 'appeared to take little or no
interest, either during her life or at her death, in the healthy, good-
looking, good-humoured army of her step-children', but this may not
be quite fair. Mamma offered to take Kathleen as her own child when
the others were going off to Edinburgh, and the fact that this offer
was rejected may have had some bearing on her deathbed reluctance
to leave her worldly goods to the family with whom things had not
worked out very well. Kathleen stayed on a year with her father and
big sister Irene, who 'took you for her doll', as Podge put it, dressing
her up and calling her Baby. Podge, in Edinburgh, missed her little
sister, regretted the ogre faces and cried herself to sleep at night
resolving to protect Kathleen in future. When, at the age of seven,
Kathleen joined her siblings at Great-Uncle William's, the protection
was needed. On one occasion, Podge reported later, 'we were all
jumping from trucks filled with sand (to be used for the erection of

the Forth Bridge) on to the sandbanks. You were a timid child and flunked jumping from the same height as they did who were several years older. One of them got behind you and pushed you down – your mouth, eyes and nose were covered with sand. I boil now when I think of it.'

In many ways the Bruce children's life in Edinburgh is reminiscent of E. Nesbit's *Five Children and It*, only there were more of them. William Skene was an amiable though strictly Episcopalian academic with no children of his own. Elma and Zoe, the first twins; Irene, Douglas, Lloyd and Gwen, the second twins; Rosslyn, Wilfrid, Hilda (known as Presh), Podge and Kathleen 'generally struck out an original line of our own, and none of us were ever at a loss to know what to do with ourselves,' Podge wrote. 'We were very independent and hated to be interfered with.' One governess suffered for weeks after being so ill-mannered as to wonder whether Kathleen had brushed her hair properly. (Brushing hair was a subject fraught with pitfalls. One of the worst accusations you could make to an Edinburgh child of the time was that she 'brushed her hair underneath' – presumably to do with vanity, or laziness, or both. Kathleen's hair was so long and thick that she was called 'lanky locks, chatterbox' even though she was rather a quiet child.)

Ostensibly well brought up, in navy blue jerseys with white lace collars, a neat ribbon at the neck and always a hat, they were in fact a bunch of little monkeys – Elma, Zoe and Irene excluded. The eldest brother Douglas is remembered with his feet up on the nursery mantelpiece eating sweets; Presh christened their black straw Sunday hats the Flyaway Hats and would do her best to ensure that hers did; even Wilfrid, the kind and gentle one, had such a terrible fight with a nursemaid over the washing of his neck that blood was drawn. Rosslyn was first expelled from school at six for lifting the lady teachers' skirts: 'I only wanted to see if they had legs,' he explained. Later he made a habit of getting expelled, largely because he insisted on keeping his animals with him at all times. This habit stayed with him all his life: as a full-grown clergyman he would preach with a lemur peeping out of his pocket; produce a grass-snake in Sunday School to illustrate the story of Adam and Eve (prompting one small pupil to tell his mother that Rev. Bruce kept the devil in his pocket) and unloose a white dove during a sermon on the Holy Spirit. His middle name was Francis, and his nickname d'Assisi.

The young Bruces delighted in tormenting their great-uncle and their governesses. One, a Miss Sandeman, arrived the same day as Rosslyn's new incubator. (Rosslyn liked to breed mice; in later life his ambition was to breed green ones. It took him fifty generations, he claimed, and was reported in the *Daily Sketch*. He also bred a terrier for Queen Victoria, when he was six.) The children decided to interchange their names, and the height of their success was when their great-uncle came into the schoolroom and said 'Good morning, Miss Incubator.' They used to hide from her and tease her: 'She, poor soul, suffered much, and was powerless,' admitted Podge. Another was a Presbyterian but agreed to take them to their (Episcopalian) church: 'We knew she would know nothing of the service so we made up our minds to astonish her with every form of ritual we could imagine, finally arranging that at the second last prayer (St Chrysostom) we should kneel with our backs to the altar . . .' Kathleen had a black velvet dress (they spent a lot of time in mourning, for their mother, their father, their grandfather, their uncle the Archbishop of York) which was very stiff and would stand up on its own; Podge would sit it up on the bed with shoes and stockings dangling and invite Bertha the maid to come and have hysterics at the sight of Kathleen's headless body.

The highest mark they could get for schoolwork was 3; if they got enough 3s they would have a treat. Feeling that the 3s were not coming fast enough, Podge and Kathleen stole their mark books and took them to the Botanical Gardens with a pencil and an india rubber, where Podge practised and practised to form a 3 like Miss Incubator's, and then awarded 3s wherever the children felt they were deserved. The ruse was not discovered, and Podge claimed that she wrote her 3s like Miss Incubator's till the end of her days.

When they started school Podge used to play truant regularly; she would lurk in the 'Botans' and when spotted (one of her brothers told on her) she claimed she had gone in there to do up her petticoat. In the end she and Kathleen both were hauled up before the curator of the Botans for consistently breaking rules – they had a running feud with the head gardener there, Foxy – but managed to get off because Great-Uncle William was a friend of the curator. They used to fiddle the accounts for their school-book buying in order to have more money for sweets, and at one school at least children were warned against 'those awful Bruce girls'.

In a religious Victorian family all this naughtiness was rather more serious than it might be considered today, but there really was nobody to keep track of all of them. Elma, who had become what Kathleen described as 'rather unwholesomely religious', perhaps on account of her responsibilities, certainly tried, but she could not always succeed. She took her small siblings on religious retreats, which simply made them naughtier. She would listen to them read their collects every Sunday, and ask them questions. 'Who was David?' she asked Kathleen. 'A ma..a..a..n,' replied Kathleen, irritatingly if accurately. 'Well, did you think I thought he was a pig?' Elma snapped. She also tried to make Kathleen eat mutton fat; Kathleen just developed a technique of hiding it in her pocket. 'Kathleen has got quite sensible about her food now,' Elma would say. 'These things, of course, only need a strong hand.' Kathleen, meanwhile, was slyly dropping little packets of mutton fat in the gutters of the streets of Edinburgh.

Great-Uncle William had poor sight: he didn't notice when they used a red-hot poker to brand numbers on the backs of a set of polished mahogany chairs (the chairs were being pupils in the children's school, and they needed to be able to tell them apart, so they knew which one had taken its turn at reading, and which one was due to spell). There was an ancient chest, a family heirloom through the Skenes, which had belonged to Bonnie Prince Charlie; the little girls labelled each drawer of it with the names of their dolls, and on one occasion cut a piece of cloth off the old kilt that lived in the secret drawer to make a plaid for their doll Gerald. The kilt too had belonged to Prince Charlie, he'd worn it on his escape to the Isles, so it was said. Uncle William never noticed any of these things. He didn't even always notice whether or not the plates were in place when he dished out the stewed prunes, much to the children's delight. He was not a fool about the children, though. When they waylaid the serving staff, hijacked their uniforms and served up dinner to the grown-ups Uncle William would never quite let on whether or not he had noticed.

On one occasion while Elma was away Podge devised a way of

missing church. Uncle William asked her if she would like to be punished now or wait for Elma to return; Podge was scared enough to prefer to wait for Elma. In fact Uncle William was not strict. There was a tawse in the house, but it was more often used on him in play than it was on the children. Podge had merely been infected with something of Kathleen's fear of men.

Although later in life Kathleen would say that she had only ever been interested in male creatures, this was not true. She recalled herself having had girl dolls, but having 'put all kindly but firmly to bed with measles. So, through life, let all females be kindly and comfortably disposed of, so that my complete preoccupation with the male of the moment be unhampered!' Her boy doll (Gerald – he of the plaid), 'a sailor boy with blue eyes and brown curls', went 'everywhere with me', and was 'my idol, my baby, my love', so Kathleen recalled. Podge, on the other hand, clearly recalls a small Kathleen trailing her beloved girl doll Rosie around. Certainly Kathleen, however she may have seen herself, was not one to dispose of women. Far from it: she spent a great deal of her adult time delivering babies, caring for their mothers and looking after her female friends in trouble. At this stage she did not like men at all.

When she was quite small she had a frightening experience on the way home from school – a 'drunken ruffian' grabbed her on the street and tried to make off with her. Presh ran after to try and kick him, but by then Kathleen had bitten him hard on the hand and made her escape. Podge was more horrified by the idea of biting someone so dirty; but for Kathleen it was the root of a fear of men which lasted into her teens, and of a lifelong distaste for alcohol and its effects. 'Should someone lurch, or the slightest bias appear in his gait, my blood ran cold with terror,' she said. Her later line was more sophisticated: 'A man is disreputable who can deliberately risk losing his self-control in public.'

In Edinburgh at that time it was very difficult to avoid drunks, and perhaps Kathleen imagined that all men were likely to behave in a frightening and drunken fashion. Certainly when she was seven and their uncle took them all aside to tell them that he had bad news for them, she and Podge both assumed that he was going to tell them he was going to prison. Kathleen quite expected that any man might have to go to prison at any time, being as they were the embodiment of evil. In fact the bad news on that occasion was the death of their father.

The Canon had tried hard to put things in order for his children before he died, but, as he wrote to William three months before his death, knowing that he had not long to go: 'I have no notion what my young ones are to do by and by, unless the Mrs (who is in Sheffield and very poorly) takes them under her protection more or less ... Before she went abroad she very positively declared she would have nothing to say to any of them ...' He was buried beside Janie at Carlton, and Rosslyn had a ferret in his pocket for the funeral. Mrs Parker continued to have nothing to say to them, but she made good some years later when she paid for Rosslyn to go to Oxford (where, legend claims, he kept a baby elephant, because the rule of Worcester was 'no dogs').

When Kathleen was about twelve another frightening man appeared in her life, her cousin Willie. He stayed at Inverleith Row for about a year, and he was old enough to have a latch key, and wicked enough to stay out at night after the front door had been double-locked. Kathleen's bedroom was on the ground floor overlooking the garden, and Willie would tap at her window in the small hours, demanding entrance. She would have to creep in silence across the dark dining room and the cold marble-floored hall, and silently unlock the door for him. 'The rage of the young man was terrifying if the bolt, bar or chain made the slightest sound. More strange and terrifying was he when in the dark and silence he would be ingratiating and affectionate.' Kathleen feared, hated and adored him in equal proportions. He would do an alarming impersonation of a hunchback and tell her it was useful in avoiding the police. 'Neither then nor when I grew up did I have the faintest notion why he wanted to avoid the police ... I thought it meant that he was some unthinkable evildoer.' What form his ingratiating affection in the dark hallway took is unknown, but whether out of fear or loyalty she never betrayed him.

Presh had rather more of a secret relationship with Willie. They became friends during the year he spent in Edinburgh, and after he went back to his own family (Janie's elder brother Felix Skene, a clerk in the House of Lords, was his father) in London they wrote to each other. In one of his letters, he wrote:

Hotel des Iles Britanniques
Monaco
10 October 1893

Hello Prechie

Here I blooming well are – beastly drunk and dead broke – so [sic] my pal. We've been here four days. We came with a thousand and forty pounds between us. He brought £1025 and I £15. I won £55 the first night lost £80 the second and now am dead drunk [crossed out] broak. So's my pal. Don't tell your brothers where I am my people don't know. I've not paid a bloody sou for my hotel bill. It's come to 30 frcs a day. Writing to a pal to send me thirty, Don't suppose he'll. Applying for a situation as a waiter at the hotel here. Lovely women here Russian princesses by the score. One very smart one to whom I was sufficiently attentive when I first came down lent me forty Louis – plunged on rouge and lost then she wanted to save me hotel expenses by – well you know – sort of marrying me but I heard she was already married and well it wasn't my fault and I was drunk at the time the wine's so beastly cheap and good here and we get it for nothing as we don't pai. Like a sweet Prechie rit me a long cheering wholesome letter to do me good and I promise not to be drunk when I write again . . . ever . . . Willie.

Willie was always a reprobate, and Kathleen was not so sporting about that as Presh, who wrote back to Willie sending him five pound notes she could ill afford and, on one occasion, repeating a 'pretty thick' story about 'Oscar' and 'the pit'. 'Where did you get hold of it?' wrote Willie. 'Your character's done for.' Later he told her of 'a rumour about in Scotland that Oscar Wilde has been released and all the Highlanders have fled to the hills. I wonder why.' Oscar Wilde fascinated them all – they couldn't work out what he'd done. Kathleen assumed he'd had an illegitimate child. Willie probably knew what it was – he was doing it himself not so many years later. For the time being, though, he satisfied himself with girls, and reported it to Presh: 'I disgrace myself at dances,' he wrote, 'sometimes successfully'; and 'She kissed me as the French kiss, and must face the consequences.'

No wonder such an evildoer was a shock to Kathleen, accustomed as she was to their childish naughtinesses and Great-Uncle William's proper household. She remembers life there with less jollity than Podge: 'Here the blinds were kept down of a Sunday until dinnertime,' she wrote in 1932 of Inverleith Row. 'Here no book save the bible might be read on the holy day. Here at meals no child might speak till she had finished her meat course. Here surface order and decorum were of the strictest.' Podge did recall that although Kathleen was pretty 'for some years it was obliterated by a perpetual frown'. (Irene referred to her as 'an ugly little maid'.) 'I think you can't have been at all well,' Podge surmised:

> From this age onwards you had no one to mother you or shew you any affection of any kind and more and more you shut yourself up and became reserved and chary of shewing any feeling whatsoever, partly due to our somewhat spartan bringing up but more I think from fear of being laughed at. Once however you began to cry and nothing and nobody could stop you, you sobbed and sobbed, no one knew why and no one could console you, you lay on the bed inconsolable. At last Elma came in and Hilda told her. I shall never forget seeing the determination in her quick walk as she went to your room and came down like a thunderbolt. 'Get up AT ONCE, wash your face and stop this minute.' Implicit obedience and not another sound!

As a young child Kathleen was rather bereft, seeking affection and attention, and getting not much. If anyone complained of a headache, Kathleen would have one too. Mother figures came and went; the continuous one, Elma, was clearly unsatisfactory. Men were frightening. As she grew older, she learnt her worth and her independence. The imagination which Podge once called 'ridiculous' became a source of fine games for both of them. She had an outwardly rebellious period, when she would go off to the sea without permission (and in the middle of the night, if she could); but she soon learnt the subtle art of doing exactly what you want without anyone noticing. She quietly avoided being confirmed for some years – she did the preparatory lessons, but avoided the ceremony. Her form mistress at St George's School in Edinburgh reported her as having original ideas, but tending to keep them to herself. A contemporary, a Miss Baily, remembered her as: 'a sturdy, indomitable little figure . . . bright blue eyes, a mane of thick brown hair and a clear-cut classical profile and . . . a certain attractive exuberance of temperament. Sharing a desk with her in the Upper IIIrd Remove of 1891–2 was anything but dull. Merriment reigned in her neighbourhood.' At some point when she was quite young, Kathleen decided to be happy, no matter what.

In 1892 Great-Uncle William died. The house in Edinburgh was sold and the proceeds divided among his fifty-four nephews and nieces. Each of the Bruce children got an allowance: Kathleen's was £72 per annum, to pay for everything: education, clothes et al. Douglas, now twenty-five, took over as nominal head of the family, and Kathleen went to live with Elma and her husband Canon Keating (who wore pince-nez). Cousin Willie described their household after a visit in 1892:

> Found them pretty gloomy . . . the gas was not turned on at the main so they borrowed a lamp from the Theological Hall, but like the Biblical virgins' it hadn't got no oil so 'they sat in solemn silence in a dull dark etc.', cussing inwardly at each other. It was too dark for either of them to reach the poker otherwise there might have been 'another 'orrible murder'. They're a rum couple . . .

After a year of this Kathleen went to boarding school. It is hard not to surmise that she was 'packed off'. Podge had already been (in her own words) 'sent away'. Kathleen's first boarding school was 'a cheap convent', as she called it, where she had to bathe in a chemise; 'I was carefully initiated into the tricky art of changing from a wet chemise into a dry nightgown without one dangerous moment of seeing my own person.' There was chapel three times a day and five times on Sunday, and the girls were given to having visions due to religious over-excitement. A popular one was for Christ the man to come down from the cross; for Kathleen, Christ the baby clambered from his mother's arms and lay in hers. She loved it, and was late for dinner. She and Podge had had baby friends in the Botans and at Pettycar, where they went on holiday. 'Babies were our chief amusement and interest,' wrote Podge, who went on to be one of the first Norland Nannies, and to run a children's home. There was Mary Ann Frew, for example, aged eight months, whom they shared between them in hourly shifts, and a two-year-old named Arthur to whom Kathleen had given a toy horse. He had a very grand nanny, and the next day the horse was sent back because Arthur was not allowed to accept presents from people his mother did not know. Religion was important to the Bruces – three of the four brothers took the cloth (Wilfrid alone didn't, he became a sailor); two of the sisters married churchmen and one, Gwennie, lived her whole life with her twin brother Lloyd as his housekeeper – but for Kathleen the miracle was not so much God as babies.

Though Douglas was now her guardian Kathleen had, in effect, no one to look after her. She was reunited with Podge at a second boarding school, St Michael's, at Bognor, when Podge was called to look at her little sister's vests. There were nine, and they were all in rags. 'Absolute rags,' wrote Podge, 'in fact no underclothes fit to be seen, and Mrs Sparks had spread them all on the bed for inspection.' This doesn't seem to have made Kathleen sorry for herself – no one to look after her also meant no one to tell her what to do. Podge wrote to Presh about 'naughty little Kathleen'. She was 'always in hot water' at school, so Podge said, but she knew (because she'd been told, after Smith's *Classical Dictionary* and a book on Christian Science were found under her mattress) that she wouldn't be expelled, because she was an orphan. Her siblings were largely grown-up, and she was beginning to think that so was she. Douglas would send her patronizing letters about how he had arranged for an aunt to be so good as to take her for the holidays – this was how she saw it, at least. At sixteen she wrote back saying, in effect, no thank you, I shall go and stay with my friends, who want me. One such was Milly, who had been on holiday to Italy, where a musician had kissed her. She wasn't certain that she might not be going to have a baby; Kathleen rather hoped she would, but thought it unlikely.

But perhaps Kathleen had once again misjudged her relatives. One, a vicar's wife from Buxted, Surrey, wrote rather sweetly to Presh in March 1895: 'I hear from Kathleen this morning that prearrangements will prevent her coming to us for her Easter holidays. When she could not come at Christmas we looked upon it as a pleasure postponed . . . so perhaps she may be able to come to us for a bit in the summer.' But Kathleen had more exciting invitations than a vicar's wife in

Sussex. She was going to London to stay with wicked Cousin Willie.

She'd been to London before, in passing; she and Podge had had to cross it on their own on their way to Bognor. Podge had cried out, 'We shall never get across London alone!'; to which Kathleen had replied, 'Shan't you? I shall.' Unlike their Skene ancestors, most of the Bruces did not care for travelling. Podge thought Kathleen tremendously brave and cavalier in her attitude to the metropolis, and this view was confirmed throughout their lives.

It was arranged that she should stay a night or two with Willie's 'ramshackle, happy-go-lucky family' at their house in Addison Gardens,

> and that we should dine together in a restaurant, and that he should take me to a play. Seventeen, but a pantomime was all I had ever seen, and never at all in all my life had I ever had a meal in a restaurant, not even at a station. First problem – what should I wear? Next – would I know how to behave as though it were not the first time? There were the agonies of cutting down the neck of my prettiest day blouse; and agonies again, lest it be too low. And the dark serge skirt, how clumsy it looked! Well, I must tie a ribbon in my jolly hair and hope no one would look below my nice clean face. Oh, heavens, one must wear a cloak! What could I do? Lucky if the odd two pounds were left over for clothes. A cloak, an evening cloak? Quick, quick! I had an idea. One yard of a coarse, unbleached stuff called workhouse-sheeting, costing a few pennies a yard, a square of blue dye, and a bottle of gold ink. Secretly I went about the business, dyed the stuff, cut it in a cunning circle, and then made a bold, mad design in gold over it. The result would doubtless not be durable, but it looked not unlike a Fortuny cloak, and it would serve.

The evening was a success – Kathleen got the hors d'oeuvres all wrong but it didn't matter; Willie had chosen the play because 'the heroine is just like you, and it will do you good to know what you are like.' Kathleen didn't think she was like her at all, but rather hoped she was. Back at Addison Gardens there was an exotic brother, Hener, playing the piano 'with great vigour and grandeur'. He was younger, wilder, stranger and more beautiful than Willie, and Kathleen was delighted with him and his thick black hair and wild gypsy-black eyes (Willie's hair was red). She asked him to play Bach, the only composer she had ever heard of, but he played Liszt which she found quite delirious and intoxicating. (Their Great-Aunt Carrie had been taught to play the piano by Liszt in Paris: 'a wild-looking long-haired excitable man,' Great-Aunt Fifi had called him. He liked giving girls one or two lessons so they could say they had been taught by him.)

The next morning Kathleen saw Hener out of the window, swinging a live cat by the tail, hitting its head against the wall, and was less delighted. She poured the water from her jug over him and threw up in her basin. Felix Skene did try to discipline his wayward sons. 'I have had the hell of a row with my guvnor,' Willie wrote to Presh. 'He told me to leave the bally hovel and I said I wouldn't and threatened to get him expelled from the Athenaeum.' Willie was always short of money to lose on the horses: at one point he considered blackmailing Aunt Zoe, the Archbishop's wife, by betrothing himself to a chorus girl.

It was Willie who sowed the seed of art as a living in Kathleen's brain. She wanted to make up to him for being so taken with his brother when after all it had been Willie who had taken her out, so the next day, after the cat incident, she showed him some 'very feeble but pretty' watercolours that she had done, as a gesture of friendliness. At this stage she was meant to be going to be a teacher, like Irene and Presh – it was respectable, and would keep her out of trouble. 'Why on earth go in for teaching?' said Willie. 'Why not go in for art?' He probably forgot all about the suggestion. In 1900, after his wicked life had resulted in him 'absquatulating' to Bombay (where he worked for a bank, lived with an Indian boy in a tent, shot vultures, shocked the memsahibs and wrote scandalous letters to Presh asking her to send him 'naughty French papers'), he wondered whether 'pretty little Kathleen' had become a duchess yet. But in 1895 he told his seventeen-year-old cousin to hell with mathematics and Latin, she was lovely and should have a lovely life. Nonsense, she replied, but she didn't think it was nonsense at all.

'IN THE FIRST YEARS of the twentieth century to say that a lass, perhaps not out of her teens, had gone prancing off to Paris to study art was to say that she had gone irretrievably to Hell.' Kathleen didn't write these words until thirty years later, but she knew at the time that they were true. To say this had no effect on her would be inaccurate; to say it discouraged her would be more so. Despite having every respect for education, and very much regretting that women could not take university degrees – she asked Rosslyn, when he had been to Oxford, to 'pass on anything that he had picked up there' – Kathleen did not want to teach. Though it was not apparent to everyone, she was going to be an artist.

Kathleen left school at eighteen, and the world was quite clearly, to her eyes, her oyster. To the relatives, it was more the case that something had to be done with her. One option was that she go and stay in Ulster with another old uncle, Sir Hervey Bruce. His father, Tory true-blue and Ulster Orange member for Coleraine for many years, used to stand up on his seat in the House of Commons and crow like a bantam cock whenever a Liberal or Irish member got up to speak. The son, Kathleen's uncle, was noted for contributing to the collection plate in church in inverse proportion to the length of the sermon – a sovereign for ten minutes, half a sovereign for twenty, and so on. Like Rosslyn, he had the Bruce weakness for animals: he once offered to peel a peach for a dinner guest, saying it was 'too ripe for the monkey'. Kathleen stayed with Sir Hervey for Christmas 1899 at Downhill, his house in Ulster.

Downhill was huge. Sir Hervey's son Benjie, who was brought up there, described it as 'a fantastic place . . . a flawless gem . . . a great granite bathing box . . . a sombre grey granite mass, perched on an Atlantic cliff with nothing but the distant Scotch Isle of Jura between it and the North Pole. On the bleak down on which it stood no tree, shrub or flower could survive. For flowers we had seagulls, assembled in hundreds on the grass and all facing the wind.' Often it was too windy to leave the house; Benjie's diary records an occasion when 'Some of the servants went out but couldn't get back except on their hands and knees. Seagulls tearing past the windows.'

Kathleen liked all that, and the sea and the lake and the wild country, but she didn't much like her uncle.

> He seemed to me an incredibly coarse and vulgar old man, and in my innocence I did not think baronets should be so. But we must remember that I was brought up in a convent, and he at Eton some sixty years before, where shirts were probably not the necessary outfit for a weekly bath, and chastity and propriety were less rigid. My puritanical rearing made me cringe with shame at his playful taunts. Nearly I loathed him, until one fine afternoon he took me across to the church-yard, and showed me his wife's grave, a wife who had died some thirty years before. 'I miss her, my dear,' he said, and I was ashamed that I could not express the spontaneity of sympathy that I would have expressed to a young male creature.
>
> That evening after tea he said to me, 'Look here, my dear, would you like to live here? You would pour out the tea and mend the china and things, and there's no one here for you to get into mischief with. Think it over. You wouldn't be in my way.'

She thought it over. She tossed and turned in her four-poster bed, and she concluded: 'But I want to get into mischief!'

Kathleen declined Uncle Hervey's offer, and went instead to London. She joined the Slade art school – not yet Paris, but in the right direction. She did stay with relatives, but she fantasized constantly about flats in Chelsea that she might take, either with another girl or – if only – on her own. But twenty-year-old daughters of the clergy did not live alone in Chelsea in 1900.

She managed to have an extremely jolly life all the same. It was made up largely of work, social fun and extra-curricular self-improvement. Work was the Slade. She studied under Henry Tonks, whose face, she said, was 'full of grey old miseries'. He was by all accounts a strict but rewarding teacher. His great respect was for draughtsman-ship, and as a former medic he had considerable knowledge of anat-omy. Another of his early pupils was Augustus John, whose work Kathleen greatly admired. She studied drawing, painting, criticism, and on 14 November 1901 her diary notes 'modelling – first clay from life'. She was good at it. 'Tremendous praise, I wonder why, I can't really be doing it well I should think,' she wrote. And 'Went to modelling. Same as ever, "Very good indeed", "excellent", "you'll make something of this" and so on.'

She loved her studies. 'Oct 9: Oh how excellently do I want to go back to the Slade,' she wrote, before term began again, and 'Monday 14: First day of Slade very pleasant.' But they were not enough for her. On a visit to the Royal Academy she had come across a quotation from Walt Whitman under a painting: 'It is not enough to have this globe or a certain time. I will have thousands of globes and all time.' On the strength of that she invested in a copy of *Leaves of Grass*, and, she said, 'life began'. That was the state of mind in which Kathleen lived. The immediate globes she went for were art, music, theatre, philosophy, and people, but that was not all. Her diary records her eclectic interests: Wagner's reaction to Beethoven's Fourth Symphony (he fell into a fever and took to wearing silk and satin to compose in); the fact that codfish lay two million spawn for two to come to maturity; Nietzsche; Herbert Spencer's *Data of Ethics*; developing photos; Baudelaire; Swinburne 'till satiated'; Goethe; Hegel; *Hedda Gabler* (with Max Behrens – 'Immense'); the British Museum; meta-physics; Egyptology; Rossini. In the late summer of 1901 she was visiting Edinburgh, and she went to the Glasgow Exhibition, which included Rodin's *Burghers of Calais*. She thought it 'marvellous'; and also admired an *Adam and Eve* by Frank Taubman; and the work of 'Chas Ricketts and C. H. Shannon', 'one of which is a beautiful young man. Must be Ricketts – ask Albert. It's Shannon.' In 1901 she was a craning, admiring student, but within five years she was friends with three of these four: Rodin, Shannon and Ricketts. Rossini she never met (though Benjie Bruce met Puccini, who played him parts of *Madame Butterfly* on the piano, explaining it as he went. 'Ça, c'est japonais; ça c'est moi (That is Japanese, that is me),' he said).

Interspersed with the self-improvement were the people: fellow art students, Rosslyn's theatrical friends (he was now curate of St Ann's, Soho, and knew all sorts of people who were generally held to be rather too interesting company for a clergyman), dashing young things about town. Again, Kathleen's diary speaks: Ernest Thesiger came up; Aveling walked her home; more hysterics from Dolly; awful letter from Evelyn; Stella has dyed her hair; Rothenstein gave her Sappho; gruesome fog; Rover had a stroke; dined with Skenes; long talk with Victor Reynolds about mortality, Aubrey Beardsley, etc; 'Drank champagne and were amusing' before seeing Millicent off to Capri; kept meeting Aveling, 'felt rather a cad about that'.

She became friends with Mabel Beardsley, sister of the late Aubrey. Mabel and Aubrey had been the subject of scandalous rumours of incest, and Mabel had an illegitimate child who some said was his. Kathleen 'played' with Mabel after they met in adjoining boxes at *Two Little Vagabonds*, and later they helped to organize a masked ball, which was a great success although Max Beerbohm didn't turn up. They forgave him, and went to the private view of an exhibition of his caricatures. She took Rosslyn to 'pinafore parties' in studios, where the guests stayed till 5 a.m., and the day before Queen Victoria died in January 1901 Rosslyn took Kathleen to a play at the Garrick, and to a party given by the actress Madge Titheradge.

There were admirers, and admirees. In November 1901 she went to a play of Sherlock Holmes. She noted that the lead was forty-five, and 'oh so gorgeous, could love him heaps and heaps'. On December 5 she 'met the Russian Goldarbeiter in a bus. Clever of him to contrive to make such a meeting romantic.' One Watts had no such trouble at the Slade ball that Christmas: they danced many times and he proposed to her 'with great élan'. 'Percy' merited only the comment 'well I wonder'. Cousin Hener the pianist was reduced to 'oh the silly ass of a child'.

Someone by the name of Wilfred, however, caused her slightly more grief.

> *Oct 3:* Hideous jealousy. She's not as fair I know, nor is her intellect to be compared. Had I modelled the statuette I would not have been so far inferior. It's not severe enough to be unrequited love and thus an experience, simply irritating. Still it has the virtue of being the

only thing so far that has occurred, and it has occurred in most lives that have been lived, and tis best to know and feel – it's really only a pity that it isn't more.

She was too proud, and too strict with herself, to allow much in the way of girlish moonings. Besides, as Herbert Spencer said and Kathleen copied down in her notebook: 'Every pleasure increases vitality, every pain decreases vitality.' Suffering was never her idea of a good time, and this is the only expression of jealousy of another female in all her diaries.

In August 1901 she went to Germany with her sister Presh. 'Every prospect pleases, only man is vile,' she wrote in her diary. 'Here alas there are women too, they are worse.' Not Presh, of course. Kathleen was very fond of Presh. This is typical of her 'dislike of women' throughout her life: she would claim to dislike all women heartily, and yet there always seemed to be a couple present whom she liked very well.

For Christmas that year she went to the Hervey Bruces at their English pile, Clifton, near Nottingham. Sir Hervey's late wife had been Marianne Clifton, whose family had lived there since Domesday, and the house included a renaissance 'pages' hall', redecorated with Dutch painted panels in honour of a visit by Charles I; an octagonal Georgian hall; a Chinese drawing room; a scaled-down copy of the Crystal Palace as conservatory; two dozen bedrooms and no bathrooms, peacocks, bestatued balustrades and seven terraces. 'Uneventful, physically and mentally,' Kathleen wrote, which was about as damning as it could be. The only high spot was on 28 December when someone was overheard to say: 'Heavens, child, be careful not to marry a Bruce, they are dreadful people with scarcely a redeeming virtue.' Kathleen rather agreed. It was time to get away from all these Bruces.

'I wish it were correct to live all alone,' she wrote in her diary. 'It's far the best form of existence.' It was the sort of thing that you could do in . . . oh, Paris, say.

THREE

◆

A Badly Dressed Virginal Anglaise in Paris

◆

1901–1902

IT WAS UNUSUAL for young women to head off to Paris with artistic intent, but it was not unheard of. (Gwen John, sister of Augustus, went there in 1904, and posed for Rodin and for English women artists as well as making her own name.) On the one hand was the very good reason that Parisian art schools were largely better than the English ones at the time, with more opportunity to work from life, more and better models, a more individual approach to the teaching, more study of the anatomy. On the other was the seductive reason that Paris was Paris: you could live in the Latin quarter, be Bohemian, meet other artists, go to the cafés and get away from your parents. This is not to say that the schools were filled with young dilettantes with no interest in art. The work was hard, and though unsuitable companions for a young lady were readily available they were not obligatory. There were ladies-only *pensions*, ladies-only classes, and it was also allowed for a young woman to take a chaperon to any individual classes she might have.

And so Kathleen went to Paris, to study art. She did not go alone: two girlfriends, neither of them close, also thought it was 'a fine idea'.

They lived initially at a *pension*, run, of course, by Madame. Madame was in her mid-fifties, 'dark and squalid', fussy, with a wig. She had about a dozen young women staying, whose grammar she would correct rudely over meals. They enrolled themselves to study at the Académie Colarossi, a studio popular with art students from all over the world. Clive Holland, a journalist writing in 1904, reported 'A pretty Polish girl', 'a Haytian negro', 'a merry-faced Japanese', 'an Italian girl of whom great things were expected', half a dozen Americans and 'a sandy-haired Scotsman'. Classes here included life drawing and painting both nude and clothed, watercolours, sketching, black and white drawing, 'decorative composition' and sculpture.

Kathleen was rather afraid of both her friends. 'I was younger than they, shorter than they, poorer than they, shyer than they, less well dressed than they and much less dignified than they. They were both very pretty.' Whether or not Kathleen was pretty is almost impossible to say. She was athletic, not tall, with particularly strong shoulders and arms. Her hands were still large, and she never sat still. Photographs show a strong face, quite masculine, with a firm jaw and a definite nose. Descriptions say she was pretty, mentioning bright eyes, masses of hair and *joie de vivre*. Her dress sense never improved very far beyond the holey underwear of her boarding-school days and the home-made almost-Fortuny cloak. Certainly she was attractive.

'Jocelyn' was tall and dark; 'Hermione' was fair and beautifully dressed. (These are the names Kathleen gave them when she wrote about them later; their identities are lost.) Hermione won Kathleen's heart with a touch of melodramatic exoticism – she told her that she lived her whole life in terror because there was madness in the family. This made her wonderfully romantic. Kathleen thought perhaps she should meet romantic cousin Hener.

It seems likely that Jocelyn and Hermione were as nervous of Kathleen as she was of them. It was Kathleen who got the male attention, but this was a double-edged advantage: 'As weeks went on I found various young men waiting at the doors for me, and the two other girls would go on with a glance of mockery. This made me feel incredibly ill-bred. I wanted the nice boys to walk home with me; I wanted them to because I liked them and it was fun; but I would tell my two dignified friends that it was a good way of learning French.' (Kathleen had learnt French at school, but had what Podge called 'the most atrocious accent I ever heard. Where you got it from I can't imagine.' This may be why Kathleen's version was that she spoke no French at all when she arrived in Paris.) 'I thought their expressions accused me of behaving like a kitchen maid. In any case, no young men hovered around them, I had no notion why; and I thought them very nice and well-behaved, and myself very inferior. The nuns would approve them and reproach me, but it was all so exciting, so stimulating, and so sunshiny.'

Her song for leaving Britain, her childhood and her family behind went: 'I won't be my father's son, and I won't be my mother's son, but I will be the fiddler's son, and have music when I will.' For an orphan, this was realistic as well as romantic, but it was only for when she was feeling brave. In weaker moments she would quote: 'To bear all naked truths and to envisage circumstance, all calm, that is the top of sovreignty' (Keats, 'Hyperion'). She found herself, in Paris, to be naive and innocent.

> Everything and everybody seemed rather ugly and terribly wicked, but I was fully determined there must be no half measures. I must appear surprised at nothing. I must allow no one to suspect my pitiful ignorance, my still more pitiful innocence. When strange, unknown things happened, I registered them, but from no one did I ask an explanation, and of many things the explanation did not occur to me till twenty years later.

One such episode involved Madame from the *pension*. To Kathleen 'this repellent woman was a formidable pillar of propriety and austerity', but with hindsight perhaps she was not. 'Madame slept on the ground floor, her window giving on to the street. I slept directly above this, and used to drag my bed across to the window to get the maximum of air. One night in the small hours I awoke, hearing a disturbance below. Looking down, I saw a quite young man jumping out of Madame's window. "A burglar," I thought, and was about to fly to the rescue when Madame's head popped out of the window, pleading, noisily, "Ah, Marcel, si tu reviens, je te donnerai encore un louis!" ' (Marcel, if you come back, I'll give you more money.) Very Anaïs Nin, but it made no sense to Kathleen.

One of the first things the convent girl with her bath-time chemises had to accept was the nude model. On her first day at Colarossi's:

> Passing an open door of one of the studios, I saw Hermione standing at the back of the room near the door and went to join her. Hermione was standing composedly with her head critically on one side. At the end of the studio passed, one by one, a string of nude male models. Each jumped for a moment on to the model throne, took a pose, and jumped down. The model for the week was being chosen. Before reason could control instinct I turned and fled, shut myself into the

lavatory, and was sick. How could my lovely Hermione stand there, so calmly appraising? How could she, how could she? Then I shook myself. 'Fool! Puritan! They'll guess how you feel if you're not careful. Go back this moment and copy Hermione's nonchalance, you vulgar little thing!'

To begin with Kathleen painted. Though there were classes for men and women together, she started out with the *dames seules*. It didn't last. 'What are these folks?' she found herself thinking. 'Middle-aged women eating their hearts out year in year out, and for what? In order that on some day of an impossible future she may have a picture in the salon. In ten years I shall be like that. Exactly like that.' The nickname for the *dames seules* was the 'damned souls'. Enough! she felt, and packed up to leave.

As she was walking out of the building she heard the cheerful sound of Norwegians singing from another studio, and looked in to see what was going on. It turned out to be the sculpture class, and she thought it looked rather fun. So it was, once she had overcome the initiatory trauma of 'tous les nouveaux payent un ponche'. This mysterious rule had been chalked up on the wall; there was also laughter (not entirely friendly) and looks (knowing, in her direction). 'All the news pay a ponch,' she thought. What on earth was a ponch?

Presently a courteous Norwegian approached me and said, 'It is a custom that any new student stands punch to the others,' and returned to his place. What an unexpectedly grim affair! How on earth was it to be done? Was I to take them to a café? Oh dear, this was terrible; and how much would it cost? Would I have the money? What a well-thought-out torture for a terrified puritan! There was only one other girl in the class, a German with lank hair, I was not going to consult her. While I hesitated, an ill-bred little Italian started in a half-singing drone 'tous les nouveaux payent un ponche'. One by one took it up until a great chorus of it filled the room. Suddenly, nearly crying with uncertainty and my heart in my mouth, I too joined in the chorus. 'Tous les nouveaux payent un ponche, je suis nouveau, je paye (I am new, I pay).' A general bravo, and much good-humoured laughter.

The kind Norwegian arranged for the punch to be sent in from a café, and lent her the money to pay – six francs.

At a quarter to eleven someone called 'c'est l'heure' (It's time). The model, an Italian youth, got down from the throne, stretched, yawned, and went over to the stove. The door opened, and a large bowl of steaming alcohol was brought in, and sixteen glasses. Thank goodness, there was enough to go round and some left for the model. Hoping so much I was looking quite normal and at my ease, I took my glass and tasted it. It was the first time in my life except at Communion that I had tasted alcohol, and rum was rather a stiff beginning. How it burnt! At Communion one had to take such a tiny sip of the horrid stuff, but this I must drink to the dregs. But no! As with my mutton fat, so with my rum. I found a way.

She seems to have forgotten, writing in 1932, 'drinking champagne and being amusing while seeing Millicent off to Capri' in 1901, but that one lapse with Millicent does seem to be the only time in her life that she found alcohol at all amusing.

Sculpture proved a success. She liked it and it liked her. Within three months she had a statue of a woman and child accepted for the Salon. Though in later life her portraits and larger-than-life public monuments were well-known, it was her naked mothers and children, or fathers and children, which were the most beautiful and most touching of her work, the result of what she called 'a tender quality' which made them 'personal and lovely'.

That early mother and child won her a medal and the desirable post of *massier*. The *massier* would select the model for the class, pose him (or her), stoke the fire and open the windows at lunchtime, and call 'C'est l'heure!' a quarter before every hour, for the model to rest. In exchange for these duties, the *massier* was relieved of class fees. To Kathleen this made a big difference. A reasonable estimate of expense for an unextravagant art student at the time was £95 per annum; she had but her £72. Her daily expenditure on food was:

Breakfast:	a croissant – 5 centimes
Lunch:	two sardines and butter – 15 centimes
	gâteau de riz – 15 centimes (20 with apricot jam)
	bread – 15 centimes
Dinner:	a *demi-ragoût* (stew) – 25 centimes
	mendiants (nuts and raisins) – 15 centimes
Tip (once a day):	10 centimes
Total:	1 franc, or 1 franc 5 centimes with jam

Six francs on punch was nearly a week's food allowance.

Once acclimatized, Kathleen and Jocelyn 'made so bold as to emancipate ourselves, and took a tiny flat together'. Taking a flat was a symbol of freedom; the first step away from being one of the protected group of foreigners; an escape from the art-student ghetto. Kathleen and Jocelyn had two rooms and a kitchen.

> It was unfurnished, and so it really remained until the end of our tenure. The front room was small and light and looked on to a court; the back room was larger and dark. By common consent I was to have the small room and Jocelyn the dark room; but my room must serve as a sitting room and be kept neat. Very resourceful was I. A second-hand box mattress on the ground served for bed by night and seat for ourselves and our guests on the very rare occasions when we entertained. With a pot of blue paint I stained the floor and round the drab wall I hung posters. It sufficed. For several months we two lived together, but our friendship in no way developed.

Jocelyn used to visit Hermione a lot in her rather grander quarters; Kathleen used to work, either at home or taking the evening classes at the studio. Most evenings she would eat quickly, cheaply and alone. 'I almost always had my meals in the same restaurant. I took a book. I always sat at the same table. Opposite me, two tables away, sat a romantic-looking, upstanding, dark, very wavy-haired American artist, Edward Steichen, a photographer. He also brought a book.'

Steichen was the same age as Kathleen, the son of Lithuanians who had emigrated to Michigan. He was living in Montparnasse, studying, painting and photographing. At the time that Kathleen first met him he was doing a series of portraits for Alfred Steiglitz's magazine *Camera Work*; and had photographed the artists Alphonse-Marie Mucha and George Frederic Watts, the symbolist poet Maurice Maeterlinck and the sculptor Auguste Rodin. His portraits are as far removed from the average turn-of-the-century photograph as Robert Mapplethorpe's are from a bulb catalogue. 'There are certain things that can be done by photography that cannot be accomplished by any other medium, a wide range of finest tones that cannot be reached in painting,' he wrote, and his photographs achieved them.

The question for Steichen was whether or not photography was art; Rodin and Maeterlinck believed that Steichen's work proved that it

was. Rodin wrote, 'I consider Steichen a very great artist and the
leading, the greatest photographer of the time,' and Steichen wrote
proudly to Steiglitz in 1901 that Rodin had described one of his
pictures (*Self-portrait with brush and palette*) as 'a remarkable photograph
and a remarkable work of art – a chef d'oeuvre'. In 1906 Maeterlinck
wrote an introduction to a volume of Steichen's work, which he
called 'une admirable, une incomparable réalisation d'art. Vous avez
discipliné directement les rayons de soleil comme un peintre discipline
ses pinceaux.' (An admirable, incomparable work of art. You have
exercised the same direct control over the rays of the sun as a painter
exercises over his brushes.) In later years Steichen burnt all his paintings (all he could find) and became the highest-paid fashion photographer of his age, working with the US publisher Condé Nast and
photographing society ladies such as Rita de Acosta Lydig, who used
to tip her dressmaker with loose emeralds.

But in 1902 Steichen, with his 'grey linen shirt with loose kimono
sleeves, short turnover collar and black ribbon scarf at the throat' and
'hair of a significant length and degree of unkemptness', as a press
notice of the time described him, ate at the same cheap restaurant
as Kathleen.

Day after day, [she wrote] lunch after lunch, dinner after dinner, for
five months, we two sat opposite each other, scarcely ever looking up
save to catch each other's eye and look down again. Never once did
we speak. Yet each knew when the other was gay or worried, had
toothache or was happy. Even in those early days in Paris any student
could talk to anybody he or she pleased, yet we two deliberately
refrained. I knew his work. It was well known. It was good. One day,
after not having seen him for a few meals, I overheard someone say
'You know Steichen is going back to New York on Tuesday.' 'As soon
as that, is it?' was the uninterested reply. My heart beat preposterously.
'He can't go back on Tuesday. It's Sunday today.' Would he lunch at
the restaurant on Monday? I went early with my book, *Le Temple
Enseveli* by Maeterlinck. No waiting, no! – hardly had I settled in the
usual place and ordered my meagre meal than Steichen passed me and
sat down at his usual table. He glanced up at me with his usual half-
smile, neither less nor more. Was he really leaving for America the
next day?

I ate my lunch slowly, wondering would he not perhaps at last speak to me? He made no sign, so I got up and quietly crept to the door. As I paused at the *caisse* for change he came up behind me, and said very quietly: 'You know, Esmeralda, that I'm going home tomorrow?'

Esmeralda – why Esmeralda? I never knew.

'I know,' I said, without turning my head.

In the street I found his tall figure walking beside me in a silence through which I dared not even look up at him. At long last he touched my yellow-covered book.

'What are you reading, Esmeralda?' I showed him. 'Oh, Maeterlinck, he's good, stick to him. Well, goodbye.'

And he turned abruptly and went back towards his studio. I tore across the road to my school without looking back. What had I said – nothing. What had I looked like? – half-witted probably. Oh dear, oh dear! – his voice was gentler than I expected, and he was going away tomorrow.

There was dinner! Would he come to dinner? Probably not, he would be packing, but I went early . . .

He did come to dinner, in his cloak and wide-brimmed black hat, and as he left he mentioned that he happened to have a picture he'd taken of Maeterlinck, and would she like it? He knew where she lived, he said, and he'd drop it round later.

Kathleen spent the evening tidying her room, doing her hair, straightening her books, changing her dress, looking at her watch, wondering if he were making fun of her, wondering why she always thought people were making fun of her, imagining reasons why he wouldn't come. And he came, and said things like, 'What will become of you, Esmeralda?' and 'Why didn't I find you before, Esmeralda?' and 'You oughtn't to be here by yourself, you're not like the others.' Then he kissed her on the doorstep.

No notion had he that this was the first event of my prudent little life. The clouds of convent faith had long been dispersing – all but gone by now. Nevertheless I flung myself on my knees by the friendly old box-mattress. Glory and gratitude must be expressed to something '. . . in the heights and the depths be praise!' The odd thing is that it was all I wanted. I was glad, exhilarated, with the knowledge that he was going away. I was drunk with the joy that this one hour had come as the climax of those five months of reticence, and that it was finished. For four stormy years I was faithful to that hour.

Steichen returned to New York in 1902, the same year that Aleister Crowley, the notorious decadent and practitioner of black arts, first met Kathleen, according to his *Confessions*. Crowley's view of Kathleen is wildly different to her description of her first kiss:

> She was strangely seductive. Her brilliant beauty and wholesome Highland flamboyance were complicated with a sinister perversity. She took delight in getting married men away from their wives, and the like ... Love had no savour for her unless she was causing ruin or unhappiness to others. I was quite ignorant of her intentions when she asked me to sit for her, but once in her studio she lost no time, and 'The Black Mass', 'The Adepts' and 'The Vampire' describe with ruthless accuracy our relations. She initiated me into the torturing pleasure of algolagny on the spiritual plane. She showed me how to intensify passion by self-restraint ... She made me wonder, in fact, if the secret of puritanism was not to heighten the intensity of love by putting obstacles in its way.

Either immediately after her first kiss with Steichen she changed from a chaste though romantic ex-convent girl into a rampant vampire man-eater and practised pricktease, 'a devil gloating on the pain', 'playing the whore' to 'her troth-plight lover', with the blood of her victims 'glittering a diadem upon [her] dazzling brows', as Crowley described her in his poems, or their world views were simply miles apart.

The only point which coincides is that of 'reticence' and 'restraint'. Kathleen was puritanical, partly by upbringing but enough too by personal taste that, as she shed habits of her upbringing, the puritanism remained. In particular, she was sexually puritanical. The reasons for this are manifold. It was the habit of her class, her sex and her time. She was romantic, insecure and self-protective. The most individual reason was her intensely idealistic attitude towards motherhood. Her passion for babies in general had matured into a particular passion for a particular baby – her future son. This was very important to her. Her ultimate interest in men was to find the one, the fine, heroic one, who would father the fine, heroic son of her dreams. She might flirt, fall in love, have long and intense platonic relationships with men. Certainly young men became very worked up about her, but that does not prove that she had or did not have any physical relationship with them. She might, after her loyalty to Steichen had run its course, have run her fingers through their hair and let them kiss her, but she did not sleep with them. She was a virgin when she married, and by her own account her love for her husband took off on to new planes when her son was born.

All this need not preclude an intense unfulfilled sexuality. It is hard to know what Crowley meant by 'algolagny on the higher plane' given his habit of inventing words and not explaining them, but it may have a root in the Greek *algos*, pain, and *lagnos*, lasciviousness. Although she mentions a great many people, Crowley is not mentioned in any of her diaries until 1930, when someone tells her he has become very fat and she is not at all surprised. The suggestion of marriage-breaking may be a misdated reference to a later development in her friendship with Steichen, when in the early 1920s his wife (Clara Smith, whom he married in America in 1903) pretended to attempt suicide, and his attentions to Kathleen were cited as one reason for it. 'Our affair', Crowley wrote, 'was too much ginger for the hoi polloi,' but it sounds rather more that she wouldn't have him.

At the end of 1902 Kathleen was back in London on a visit. On 12 December she went to the Slade arts ball with Rosslyn and their friend Nigel Playfair. He tells (in *Hammersmith Hoy*) how he arrived late at the party having been to review a play, and found that Kathleen had broken her leg.

We brought her back to Gray's Inn, [where Playfair lived] and sent for a doctor who promptly decided that she must stay where she was for at least six weeks. Her brother, most Jesuitically I thought, decided that he could return to his own rooms in Soho Square, Mrs Brooks my housekeeper, plus a leg in plaster of Paris, being ample chaperonage, and there we were, a fortnight before Christmas. [Another version says that Rosslyn came back and stayed too.]

My own family were to spend the holidays in Hampshire, but I thought that I must not neglect my guest and that I would give a dinner party in her honour, she being by then able to hobble. But though her brother and Mabel Beardsley were available, there was nobody else free, and you can't have a real Dickensian Christmas banquet for four. So it occurred to me to advertise for guests! And this is how I did it, in the columns of the *Morning Post*, to secure a reasonable social atmosphere. 'A brother and sister' (note trifling hypocrisy, but Queen Victoria was only just dead) 'living in rather pleasant rooms near the Temple invite any ladies and gentlemen who may be lonely to dine with them on Christmas Day. All ladies must prefer Lewis Carroll to Marie Corelli [a novelist whose lack of fame now is a fair comment on her talent] and the gentlemen must not wear made-up ties. Reply box xxx.'

It does not seem very daring today, but the sensation this advertisement caused was immediate and tremendous. I think it was the *Daily Telegraph* had a leader on the subject, and I don't think any, unless it were *The Times*, refrained from comment. We had over four hundred replies, written with varying wit, and we chose eight or ten guests who promised to be the most amusing, writing (a heavy labour) polite regrets to the rest.

They were so busy they forgot to order any food, so at the last minute a local restaurant, Café Roche, was asked to send in the dinner, and although Rosslyn had been busy in church from 5.30 that morning Nigel found it 'a most amusing evening. . . . we played snapdragon and charades and whatnot, and parted with vows of eternal friendship at two in the morning'.

When her leg was better Kathleen went to Spain with Hugo Law and his family. They were friends initially of Rosslyn – Hugo's father, the Chancellor of Ireland, was a neighbour of the Bruces at Downhill. Kathleen thought Lota Law, Hugo's wife, 'the beautifulest woman of all', and took to Hugo when he tried to teach her to drive. She had two pieces in the Salon in Paris and learnt that 'the papers have given me some rather nice notices . . . what they really appreciate was done in three hours so I think I shall give up working very hard,' as she wrote to Rosslyn. Despite a fever and her new resolution of laziness, she was busy on this holiday learning Greek and sculpting the friends who came to stay.

Back in Paris, the company Kathleen kept was pretty mixed. On the one hand were the British: Jocelyn and Hermione and cousin Hener Skene, who had arrived in Paris knowing no one but Kathleen, and who played the piano to her for hours on end. He soon entered into Paris life: he met Crowley, and introduced him to Isadora Duncan's companion Mary Desti. She became Crowley's lover and his 'seeress' under the name of Sister Virakam, and wrote a biography of Isadora. It was probably Kathleen who introduced Hener to Isadora (whom, as we shall see, she met through Rodin) and thus Mary Desti, and it could well have been Hener who introduced Kathleen to Crowley.

Hener had been in Vienna, ostensibly studying the piano with Leschetizki, though in fact he never met him. He had given away his lessons with the maestro to a German girl called Else: after three years she said, 'You have compromised me,' so he married her, shook hands at the church door and left her. 'She was a better pianist than me,' he said. (Willie Skene, who had by now 'absquatulated to the colonies', thought Hener's marriage shocking, and that Hener should have been made to do more sport at school. 'He would have learnt that . . . one can't compete with anybody without training,' he wrote rather pompously to Presh, which coming from him was a bit stiff.) Hener had discipline, though. On one occasion he locked himself into his room for a week with an enormous bunch of bananas, to prepare for a concert. He became Isadora's pianist, playing with her all over Europe; Jocelyn and Hermione took him up too, but Kathleen could never forget the cat being bashed against the wall.

Other foreigners she knew at this time included Gertrude Stein, whom Rosslyn described as 'a bookish American lady writer who talks and writes any way she likes, mixing her tenses and first and third persons at will', and 'her odd companion and sounding-board Alice B. Toklas'. Stein was rather taken with Kathleen: she described her (in the *Autobiography of Alice B. Toklas*) as 'a very beautiful very athletic English girl, a kind of Sculptress, [who] had at that time no money to speak of either but she used to bring a half portion of her dinner every evening for Penelope.' (Penelope was Isadora Duncan's sister-in-law, who was then both pregnant and impoverished.) Kathleen knew Picasso too, slightly; she introduced him to Rosslyn, who sold him a terrier.

On the other hand were the French. Her closest French companion was a successful painter seven years her senior, named Hofbauer.

He was suffering slightly from resting on his laurels and spending more time on the town than in his studio. 'He had dozens of mistresses', but Kathleen confounded any improper intentions by agreeing to meet him only at six in the morning for her daily swim in the river, and calling him a coward when he didn't turn up. She would meet him for breakfast, for a dawn stroll in the Luxembourg Gardens or on the roof of Nôtre Dame (when she could persuade the custodian to let her up) but she wouldn't meet him indoors or in the evening. He was rather embarrassed by it. What would his friends think of 'this subjugation to a badly dressed anglaise with virginal tastes', as Kathleen described it? Luckily they would never see them together, because they were always still asleep at the times they met. And if they did see the couple together at six in the morning, they would assume they had spent the night together. Kathleen didn't like to think of that, but recognized that it was unavoidable.

Hofbauer became jealous of Hener ('Ha ha! That was it! There was a cousin!') and started following Kathleen about. Finally he lost his temper, and she explained her reasoning: 'I wanted to learn French, I've done that. I wanted to get you to work in the morning, you've done that. And I wanted to get our friendship on to a proper sort of foundation. We've done that.' Later on when his laziness was again being a problem she borrowed Hener's idea and locked Hofbauer in his studio every day, bringing him food and not letting him out until the day's work was done. The painting he produced under this discipline won the Prix du Salon.

Her other French friends were Monsieur and Madame P (though Madame was in fact South American), at whose house she met writers and poets, Henri de Régnier, Paul Adam and Anatole France. 'It was quite useless really, for my French was so poor that I dared not utter a word of it, and their French was so flashingly fast that I scarcely followed a word.' The Ps were 'rare friends', 'young, rich', with 'charm and wit', her 'skylight to a different Paris'. Kathleen introduced Jocelyn to the Ps – she had still not realized that her nervousness with Jocelyn and sense of inferiority were actually a nascent dislike, and tried to please her with introductions and attentions. 'I was baffled about Jocelyn, and made repeated efforts to disperse that intimate, slightly scoffing regard with which she seemed to look with mockery into the deepest recesses of my heart, and find there nothing but the commonplace and the trivial.'

She did, however, realize that it was time to get a place on her own, but not before Jocelyn had played a trick on her of dressing up as a boy. She announced the arrival of a cousin; could Kathleen entertain him for the evening because she Jocelyn was otherwise engaged? Certainly Kathleen could. She was completely taken in by the slender youth in a baggy Norfolk jacket, and when Jocelyn made her true identity known Kathleen's reaction was mixed. She laughed, she claimed to have thought it was fun, but she felt sick too. Her love of her own freedom was always slightly charged by her distaste for the way the people around her in that easy-going milieu used theirs.

The day after Jocelyn's trick Hener gave Kathleen vicious Chinese burns, demanding to know what had been going on. Jocelyn had sworn Kathleen to secrecy, so she didn't tell. Hener got his own back by telling Kathleen that there was a Swede about who wanted to kill her, who was at that moment asleep in a drunken stupor on Hener's studio floor. Hener had discovered him lurking with a revolver, threatening to shoot Kathleen. 'What have you been doing to Sternstrom?' Hener demanded. 'He said he loves you, and that he is a god, and that it's not fitting that a god such as he should be slighted. Later he wept and said you were so lovely you had better be killed before you got less so.' Kathleen was less upset about the revolver (she knew about that anyway, and only hadn't told Hener because she thought it might put ideas into his head) than about the drunken stupor. She decided to bolt to Chartres, which is what she did when things got a bit much. She would read at night in her room at the Chariot d'Or, and spend the day at the cathedral, communing with the statues on the west face, loving the stained glass, far away from 'violent cousins, jealous painters, sinister Jocelyns and murderous Swedes'. Cathedrals gave her great pleasure. Such religious beliefs as survived her childhood had been waning for some time, but cathedrals were something else. 'Could worship anything of which Cologne was emblematic,' she wrote after a visit in August 1901.

When she got back to Paris she moved house.

On her first night in her new room, a long narrow studio overlooking a courtyard with a pump, she observed her opposite neighbour

across the yard. 'He was a young bearded Frenchman, animated and
rather good-looking, and despite the beard I thought he might be an
amusing neighbour.' He seemed to be giving a party; there were a
lot of people, a lot of late-night toing and froing. In fact he was
doing a moonlight flit. She was rather disappointed.

The next occupant of the opposite studio hanged himself: she saw
his dark figure through the window, fixing something to the ceiling.
The afternoon before he died she had had her first conversation with
him, and she tormented herself with feelings of guilt. 'He could have
been planning these ultimate measures while I stood beside him
unawares. How dreadful were these unawarenesses! It is impossible
to take on the responsibility of intimacy with everyone who stretches
out a hand . . . I found it difficult to believe that my sympathy had
been so dormant. I was well, healthy and happy. How unspeakably
grim.' Quite soon she moved again.

Her new studio had a flat roof; she rigged up a mackintosh awning
and slept out, rain or shine, pulling the mackintosh this way or that
according to which way the rain was blowing in. It was in this studio
that she entertained Rodin to lunch.

She had taken to visiting the great sculptor in his studio on
Saturdays; though he had no official students at that stage he liked
her and allowed her presence. The lessons she learnt from him were
simple and essential, and she followed them all her life: to love the
great masters, to have absolute faith in nature, and to work relentlessly.
He wrote, and she followed: 'All life surges from a centre, expands
from within outwards. The main thing is to be moved, to love, to
hope, to tremble, to live. Be a man before being an artist!'

I would walk with him round his studio, he would open small drawers,
such as one is used to finding birds' eggs in, and show dozens and
dozens of exquisitely modelled little hands or feet, tiny things of a
delicious delicacy to compare with the grand rough *Penseur* or his
Bourgeois de Calais. He would pick them up tenderly one by one and
then turn them about and lay them back. Sometimes he would unwrap
from its damp cloth, generally an old shirt, his latest work and,
spreading out his hands in uncritical ecstasy, exclaim 'Est-ce beau, ça?
Est-ce beau? (Is it lovely, that? Is it lovely?)' Sometimes he would call
a model to pose for him, and taking pencil and water draw, never

taking his eyes off the model, never looking at all at his paper. Sometimes he signed one and wrote my name on the back and gave it to me.

Rodin asked if he could come and have lunch in her studio. She improvised a lunch table from a couple of boxes, fried some eggs, provided 'some lovely coloured pomegranates' and hoped he would not be too hungry. 'Brave peasant that he was, he would eat bread and cheese.' He did, but he also ate a pomegranate. 'Suddenly I became aware that he appeared to be eating the pomegranate hard pips and all. Anxiously I watched. No pips appeared. I was deeply concerned, but much too shy to comment. Long after lunch I saw in a looking glass the old man hastily approach my open window and rid himself of the million seeds. But for his beard he could never have kept up for half an hour such good manners!'

On another occasion when he was to visit she was distracted by a neighbouring student threatening suicide: she rushed off to help dissuade him, squashing the clay statuette she had been working on as she went, and by the time she got back Rodin had been and gone.

She kept very quiet about her friendship with him, learnt from him and treasured his compliments to her work. One of her most valued possessions was the first letter in which he addressed her as Cher collègue (Dear Colleague) rather than Chère élève (Dear Pupil). He called her 'un petit morceau grec d'un chef d'oeuvre' (a little Greek fragment of a masterpiece), 'and I would look at my stalwart arms and legs and not feel at all fragmentary. But I looked for the days when I was allowed to lunch with him at Meudon and watch him work. Those were days not wasted.' She had no desire, however, for a mentor, such as many female artists found themselves lumbered with. And Rodin was notoriously amorous. Gwen John had gone to Paris to escape the influence of her brother Augustus and had ended up with Rodin, who rendered her (in her own words) 'un petit morceau de souffrance et de désir' (a little fragment of suffering and desire); Camille Claudel's reputation both personal and professional was inextricably tangled up with him. Marie Laurençin had a similar problem with the writer Apollinaire. Kathleen remained independent. Many years later some people assumed she must have 'more than studied' with Rodin; it would have infuriated her had she known.

On a special train taking guests to a picnic to celebrate Rodin's birthday Kathleen noticed a young woman talking 'exceedingly bad and ugly French'. She was most upset when she realized that it was the great and revolutionary modern dancer Isadora Duncan. Only days before she and Hofbauer had seen her perform and had wept aloud at the beauty of it. 'The dancer had seemed the most remote, the most intangible expression of ultimate beauty. And here she was sitting in a crowded railway carriage talking the most Barbaric French.' Kathleen closed her ears and looked out of the window to deny that her 'vision glorious had been made flesh'. Later, at the picnic, someone played the fiddle and Isadora danced in her petticoat and bare feet. Kathleen was 'blinded with joy'; Rodin was 'enchanted'; 'everyone was enchanted, save the few inevitable detrimentalists who seem to creep in almost everywhere.' If there was one thing Kathleen could not abide, it was a detrimentalist. Then 'Rodin took Isadora's and my hands in one of his and said "My children, you two artists should understand each other." And so began a long-lasting relationship of the most unusual order.'

FOUR

✦

Babies Are Being Born

✦

1902–1905

'AS AN ARTIST I thought of the dancer as a resplendent deity,' Kathleen wrote, 'as a human being I thought of her as a disgracefully naughty child. As an artist I exulted in her; as a tiresome child I could not abandon her.' In 1902 Isadora was twenty-four, and well on her way to becoming 'a household name in St Petersburg, Berlin, Paris, Vienna, Munich, Copenhagen, and Stockholm', as Martin Shaw described her a couple of years later. She hadn't yet had a duel fought over whether her free, unfettered modern form of dancing was better than the classical ballet, but she soon would have.

Their friendship was based on idealism, but though their ideals of independence, love, joy and art were similar, Isadora and Kathleen had very different ways of manifesting it. In the beginning this did not matter. They both believed that inherited money limited a child's freedom; that marriage limited a woman's freedom; that adventure was the root of true wealth; that art and babies were the greatest achievements. Neither could understand why, in Isadora's words, 'if one wanted to do a thing, one should not do it'. In the end their different ways of treating these ideals drew them apart. Kathleen grew up; Isadora didn't.

Even those who wanted to dislike Isadora's dancing found it difficult. Some, because she had bare legs and loose tunics, wanted it to be lewd, and came away having to admit that these bare legs were the most innocent. Kathleen's brother Rosslyn was very impressed by the fact that she 'could dance in her petticoat without it seeming improper'. Some, because she was American, wanted it to be naive and pretentious, and came away admitting that it might be genius. Kathleen had no such problems. She wanted it to be art, and it was

art, and for love of the dance she loved the dancer, and travelled with
her across Europe. Hers was one hand held out from which Kathleen
did not turn away.

'Come with me to Brussels,' said she, and I went. 'Come with me to
the Hague.' At each place and many more she gave her grand performance. The greatest conductors led the finest orchestras for her; the
houses were crowded out. At Liège one night the audience stood up
in their seats and waved their hats and roared. I sat quietly on my
seat, disposing of my preposterous tears, before going round to see
that my dancer had her fruit and milk, and a shawl over her whilst
she cooled off, before facing the wild enthusiasts who surged around
the stage door and yelled their delight.

We got up early, ran in the park that was near, and did a few
gymnastics. Whatever happened later, and terrible things did happen,
at that epoch the dancer was a healthy, simple-living, hard-working
artist, neither beautiful nor intelligent apart from her one great gift
for expression. She was open handed, sweet tempered, pliable, and easy
going. 'Oh, what's the difference?' she would say if I, who hated to
see her put upon, wanted to stand out against over charges etc. 'What's
the difference?'

Kathleen mothered her, and she needed it. At that stage Isadora
was more or less keeping her family (mother and three siblings – her
father had not been in evidence for years) financially; later she would
keep her lover and her dancing school too, all on the money made
from performing. She had a wild, romantic imagination and a saleable
talent, but she was not practical. When the 'terrible things' started
to happen, it was to Kathleen that Isadora turned.

Though she loved travelling about with her friend, Kathleen did
not wish to become 'vicariously engulfed in dancing'. Back in Paris
she worked hard at her own talent, but Isadora's life touched upon
hers in more ways than one. Among Isadora's disciples was a pair of
German Jewish brothers with whom Kathleen was rather impressed,
as they seemed very literary. The younger, aged about twenty-eight,
'hung himself round with mysteries' and wanted to involve her in a
'grand scheme he had' for shipping revolvers to Russia hidden behind
false bottoms in petrol cans. Writing in 1932, married to a cabinet

minister (her second husband, Edward Hilton Young, later Lord Kennet), Kathleen claimed ignorance:

> I thought this great fun and most exciting. I had no notion of the purpose of the firearms, nor why they should be sent thus. One day when the young man came round to my studio with a couple of suitcases full of I knew not what, saying that the police were going to search his rooms, I very gaily said, 'Rather, leave them here. Stuff them out of sight somewhere.' Later these young men introduced me to a middle-aged Englishman who, they told me, shared my enthusiasm for the Greek dramatists and philosophers. He was a prim little man, always neatly and conventionally dressed, but he seemed even poorer than me and I therefore took to making an evening meal at home and letting him share it, in return for which hospitality he would read the Greeks aloud to me. I knew little, indeed nothing, about him, so I was not in the least ruffled to hear that a bomb had been thrown at the King of Spain in a Paris street and that the Englishman had been arrested as the maker of this murderous bomb. All my standards of right and wrong had suffered such an upheaval since I left England that this seemed no queerer than many other things. Perhaps this sort of thing was quite usual, like having lots of mistresses and yet being quite nice. Perhaps it was only a matter of getting used to it. Still it was rather a ruffling affair to get a letter from the courts of justice to ask me to appear at the trial as I was understood to be one of the accused's few friends in Paris. The trial lasted several days. I crept off each morning, returning in the evening. I dared tell no one what I was up to. I was terrified that my name would get into an English paper, and I imagined aunts and uncles toying with the word anarchist. I hadn't the foggiest notion what the word meant, but it made me feel uncomfortable.

This sounds to modern ears almost unbearably naive, but Kathleen was not political, not a newspaper reader. Her world was apart from such things, and she was dangerously cavalier about it all. 'I was young enough not to have discerned the difference between knowledge and wisdom,' she admitted later, 'and nearly got myself into very hot water.' As it was, all she had to do was stand up in court and say yes, she knew the accused, that he visited her studio and read Sophocles. Laughter in court. Did he ever talk about the King of England? Oh dear no. What did he talk about? Socrates. More laughter in court, and it was all over.

Her other adventure with the mysterious German Jew was a trip to the hotel where Oscar Wilde had died. Kathleen had read some Wilde, and found it 'very amusing'. She still didn't know what it was that he had done. Rosslyn had known Wilde's lover Bosie, Lord Alfred Douglas, at Oxford (he had once appeared on the football pitch wearing a wreath of flowers and patent leather shoes) and had met Oscar Wilde, but he had not enlightened his little sister. Nigel Playfair told a story of how in 1894, when Kathleen had been visiting Rosslyn at Oxford, a clergyman had been hideously embarrassed when she, aged sixteen, had asked who Holman Hunt had married. 'My dear fellow,' said the clergyman later, out of her earshot, 'I could hardly tell a young lady that Holman Hunt had married his deceased wife's sister!' 'Deceased wife's sister' became a joke term among them for something unmentionable. Times had changed and she was in very different company, but homosexuality still dared not speak its name.

> The German talked about Wilde with awed voice as about a prophet or a martyr. I, amiable and acquiescent, said I would love to come down with him to the little place, where he was acquainted with the hotel keeper. After a few preliminary civilities we were shown a rough wooden box full of books with a coat and waistcoat on the top of it. These were Oscar Wilde's. In the coat pocket was a hypodermic syringe and a used handkerchief. Underneath were several signed photographs, and about fifty books, many of them signed by their authors. The hotel keeper said, if the English lady would like the contents of the box she was welcome. I hesitated, and then went through it and took a selection of half a dozen of the most interesting. Would I not like the syringe? No thank you! It would be better to throw that away.
>
> This adventure I innocently recounted to Hofbauer, who, to my amazement, detonated in violent rage. What right had the damned German Jew even to speak of Wilde to me, and to let me rummage about with his disgusting possessions, that, it seemed, was too much. *Sales gens!* (Disgusting man!)

Not unreasonably, Kathleen thought that her Rabelaisian painter, with all his mistresses, might be the person to clear up the mystery.

'Oh, ne demandes pas ça à un français (Oh, don't ask that of a Frenchman),' he replied, with a 'furious gesture', and she was none the wiser.

Kathleen was to spend the rest of her time in Paris in the studio with the roof and the mackintosh, but that is not to say that she was always there. She had already acquired a taste for 'vagabonding': putting some hard-boiled eggs in a bag and going off for a long walk – preferably one lasting several weeks. Given the choice between sleeping indoors or out she would take out any time, and travel and adventure were next only to sculpting as her pleasures.

Late in 1903 a new adventure, a major one, opened to her. Noel Buxton, a young and fervent English politician (later a Labour MP and Lord Noel-Buxton), a friend of Rosslyn, visited her in Paris and made her feel that her existence there was something of a waste of time. He talked to her of the troubles in Macedonia.

National and religious struggles are nothing new in the Balkans: not for nothing is *macedonia* the Italian for fruit salad. The current wrangles among Christians and Moslems, Serbs and Bosnians, Bulgarians and Turks and Slovenes, Montenegrins and Albanians, Slavs and Croats, Catholic and Orthodox and people who up until a few years ago were Yugoslavs (if there ever were any such thing) have been going on in one form or another for a thousand years. In the first years of the twentieth century Macedonia was under Turkish rule, and armed bands known as Komitadjis had been supporting Bulgarian nationalist priests and teachers in Slav Macedonia. The Internal Macedonian Revolutionary Organisation, formed in 1896 for all Macedonians 'regardless of sex, nationality or personal beliefs' was basically pro-Bulgarian and anti-Turkish. On the night of 2 August 1903, 750 of these rebels took over the small town of Krusevo, fighting under the skull and crossbones, the symbol of the uprising. When the Turkish garrison fled, the red flag was raised instead and Krusevo, population 15,000, was declared a socialist republic, the first in the Balkans. The republic lasted nine days: on 11 August 15,000 Turkish soldiers, plus the Bashi Bazouks (irregulars), moved in to put a stop to it. Despite deeds of heroism the red flag gave way to the white.

The whole uprising was suppressed within three months, and a bitter vengeance taken: according to conservative Bulgarian figures,

9,830 houses in Macedonia were burned down and 60,953 people
were left homeless. Whatever the true complexity of the political
situation, to the West Turkey had put itself deeply in the wrong and
the Bulgarians were innocent victims. And winter was drawing in.

Buxton told Kathleen of disease and starvation, torture and cold.
He told 'how the Turks were massacring the Bulgarians, how direly
they were in need of help, how good was the organization in London
to collect necessities for them but how there was nobody on the
spot to see to the distribution of food, money and clothes.' He told
her that 'the plight of the people there is unspeakable. Babies are
being born, quite untended, that nobody wants, and quite unprovided
for; terrible cases . . .'

Well, to Kathleen that was it. Babies, untended, unprovided for,
unwanted? She would tend and provide for them. She wanted them.
'My heart beating loudly against my chest, I said, "Couldn't I go?"
And so it came about that the very next day my work was again
discarded, the key turned in the studio door, and off I went to England
to see the austere lady who was looking for an assistant to undertake
on-the-spot relief.'

Lady Thompson was 'more than twice my age, and very sad' – her
husband had dropped dead a year before. She engaged Kathleen 'as if
she were engaging a kitchenmaid', and on 4 December they were on
their way to Salonica, Kathleen teaching herself Turkish and writing
to Rosslyn: 'Lady Thompson is fagged out . . . but I could face a
massacring Turk with a cheerful rebuff.'

Dec 12: Set off about daybreak with Mr Hazkell, the American
missionary, to Monastir. All the way from Uskub the line was guarded
by poor miserable-looking soldiers in tents surrounded by mud and
water, they had been there some eight or nine months. Trains are not
to run at night, as frequent attempts are made to blow them up. The
day before we crossed the frontier 2 Servians (*sic*) being searched in
the customs were found to be stuffed with dynamite. There is much
smallpox in various districts. Dined excellently in a corner of the bar
room at the Hotel Constantinople, where quantities of Turks were
smoking, playing billiards and backgammon, and drinking. A Mussul-
man, mark you, may not drink wine, but he may drink spirits, for
that was not mentioned in the letter of the law, not then being known.

Much nonsense is talked of the dirt of these places. The cabinet is truly not pleasant but in no way worse than the Paris studio ones, and the rooms are perfectly clean and fresh. Doubtless my opinion might undergo a change in the warmer weather.

One of their first duties on reaching Monastir was to call on Hussein Hilmi Pasha, the Inspector General: 'He was supposed to be omnipotent in Macedonia, and he fondly believed the supposition,' wrote Henry Nevinson, a journalist who had also been inspired by Noel Buxton. Nevinson rather fell for Hilmi Pasha.

His dark blue uniform was drawn tightly around his tall and graceful figure, his fez thrown rather back from his pale and weary face, relieved so effectively against the carpet of deep purples and crimsons that further darkened the wall behind. It is the face of a tired but unflinching eagle, worn with toil. On each side of the delicate eagle nose, the deep brown eyes looked into yours with a mournful but steady sincerity that would carry conviction of truth into the wildest tale of Arabian Nights. A grave charm hangs over his face, sometimes broken by a shadowy smile . . .

Kathleen was less impressed. They had been advised to call on Hilmi in the evening, it being Ramadan:

he would have broken his fast and regained his good humour. Therefore at 10pm we drove to his dwelling and were ushered along passages by countless flunkeys. The great man was sitting at his writing table . . . for a long and weary time we discussed trivialities in French. I thought we should never arrive at the point of our visit; the heat of the room was excessive ['a genial warmth', Nevinson called it] and tho' he plied us with lemonade and tea I was scarcely able to control my impatience. Numerous servants were rung for, for various causes, each retiring backwards, never turning his back upon the Pasha.

When it came to talking business Hilmi told them that three or four thousand hamlets had already been rebuilt. He gave them permission to travel in a particularly dangerous district; he would organize a guard for them, with a French-speaking officer; he would send word ahead that they were coming and arrange for the hospitality of the local bey. 'His affability and foresight were amazing, but in spite of it all I was in no way attracted to him. I in no way distrust his intelligence, but he inspires me with no confidence and very little interest,' Kathleen wrote in her diary. Her reaction proved right. Hilmi was not 'capable, just, and inspired with a benevolent zeal for reform' as Nevinson had hoped. He was a bureaucrat, master of the gap between an order given and an order carried out. His speciality, as all the Macedonian relief workers were to find out, was allowing everybody everything they wanted – in theory. Nevinson, on further experience of him, reported how he would smile and say, 'But all must be well, I gave the order!' 'Of all the incarnations of State that I have ever known in any land he was perhaps the most complete,' Nevinson concluded.

Kathleen had not even started work yet, and she was riddled with impatience. In Monastir 'The depot house is stocked with blankets, which makes me even more anxious to get to work, they seem to be wasting their warmth.' As the winter set in women with hungry babies and men with gangrenous wounds were coming down from the mountains to which they had fled during the fighting. Their need was great, and so was the desire of the relief workers to get on with it.

Then arrived Henry Brailsford, agent of the Macedonia Relief Fund, and his wife Jane, a very fine couple by all accounts: 'extraordinary mental energy ... accurate mind ... unfailing memory ... sensitive and sympathetic temperament ... unflagging industry,' said Nevinson of Henry, and of Jane '... much the same qualities, beautified by the further touch of feminine delicacy and imagination; beautified also by Celtic blue-grey eyes, dark hair and a smile to soften the heart of any infidel.' Kathleen too found Brailsford to have 'enormous personal charm', even though he changed plans at the last minute, and she thought Jane Brailsford extremely pretty. With the Brailsfords, Lady Thompson, a guard of Turkish cavalry and an officer (ostensibly to guide and protect them, but actually to report on them and hinder them if need be – Brailsford called them 'spies in uniform'), in a party of twenty, Kathleen set off for Klissoura.

'We set out ... in a ramshackle carriage with three horses. Wonderful wild desert scenery, and a slight rather pleasant rain. After a long distance we began to rise and rise, and finally our horses could no more ...' For a while they walked, following a lamp as darkness overtook them. The cavalry, with whom they had left the carriage, could not follow. Brailsford went back to find them, taking the lamp. It was at least three miles to the village, and there were brigands in the neighbourhood, they all knew. Ankle-deep in mud on a narrow, precipitous road, they lit cigarettes to frighten the wolves away. When the cavalry finally caught up, Kathleen was more than happy to ride: 'astride a Turkish soldier's saddle is quite a comfortable thing,' she noted, despite 'perilous precipices and streams, lit merely by a lantern, climbing over slippery rocks and boulders . . .' She was even happier to arrive at the house of 'a rich Wallachian' (she doesn't seem to have mentioned to him her descent from his former Grand Postleniks) where their boots were removed and their hands washed for them, and they were provided with a 'wonderful completely Turkish room – half the floor covered with mattresses . . . we reclined by a roaring wood fire'.

At dusk they had passed a burnt-out village; the next morning they went to the monastery to which its refugees had fled. Some of the thirty-three families had returned to the village to try to rebuild it, but the Bashi Bazouks had swept down in the night and stolen the wood they had prepared for building. Kathleen admired their babies, 'all swaddled, they felt like brown paper parcels when one took them', and arranged for wool to be provided so that the women could knit socks and jerseys, which the relief workers would then buy and distribute.

At Klissoura refugees were living two or three families to a room: 'some were in excellent spirits, others wept and mourned, all were overjoyed to see us.' They had thin mattresses, a blanket, a little maize or corn. Nothing else. Kathleen was much outraged at 'a rascally doctor, a perfect brute who cheated hideously in distributing flour.' Visiting villages, burnt-out or full of Komitadji, resulted in 'considerable unpleasantness' with their officer when Brailsford spoke to men who had been beaten to give up their arms. 'I fear it may have sown an annoying seed, which may bear unpleasant fruits.'

Thence to Kastoria, where two nuns from Salonica had set up a 'primitive but good' hospital. The English ladies' accommodation was a thousand times better than Kathleen had expected, with a view over the beautiful lake, and their work began in earnest.

Dec 21st: Today I saw an old woman with a very dreadful bleeding cancer on her left breast, but the majority are merely cases of starvation . . . [The doctor told her about the patients.] One woman had died, another being in the worst plight [pregnant and unmarried – Kathleen always used this phrase] had gone mad with shame, and the doctor was undecided whether to kill the embryo with drugs or not. If the child is allowed to be born, the people will not allow it to live. The case is difficult but in this country his action would not be criminal. Another case was a little girl of ten, and many more, more or less horrible. One girl was locked in a cellar to hide her from the soldiers by her grandmother, and there she went mad. Another was brought to the hospital, but sat looking out the window, crying. She wanted to go to her Turk.

Rape and seduction by soldiers were rife, and as well a tax was levied on Christian marriages by the Turks; if the tax was not paid, *droit de seigneur* was claimed. Kathleen had not been old enough to hear the tales her mother was bred on in Athens of the basic evil of the Turk, but Rosslyn, now working in England to raise money for Macedonia, may well have remembered and passed some on. He certainly remembered their mother's visit to her brother George in a field hospital at Scutari after the Crimean War, the horrors she saw there, and the letter she wrote to her grandfather, who had sent it to *The Times*. Its publication had helped to stir up public feeling just before Florence Nightingale started to put together her troupe of nurses (three of whom were trained by Fifi Skene).

It was to Rosslyn that Kathleen wrote. Later he published her letters, along with his own from his trip to Macedonia in 1905.

Today there are 30 patients, mostly starvation [she wrote]. Last night the wife of a village priest was brought in; her eyes were fixed and staring. Her husband and his brothers had been missing for a long while, and they thought them imprisoned in Kastoria, but lately their bodies were found in the mountains, cut in pieces, and she is going mad. She wouldn't stay, and went off this morning.

Kathleen did the accounts, listed requirements, distributed blankets, applied hot cups to congested chests, and held the hands of the dying. 'Here I learnt a calmness and a lack of dread of death,' she wrote later.

In very few cases was the fearful death rattle I had read of. Almost always death came merely as a cessation, as a clock runs down. Only once did I falter. The dying patient was a boy of about 14, with large brown eyes like a raccoon and tousled black hair. He clung to my hand with a strength that made me hope that they were wrong in abandoning him, and that he might not be dying, at any rate not tonight. And he would open his eyes and say things to me, and I could not understand a word. And then, very suddenly, with his eyes still open, he stopped breathing. My religion, which had been waning and waning, went out with a spirt.

At times she got depressed. 'A miserable day. Not the weather, but uselessness, that horrid curse.' She visited a hospital with six patients, men, women and children, one with smallpox, all in together on mattresses a metre long and having had no food or doctor for three days. Two days before Christmas they were told their hospital was to be shut down, and their doctor was not to visit the villages. A woman with pleurisy was sent away after travelling an hour and a half to get to the hospital.

25th: Cheerful sort of Christmas, eh? Never mind. I had a letter, a great event. Gave out blankets, and went a tramp round the town, but feel very useless and stupid. On the hill to the back there are some fifteen corpses still lying, all horrid and dried, unburied.

30th, Wednesday: Rode to Vernik. Hideous roads. Very poor and miserable. Even the children's faces seem wrinkled with a chronic shiver. Women tell one their horrible tales, but one has heard them before. Little boys look starved, but one knows they are starved. Old old priests tell how they have been beaten, but others have been beaten. Our whole being is pity.

Her worries she kept to her diary on the whole; but in one letter to Rosslyn she said how lonely it was to have no one to call her anything but 'Miss Bruce'. Kathleen liked and respected Lady Thompson, and worried that she was miserable or sick, but as Brailsford wrote years later: 'Lady Thompson was a stiff and conventional person, and she and Kathleen were temperamentally poles apart.' One rare sunny morning Kathleen was brushing Lady Thompson's long hair, and singing a comic song: 'I cannot understand,' said the austere lady, 'how you can sing with so much sadness all around you.'

Propriety was another problem. On one occasion Lady Thompson took Kathleen aside, when she had touched their Major's knee after a long hard journey, saying, 'Why, you're absolutely drenched.' 'You are very young, my dear,' said Lady Thompson, and explained that it was really a little indecent to touch a man's knee. Later, when Kathleen had taken off her soaking hat during a rainy ride, that same man rode up beside her

and with many apologies begged me to be so very kind as to forgive him but he had something very delicate to implore me (Oh dear oh dear, my austere lady must have been right; what is coming?). He hated being obliged to ask me, but would I mind, could I please, put on my hat. It appeared that I might ride astride, ride without a skirt, do almost anything, but to have the head uncovered was terribly shocking. With deepest and most serious apology I put on my soaking cap, and never again offended. Then I turned over in my mind the prejudices of the middle-aged lady and the Turkish soldiers, and thought I had my work cut out for me: perhaps somehow, somewhere, there would come a time when it would be right to be simple, direct and innocent. But that time never came.

Her escape was to go out riding on the tough little Turkish horses, one of which she bought for £7. She became quite used to riding astride, and rather preferred it. Henry Brailsford remembered her as 'a very spirited and attractive young woman. I doubt if she had ever been on horseback before. That was like her. Nothing daunted her.' But even riding was generally accompanied by the spies in uniform: 'We are never allowed outside this little town without 12 or 15 Turkish Cavalry, an officer and several policemen. Even in the town we have always to have an armed escort, and a policeman is stationed in our passage . . .' 'Yesterday we had to pass through a favourite brigand pass – we were forty-two, all armed!' 'A real-live gorgeous staff major never leaves us,' she reported in a letter, being cheerful. When she did escape alone, she found dismembered limbs out on the mountainside, arranged like the limbs of a starfish.

No relief was found either with the wives of the local notabilities with whom they stayed when doing the rounds of the villages.

En route we stopped for half an hour chez un Bey and were forced to go to his Harem. The women there were the worst things made in creation, hair dyed scarlet, teeth absolutely black, and fat, ma chère! fat to such a degree that one became physically unwell in seeing them – barefooted, and hideously indecent in word and gesture. It was indeed a relief to go back to the rough cavalry after that den of harpies.

On New Year's Day 1904 they mounted their horses and rode to Smrds. 'Don't comment that there are no vowels in their words: there is no water in their houses, no streets in their towns and no justice in their land.' Smrds had been one of the wildest and fiercest of the rebel towns. Small boys refused to study in school; a five-year-old explained that studying wouldn't help them to shoot Turks. The ambition of the people there was to survive through winter so that in the spring they could fight the Turks again, and no doubt get killed that way. 'It seems a false economy,' Kathleen wrote to Rosslyn. 'Once begun however one must go on, so heaps and heaps more money must be sent.' It was getting very cold: Kathleen wore five layers of wool, and slept in a sleeping bag, two blankets, a fur coat, two golf capes and a fur cloak, with hot water bottles, and still froze. And it was damp. And 'Mud, mud, mud, oh dearie man,' she wrote, 'do you know you have never seen mud never in all your life.' She kept warm on the affection and gratitude of the people she helped, and longed to bring the babies home with her, but made do with supplying bundles of cloth for their mothers to dress them in.

Her other pleasure was the landscape. 'This is the most detestable country I ever knew . . . nothing attractive in all the land except the views which are exquisite.' She marvelled at the ice: 'perilous and wonderful, but beautiful – White mountains stood against a deep clear blue sky, too impressive for fairyland, but too brilliant to be true. Ice, snow, eagles, vultures, the sound of the bells of trains of mules in the valley below, the soldiers singing their weird songs, a good smell of horses – enfin, every sense gratified.' When Rosslyn went to Macedonia he taught his infidel escorts to sing hymns – they particularly liked 'Onward Christian Soldiers'.

On 17 January Kathleen heard that her brother Wilfrid was ill. On the 18th she cut out 19 shirts, 12 pairs of knickers and 16 babies' outfits, and noticed that she was covered with an extraordinary rash.

'I don't want to die out here. I can't die without seeing Wilfrid. I say "die" because I could not be ill out here and not die, of that I am convinced.'

> *20th*: Set out at 7.30. No sooner had we started than a terrible storm of wind and rain came on. Snow! It was rather great slabs of frozen horror that hit you in the face, and cut. It blinded and choked me and made me so numbed I was incapable of resisting the infuriated gallop of my little animal, who sought to extricate himself from the horror that surrounded him. This lasted for miles, over horrid ridges, streams, boulders, everything . . .

The next day 'I was a little ill, but would not be so.' That night she ran a fever of 105°; then followed delirium, haemorrhage, coughing up blood, and a temperature of 107°.

She was nursed at first by a Greek carpenter, Nico, who spoke no English and only a little French. He did his best for her, but only once did she rave in French, and all that he could make out was that she wanted him to bring her old white pony to her. The room was at the top of a steep, narrow staircase, and realizing that he really could not satisfy the only wish he had been able to understand, he wept. Rats ran around her bed at night, but they gave her comfort because they reminded her of Rosslyn's rats from her childhood.

The disease was 'a malignant type of influenza with symptoms like typhoid' as Brailsford described it; it was epidemic and many died of it. Kathleen was not one of them, largely because of the reappearance of Jane Brailsford, who 'descended as if from heaven, and the will to live was supported by the dear devotion of this young Englishwoman', as Kathleen wrote years later. At the time she wrote in her diary, 'It is splendid to have someone. She is most good and thoughtful.' Mrs Brailsford acquired clean sheets for her, and slept in her room throughout the delirious nights.

By 30 January Kathleen was writing to Rosslyn: 'Sorry I couldn't write the last week or two, I was too busy striving with death. But I won! So here goes. The Turks still put every kind of difficulty in the way of every step one takes. You think of some nice little scheme to help some people with something, and down come the authorities and put a stop to it, stating no possible excuse or reason . . .' Though her tone is jolly, the litany of misery continues: a child with a face 'which was already like that of a corpse, quite without colour or any look of intelligence'; the 'hideous, most malicious' influenza epidemic, walls falling down and burying people. She wonders rather pathetically if perhaps Rosslyn and Nigel might 'come and fetch me and we [might] go home by Athens a little.'

On 2 February she is in bed, but cheerful: 'There is a funny little Turkish girl of about fifteen sticking her nose into my letter in terrified wonder that I can write. Now she has discovered Lady Thompson's stays (for all the world walks in and out of our bedroom – our officer, the post and all). She is holding them up and shrieking for joy.' Later in the same post she reports having heard from Brailsford that soldiers were beating up 'our ill people on their way to our hospital. Can you imagine anything so horrible?' Stuck in bed, she felt useless and miserable, ashamed of not having finished her work even though all the relief workers were being warned that they would soon have to pack up and leave, as the spring approached and the Komitadji started action again. The expectation of renewed fighting was universal.

By 6 February she had had three more fevers, but by the 12th she was well enough to travel to Klissoura by 'antidiluvian cacique' and 'ramshackle open carriage'. The most upsetting thing about the journey was the moans and groans and 'Mon Seigneur, c'est pour vous que je souffre (Oh Lord, it is for you that I suffer)' of the French nun with whom she was travelling, as they passed through a snowstorm. At Klissoura she reported 'the drollest of adventures, which may not even be written in a private female note-book. But ah! I shall nevertheless not forget', which was very annoying of her.

In Salonica she stayed a week with the Sisters of St Vincent de Paul: 'nice, good souls, absolutely without self control, the most arrant chatterboxes I ever knew. I haven't had a word of religion spoken to me, and that's just as well or I should be obliged to go away. One can't help mocking a little sometimes at the things which are attributed to the almighty, and the absolute lack of logic in their exclamations. But here is a subject on which I could mock for pages . . . à quoi bon?' To get away from too much Christianity she went to a mosque:

I had taken the precaution to put myself on excellent terms with the two men who guard the mosque, having spent half an hour sitting in their garden and picking their flowers . . . Outside there is a fountain at which each man washes his feet, his arms to the elbow, his face and behind his ears. Then he enters barefoot, carrying however his shoes. From within are called prayers and instructions, amongst which is a supplication that the powers of the world may never agree. They stand, kneel, prostrate themselves in turn, and sometimes they place their thumbs behind their ears; finally they turn their heads slowly to one side and then the other, and then get up and go away. All move as one man, very much superior to their military drill. I am told it is an exceptional favour to be allowed to be present on such an occasion.

Despite this, she was still 'preposterously weak, and I get hot and cold all about nothing. But I can walk now, thank god!' At the end of February she left by sea, heading for Marseilles, looking forward to home. She felt as if she'd been away six months, but in fact it was not quite three.

Kathleen boarded her steamer for France in high spirits. But the boat was small, the sea was rough, and she was the only woman passenger. Though her health had returned 'in waves of well-being', her sea-sickness was terrible; so terrible that by Naples she could bear it no longer and jumped ship. She had little money, no Italian, and no acquaintance in Naples, so she fled for peace and quiet to Capri. 'There I engaged a tiny room at the top of a small hotel, and stayed until the earth grew steady again under my feet.'

When it did she realized that she was 'magically and unaccountably' in Italy, and decided to go to Florence to see the art. She knew students there who lived on next to nothing. After the long terrible winter in Macedonia, spring in Florence was a joy, as her autobiography tells.

At all times convalescence is a sort of delirium, tasting life again and tasting it abundantly. A slight guilty feeling that my studio lay empty, my work undone, my painter Hofbauer, Hener and Isadora, who all rather looked to me to stir them, all neglected; and neglected the Macedonian Committee, which should have been reported to personally. All these guiltinesses perhaps enhanced the glory of the weeks that followed. I found a little art school. I found too a band of lighthearted English students, some of whom I had known in London. I found Charles Loeser, a great connoisseur of things Florentine, eager to show me, to teach me, to explain to me carefully the distinguishing features of trecento and quattrocento mouldings, to make me look beyond the Donatellos and the Michelangelos which might otherwise have satisfied me. I found a grand young singer, Von Warlich, who would walk home along the Lung'Arno with me at night, singing so gloriously that even the crotchetiest old maid, woken in her *pensione*, could surely not complain. I found an entrancing dwelling on the Via dei Bardi. It consisted of one room on the fifth floor up an old solid stone stairway, one room and a terrace. The terrace hung out over the Arno with the Ponte Vecchio on the left and straight opposite a high tower which belonged to my middle-aged friend the connoisseur. When, as often happened, we had dined together in his lovely house or in some underground cellar restaurant, there was always a solemn ritual. We would wave our candle to each other across the river before turning in. I found bathing parties, dances, revels and copious sunshine. Health came back by leaps and bounds. There were queer and ugly things in Paris. There were ugly and terrifying things in Macedonia. Here, to me at any rate, all seemed as spontaneous as a Botticelli picture.

Another friend she found was Herbert Alexander, a sun-browned, bleached-haired English painter, with whom she danced by moonlight. He told her of his explorer brother who had been 'destroyed by natives, probably cannibals', and invited her to watch the sunrise from Fiesole, on the hill above Florence.

It was misty, almost foggy. Not a sign of Florence was to be seen, just an ocean of clouds, gold, blue and white, with the sun shining down on it from the east. We stood shyly, transfigured with the rare, the unusual beauty. Florence was lying hidden, 'a bosomer of clouds'. Just as that thought ran through my mind, the clouds settled a little, and the great dome of the cathedral shone out firm and clear, as though the lovely Firenze had turned in her sleep, thrown aside her white linen and bared one shining breast. The lad and I held our breath with joy and wonder.

She slept, as ever, on the terrace. Across two rooftops on the right lived Herbert and another young painter. 'One night about two o'clock, under a low crescent moon, I woke from sleep feeling something near me. I lay absolutely still; keeping my eyelids all but closed I saw kneeling by my bed, with hands together like a mediaeval saint, the quiet figure of Herbert. His hair as well as his clothes looked white under the moon, and his face very still and radiant. My heart knocked, thumped, roared in my ear, but I lay deathly still, scarce breathing. So we stayed. At last, very very stilly, with an athletic movement, he slipped back on to his bare heels, and raised himself to his feet and tiptoed to the buttress of my terrace, swung himself lightly on to it, and climbed with sure-footed agility over the roofs, his lithe figure showing up now and again against the sky.' She never told him that she had been awake.

A few days later she and Herbert set off with knapsacks and bathing costumes to vagabond in the countryside. Initially she tried to disguise herself as a boy – her hair was still short after the illness – but no matter what she put on 'I would look like nothing but a fat German boy of about sixteen, a risible figure', so she borrowed peasant clothes from a lace-maker who lived in her building. For three weeks they wandered, walking twenty miles a day, sleeping in haylofts and caves and riverbeds, bathing in lakes, hanging their clothes to dry on bushes.

'Getting meals in these mountain villages was always in the nature of an adventure. I knew no Italian and Herbert next to none.' Local people fed them: they imagined wayfarers would want meat.

When they found that bread and cheese and eggs sufficed they became, with scarcely an exception, animated and delighted to bring out their best. Almost always they refused payment at first, and often at last too. Sometimes, if there was a beautiful daughter, or an attractive child, or a characterful old man, they took pay for food in the form of a watercolour sketch. This in some places was tremendously popular. Quantities of lovely creatures presented themselves as possible models offering food and shelter in exchange.

My heaven was so many sided! Never before had I seen fireflies. In some places the woods in the early night were bright with them. They would even settle for a moment on my arm. One such lovely night we made our camp in a small wood. I spread my mackintosh sheet, wrapt my blanket over me, and turned the spare half of my mackintosh sheet over me to keep off the dew. Suddenly I felt something moving under my pillow.

It was a mole, wriggling about underground, and Herbert had to come from his bivouac, a gentlemanly distance away, to help her find what it was that could be felt but not seen. By the time they had tracked it down and laughed about it they had attracted the attention of two country carabinieri who were patrolling the road.

We simple innocents were tracked down by these vigilant sleuths, themselves even more simple and innocent than their victims. Followed a conversation that nobody understood. Finally we arranged to explain that though we couldn't explain ourselves in Italian, we could in French. 'Ah, Enrico,' said one policeman to his mate, 'you've always said you could speak French, now's your chance. Ask them what they're doing here.' A considerable pause, while everybody turned hopefully to Enrico. Finally, very slowly and deliberately, Enrico addressed me. 'Quel est le prix du beurre à Paris?' With elaborate composure I replied that butter, when I left Paris, cost two francs a kilo. Enrico turned triumphantly to his colleague. 'It's clear we must take them to the police station.'

Our detention was abbreviated by Herbert's suggestion of a bottle of Chianti in the adjoining café before it was too late. This idea seemed easy to grasp and was fallen in with. A good deal of laughter ensued, and we wayfarers were allowed to disperse, with the injunction that we must never sleep out again. To this injunction we complied for about half an hour.

'It'll be a bore not being able to tell people our lovely adventures,' she said to Herbert.

'Won't we be able to? Why not?' he replied.

'Because we mustn't tell anybody. Well, you could perhaps, because you could pretend you were with another boy, but I wouldn't pretend I'd been with another girl — too dull.'

'I shan't pretend. I shan't need to tell anyone. I'll just put it by and hoard it,' said Herbert very gently and slowly.

And so she returned to Paris, 'looking more like a sun-gilded Amazon than a typhoid convalescent'.

IN 1906 ISADORA'S 'terrible things' began to happen. Kathleen's first intimation was in a letter from the Hague, 'a queer cry, childish and pathetic. Would not, could not I come to her? Her need was very great, very very great.' (Isadora in her autobiography says that Kathleen just 'arrived', but Isadora was often inaccurate on details and the fullness of Kathleen's account makes it convincing.)

In high summer Kathleen locked her studio and set off to Noordwijk, a tiny village on the coast of Holland, where her friend was staying in a little white house called Villa Maria. She found Isadora 'very pitiful, very helpless and for the first time very very endearing.'

'Poor darling, what is the matter?'
'Can't you see?' cried the dancer, spreading high her lovely arms. Slowly, and with many a lie, the story came out at last. A well-known Englishman with a wife, a mistress, children, dissolute habits and no money had entranced her body and mind, and her baby was due in a month or two.

The well-known Englishman was Edward Gordon Craig, the illegitimate son of the great actress Ellen Terry and Edward Godwin. His accomplishment was to revolutionize theatre design, despite producing less than half a dozen complete shows in his life. Simply, he was the first to propose that the set for a forest scene did not have to be bundles of foliage, and that 'realistic' was not the only way to present artistic truth. But he could not work with other people. He tried, and it infuriated all concerned, including him. He was astonishingly attractive and remarkably talented, one of those who doesn't bother even to try to excuse egocentricity and selfishness because it is all for their work, not for them. His amours, according to Max Beerbohm, were 'almost mythological'. Kathleen in fact slightly underestimated his involvements; he had, when he and Isadora first met in 1904, seven children by three women: his wife May Gibson (he left her during her fourth pregnancy); his mistress Jess Dorynne (he left her during her first pregnancy), and Elena Meo, who was expecting her third child by him and remained faithful to him all her life. But he and Isadora fell in love, and love, to Isadora at least, was simple and all-consuming.

'This was the meeting of twin souls,' she wrote in her autobiography. 'The light covering of flesh was so transmuted with ecstasy that earthly passion became a heavenly embrace of white fiery flame. There are joys so complete, so all perfect, that one should not survive them.'

Within weeks of first meeting Craig, in Berlin in December 1904, Isadora was writing to him: 'Thank you thank you thank you for making me happy — whole complete I love you love you love you and I Hope we'll have a dear sweet lovely baby — and I'm happy forever — your Isadora.'

At the same time he was writing, in his special Isadora diary: 'Do I love her? Does she love me? I do not know or want to know. We love to be together . . . Is that love? I do not know. She says she loves me. What does that mean from her? I do not know.'

A few weeks later they were having a conversation in note form:

5.1.05, Dom-Hotel Cologne

SHE: Isadora has decided that the father of her child shall be the man she loves.
HE: A world of thought can be given to this.

'In after years,' Kathleen wrote, 'when the War had given different values to these things, she said, and probably believed, that she had done this thing deliberately, and was proud of her courage and independence, but at the time she was still nothing more than a very frightened girl, frightened and pitiful.' Isadora did have her ideals. When asked about 'free love', she had written: 'Of course, people will respond, "But what about the children?" . . . How can a woman go into this marriage contract with a man who she thinks is so mean that, in case of a quarrel, he wouldn't even support his own children? If she thinks he is such a man, why should she marry him?' Which is all very well, except that Craig was not supporting his – in fact his mother was supporting him with £500 a year.

By March 1907 Isadora's eyes had been opened enough for her to write to Craig: 'Why the very Goo of a baby makes you look for a Time Table book', but at this stage she was full of romance and idealism, and once pregnant she put a brave and cheerful face on to her conflicting and socially unacceptable desires. She can hardly have known that she was already pregnant when in January 1906 she wrote to Craig: 'I wish you would know that in all the hundreds of times you have kissed me there hasn't been one that every thing in me hasn't cried out – make me fertile – give me a child – not once – I have always had that constant longing, impossible to control.' She dreamt that 'Ellen Terry appeared to me in a shimmering gown . . . leading by the hand a little blonde child, a little girl who resembled her exactly, and, in her marvellous voice, she called to me – "Isadora, love. Love . . . Love." The divine message sang in all my being. I continued to dance before the public, to teach my school, to love my Endymion.'

Her great love and laissez-faire indulgence allowed her to see the best in Craig. Though she worked extraordinarily hard, travelling all over Europe and feeling that she 'lived on railway trains', and though her earnings were helping to keep him while he was incapable of making any practical link between the talent he had and the money he needed to live on, he would say to her, 'Why don't you stop this? Why do you want to go on the stage and wave your arms about? Why don't you stay at home and sharpen my lead pencils?' And in the same breath she writes, 'And yet Gordon Craig appreciates my art as no one else has ever appreciated it . . .' No doubt he did, in some way. And Isadora was herself perfectly capable of being dismissive of the work of others. Kathleen had fallen ill (three days of high fever due to overstrain, said the doctor) during a visit to Isadora at the Hague in November 1905, and Isadora had no respect for her anxiety about 'some statue whose clay will crack if she doesn't get back'.

So in the summer of 1906 Kathleen found her friend in a white house with a white shell garden among the sand dunes. Isadora told

Kathleen that she was all alone, that she hadn't told even her family of her situation; but Isadora was not above a little emotional blackmail. Her family did know, but her mother thought she should be married. 'But *she* had been married, had found it impossible, and had divorced her husband. Why should she want me to enter the trap where she had been cruelly bitten?' Isadora wondered. She turned instead to Kathleen, the 'nice quiet English girl', as Isadora described her to Craig, 'very sweet and gentle'.

'Kathleen was a magnetic person, filled with life and health and courage,' Isadora wrote later, but those qualities were not to the fore when Isadora's story first came out. Kathleen, initially, was shocked.

> I was torn and shattered. All my inborn prudery, strengthened by the convent upbringing, was terribly affronted. The sad queer happenings in the Balkans served not at all to soften this present experience. The girls of my nightmare winter there were of a so completely different civilisation that they had seemed like lovely wild animals. But here was the dancer, my friend, with an education limited indeed, it is true, but speaking my language, sharing my acquaintances, with recognizable ambitions and ideals. It was a shattering blow to me, who found exultation in audacious defiance of convention coupled with an assured control. So loudly and arrogantly had I proclaimed that complete independence for a lass was fraught with no dangers whatever, given there was character and intelligence to back it. I was very young. Daughters were still living with their mothers in dutiful subjection. Well, here then was a situation to be grappled with. My pseudo-maternal heart hit my head a sharp blow. 'Get on with the job.'

'Daughters were still living with their mothers,' she wrote, to define the nature of propriety. She of course was not living with her mother, and never had. She was undoubtedly aware that to be as independent-minded as she was was quite unusual, but it is not clear that she yet associated her independence with her orphaned state. She was certain that there were no dangers for her; she was interested not so much in the nature of female independence as its fruits. And to find Isadora bearing such fruit as this was quite extraordinary to her. Sexual freedom, as an option, seems hardly to have crossed her mind before. Now that it did, 'character and intelligence' precluded it for her, and at the same time required her to 'get on with the job' for her foolish, as she saw it, friend. Perhaps she felt that Isadora had in some way let down the ideal of female independence by ending up in 'the worst possible plight'.

> Vicariously I figured myself the mother of Isadora's son. It never occurred to me that the expected baby could be other than a son. For the health of this future son, the mother must be cheered and cared for. I would not let Isadora see that I was shocked, yes, quite simply and honestly shocked. Never did I let her suspect my rather mean fear lest any of my common-place standard-moraled relations should hear of my aiding and abetting, with sympathy and capacity, the arrival of an illegitimate child of a dancer. In my head I could hear the scorn with which those last words would be bandied from naval mouth to military, from military to clerical, from clerical to old maids'. 'It is easy,' I thought, 'to have the courage of one's convictions, but these are not my convictions. Well, I must have courage all the same.'

The life they led at Villa Maria was 'queer and anxious'. The wind blew all the time, gently or in such storms that the house, in Isadora's words, 'was rocked and buffeted all night like a ship at sea'. Isadora sewed baby clothes and wrote cheerful letters to Craig, who had gone to London to visit his other pregnant mistress, Elena Meo. In one letter Isadora all but invites him to bring Elena with him to Villa Maria: 'If there is anyone you care for very much who feels unhappy and wants to come with you she can have half my little house with all my heart. It will give me joy – and Love is enough for all.' Sometimes Isadora was peaceful, but at others 'a fierce cloud of doubt, fear and loneliness would descend upon her . . . and she would cry for death and plan her suicide.' Kathleen would cheer Isadora with tales of future triumphs, and herself with the thought that people who talk of suicide are not usually the ones who go through with it.

Adding to the strangeness of the situation was the attention of the press – Kathleen's first experience of it, though later she would come to know it well. The story of Isadora's pregnancy had got out, along with rumours that she and Craig were married. (Craig quoted, rather aptly, of the press: 'One said he was married, and the other he said nay, he's just a blooming lunatic that wants his blooming way.') A reporter had tracked Isadora down, and though he was refused an interview he remained hanging around the house. This added to

Isadora's misery, and to get rid of him and scotch the rumours she asked Kathleen to dress up in Isadora-esque drapery and run and dance on the beach in a very unpregnant fashion. Kathleen did it, to her 'uncomfortable shame'. Later that night, in the small hours, Isadora walked out to sea. Kathleen woke with the sense that all was not well, and followed the trail from Isadora's empty bed to the open front door to the lonely beach. The sea was calm, and there was the dancer standing in the water, with a gentle, dazed look, a faint childish smile, saying, 'The tide was so low, I couldn't do it, and I'm so cold.' Kathleen led the fully-dressed Isadora out of the water and back to the house where she warmed her and rubbed her and fed her hot drinks and put her to bed.

That night was the low point. Soon afterwards Craig made his appearance, and everything changed. 'Isadora's lover arrived without heralding, to stay we knew not for how long. Isadora was radiant and masterful. He was to be treated as a Messiah, everything was to fall before his slightest wish. Our simple fare must be supplemented, wine must replace the customary milk, everything must be turned to festival.'

Kathleen's first instinct was to fly. She says that the reason she did not was because of loyalty to the unborn child, her vicarious son, but she would have been rare indeed if she had had no curiosity about Craig, and had felt nothing at all of his notoriously attractive energy and intelligence. Almost certainly she was a little jealous. Whatever the reasons, 'I felt I must submit to the presence of this thoroughly inappropriate father. Physically, I was bound to own, he was not altogether inappropriate. He was tall and well-built, with a mass of long, thick, golden hair, just beginning to turn grey. He had good features, high cheekbones, and a healthy colour. Only the hands with the low-bitten nails betrayed the brute in him.' Isadora mentioned the nails too; when 'poor Craig was restless, unhappy, (he) bit his nails to the quick exclaiming often "My work. My work. My work."'

He was gay, amusing, argumentative [continued Kathleen]. Only once or twice did wild outbursts of uncontrolled temper pass with a wave of terror through the little villa. And I, ever mindful of the little life, wondered whether it were taking any harm from these distressing scenes. Isadora herself remained externally beautiful and serene. Endowed always with an abundance of generosity to those about her, she seemed now ready to forgive, to condone, to accept, to give herself up to ministering to this unbridled child of mature age.

There was one moment, at least, when Kathleen liked Craig. Live lobsters had been sent for, 'to feed the rare brute well', and put in a pail overnight. In the middle of the night Kathleen was woken by hair-raising noises, and rushed downstairs fearing suicide, murder or worse. The whole household had been raised, and they peered nervously round the pantry door to find that the lobsters, having upturned their pail, were amusing themselves by shattering all the crockery that shared their shelf. In the hysterical merriment, born of relief, which followed, they were all for a moment united.

Craig left, and Isadora's time came. A telegram was sent to Craig in Rotterdam and he arrived in time. Kathleen's diary gives the bare and brutal bones.

22 Sept 1906: (Sat) I. woke me at 5. Dilation pains begun. Got into bed with her and lay there till 8. Got her up – breakfast and a little walk.

23 Sun: Isadora got up suffering 2.30. Tried to walk outside – awful. Sitz bath – tremendous relief. 11.30 went to sleep.

24 Mon: 2 a.m. woke. Sitz bath. Labour began. 4.30 woke Ted [Craig] went for Dr Van Nes. 5 came Dr. Slept 5 till 8. About 10.30 forehead appeared. 11.15 pulse weakened, instruments – no time for chloroform. Alive – rupture to rectum . . . stitches. Placenta easy – buried it in sand.

25 Tues: Nurse Kist arrived. 12 walked with Ted to Nordwyck Binnen to buy things. 10pm, found her flushed. Went to interview Dr at his house. He said possibly never dance again and certainly not for 8 weeks.

Later Kathleen wrote a fuller version:

The local doctor, a little fat middle-aged Dutchman with a stubbly beard, arrived with a black handbag containing, he said, anaesthetic; this, however, he left in the hall, both then and later. Then followed the most terrible hours that I had ever experienced. I had seen and heard things grim enough in the mountain hospital, but here must be, I thought, the ultimate agony. Hour after hour I held the hands, the head the writhing body, the same hands and head and lovely body that has held European audiences enthralled. The cries and sights of a slaughterhouse could not be more terrible . . .

Isadora said later that no woman who had ever had a child would have any reason to fear the Spanish Inquisition:

It must have been a mild sport in comparison. Relentless, cruel, knowing no release, no pity, this terrible unseen genie had me in his grip and was, in continued spasms, tearing my bones and sinews apart. I have only to shut my eyes and I hear again my shrieks and groans . . . And for two days and two nights this unspeakable horror continued. And on the third morning, this absurd doctor brought out an immense pair of forceps and, without an anaesthetic of any sort, achieved the butchery.

Kathleen tried to get the doctor to administer the anaesthetic he had in the hall, but 'he seemed to reply only that there wasn't time; he could not leave her to get it ready; and so the frenzied agony went on and on and on.'

Not unusually for the time, Kathleen felt that an artistically sensitive person suffered more pain than a philistine, and Isadora believed that 'the more civilised the person, the more fearful the agony'. She thought it a nonsense to speak of any kind of female emancipation until 'this operation of childbirth, like other operations, shall be made painless and endurable', and could not forgive 'the unspeakable egotism and blindness of men of science who permit such atrocities when they can be remedied'. Kathleen, writing in 1932, expressed great relief that among the changes in women's lot this suffering, at least, was no longer expected of them.

And after the frenzy, the agony, the two days and two nights of unspeakable horror, there was the baby. 'It was unhurt by it all,' wrote Kathleen. 'It was perfect. I turned from the horror with joy to the tiny miraculous object.' She had a brief, fleeting moment of jealousy that it was not *her* son, and then a moment of shock that it was not anybody's son, but a little girl. But soon she was 'tending and purring over the queer little atom with that love that passes all understanding, the love of a woman for a new-born babe.' The mother herself felt 'this tremendous love, surpassing the love of men. I was stretched and bleeding, torn and helpless, while the little being sucked and howled. Life, life, life! Give me life! Oh, where was my Art? My Art or any Art? What did I care for Art! I felt I was a God, and superior to any artist.'

Kathleen left Noordwijk soon afterwards, but not because she felt she was no longer needed. Isadora, in her passion of romance, and also perhaps because she had been a little jealous when Kathleen and Craig had both slept out on the beach, had been questioning Kathleen about her own love life. Kathleen said she hadn't a love life, but Isadora was not satisfied. The painter Hofbauer came to visit, wanting Kathleen to go back to Paris, but she said no, Isadora wasn't well enough, and when she was, Kathleen would go to London to see Wilfrid, who was due home on leave. Isadora thought Kathleen was callous to Hofbauer – did she not love him at all? Kathleen said she loved their lopsided friendship. Isadora felt it was disgraceful not to love anybody. Had Kathleen never loved anybody? The answer no doubt encompassed the fact of Kathleen's virginity. Simple Kathleen, sentimental, romantic Kathleen, thought Isadora.

Isadora thought that virtuous people either hadn't been tempted enough, or were so concentrated on one subject that they 'have not had the leisure to glance around them'. Kathleen was in a way the latter, concentrated on the ideal father for her potential child, and not interested in physical involvement with men she 'glanced around' at. This was not good enough for Isadora. At last, perhaps to shut Isadora up, Kathleen told her about Edward Steichen, the romantic American photographer, and her long fidelity to the idea of him.

Isadora was delighted, and decided to invite Steichen to Noordwijk to photograph her. Kathleen was aghast. She tried to explain to Isadora that it was the not knowing him which had been so interesting. Isadora said that Kathleen must begin living some day, 'like me', she said. 'No, dear,' said Kathleen, 'not like you. I'll live all right, but not like you. Quite, quite differently.' This made Isadora cry, so Kathleen fetched the baby to cheer them up, and forgot about the conversation.

'Two days later Isadora, with a joyful and mysterious air, produced a telegram signed Steichen, which said "Many thanks. Leaving tonight. Arriving 9.30." I went scarlet to the roots of my hair.'

Kathleen was furious, and terribly embarrassed. Steichen was married now, and she hadn't seen him for years – since their farewell at the door of her first Paris studio, and her first kiss. She couldn't let Isadora's no doubt well-intentioned game put her in this position. So she left a note and bolted to London, to Rosslyn's flat in Soho. The journey was bad, she was seasick, Rosslyn was away, and she went to bed miserable with a wine-bottle full of hot water to keep her warm. Then came a telegram: Isadora was haemorrhaging, she was sick, please please would Kathleen come back at once? 'Of purer eyes than to behold iniquity', as Kathleen put it, she counted out her money and saw that by walking to the station, using no porters and going third class, she could. She set off back to Holland after only ten hours in London, in 'flurried self-contempt' – she felt terrible at having left her friend and the child when they needed her.

There to meet her on her arrival at the station was Steichen. 'I was so tired and forlorn, and the sight of his upstanding figure and quizzical expression was so breathtaking, that I went up to him as though he were spreading a great wing and I were taking my natural cover under it.' Isadora, needless to say, was fine, and 'childishly entranced that her ruse had succeeded'. 'No matter that I had travelled two consecutive nights, spent all my money and been thrown by a bevy of lies into renewed intimacy with a man married to someone else. She was agog with kindly glee. "Well," she said, "if you don't want him, I'll have him myself. He's lovely." I was all in a tangle . . . He talked to me as though I was then and always had been the one thing he delighted in . . .' Kathleen gave in, and 'a reprehensible light-heartedness' invaded her.

The next day she had thought better of it, and said that she would go back to London. Steichen thought that was such a good idea that he would come too. And rather than go direct, they should go via Haarlem to look at the Franz Hals portraits. Isadora was delighted, and said to Kathleen, 'You love him good now, you've got to stop being so English.' Oh no I shall not love him good, thought Kathleen, but her heart was patting away and she was not entirely sure that she could handle the situation. She fixed her attention on her ideal, the father of her child, the only man she would ever 'love good'. After Isadora's recent experience, Kathleen was not about to enter into romance with a married man. Had he not been married . . . well, who can say.

They had a wonderful trip back to England. 'He was demonstrative, enthusiastic, amazed and delighted with everything, and ecstatic over his companion. Arrived in London, he stayed a week, and then very sadly returned to Paris.' Back in Paris Steichen was still ecstatic about her – rather too much so. He would say to his wife when the sun shone: 'Oh gee, you should see Kathleen's eyes in the sunshine,' and when it rained would recall how wonderful raindrops looked in her hair. There can be no doubt what this contributed to Mrs Steichen one day swallowing a bottle of chemicals. Kathleen received a telegram: 'Clara has taken poison.'

She wanted terribly to go to him, but was fully aware of the possibility that that would make everything worse. If Clara died, there would be an inquest. 'It would all be very sordid, Steichen would be hurt, nothing would have been gained, everyone would believe the worst.' She made do by sending him an unsigned telegram asking to meet him on the steps of the Madeleine, away from her own quartier. She went back again to Paris, and they met as arranged. Clara hadn't died.

> It seemed that after hours of unconsciousness, when they had decided that she couldn't possibly survive, she had murmured weakly, and Steichen had put his ear down to her face, and she had whispered, 'Do you kiss her?'
> 'Only her hands,' he replied.
> 'Then perhaps I'll live,' she said.

Years later it turned out that Clara Steichen had had more control over whether or not to die at that moment than might have been supposed. By 1921 the Steichens' marriage had collapsed in a flurry of law suits, and Steichen testified that his wife had become jealous of 'a sculptress in Paris, and though he insisted that he was not in love with the sculptress his wife drank the contents of a phial which he thought contained poison, but really held harmless crystals.' In due course the jury decided that Mrs Steichen became jealous of every woman with whom her husband had any association in an artistic way, and some others: the *New York Times* headline on the story was 'Wife jealous of mother'.

At the time Steichen and Kathleen both felt a mixture of guilt, confusion and relief. He decided that one way to ease the situation would be for Kathleen to call on Clara. 'I believe that if she could just see you, and know that you are just beautiful and innocent and young and not some terrible creature – I believe that it would dispel the dreads and horrors from her mind.' Why he thought that seeing at first hand the youth and beauty and innocence of the woman she believed her husband to be in love with would comfort his wife only he knows; Kathleen was not convinced. He said she was unkind to make difficulties; she was young enough to be swayed by this argument. She went to call, pretending to be bringing a book. And Clara did seem comforted – enough to insist on Kathleen staying to supper, and on her husband taking Kathleen to the station when she left.

'Never ask me to do a mean thing like that again,' Kathleen said to Steichen as she got on the train.

SIX

✦

Vagabonding in Greece

✦

1906–1907

KATHLEEN HAD GLIMPSED Greece from Salonica, and had thought of her Greek grandmother and Greek-bred mother. When Isadora announced that she and her family were going to Greece on a spiritual pilgrimage ('The spirit I sought,' she wrote, 'was the invisible Goddess Athena who still inhabited the ruined Parthenon') Kathleen went too.

The 'dancing vagabonds', as Kathleen called them, camped on the 'thyme-covered slopes of Mount Hymettus' with a glorious view of the Parthenon, and tried to build either a house (Kathleen's version) or a temple in the shape of a scale reconstruction of the Palace of Agamemnon, realized by Isadora's brother Raymond (Isadora's version). Although they were all 'completely emancipated through our ideas of modern science and free-thinking', as Isadora put it, a black cockerel was sacrificed by an Orthodox priest at sunset to celebrate the laying of the first stone. They wore Greek robes in the ancient style, ate no meat, rose at dawn and tried to teach the local inhabitants to dance and sing, which they cheerfully did when the raki was rolled out for celebrations.

Each day Kathleen would walk to the Acropolis and marvel. It reminded her of her favourite bolt-hole, Chartres:

> The archaic priestesses, conscious ancestors surely of the twelfth-century saints of Chartres, the mellow marble, the exquisite drapery, and the whimsical illusive personal faces. I would walk hour after hour among the columns of the great temple, and finally come to a long rest before that loveliest of little things, the Temple of Nike. From early morning until sundown there was enough to do merely to move and live among the apricot-coloured columns.

She knew little history, but found out enough to rail against Lord Elgin – the same wicked Lord Elgin against whom her great-aunt Fifi had railed, and for the same reason. He 'had stolen one of the exquisite caryatids, and . . . the authorities . . . had replaced her with a dreadful cast of an entirely different colour to her sisters – vandal's act.' Perhaps she knew the story of how the remaining caryatids wept every night for their lost sister. When she returned to London she went so far as to lunch with Sidney Colvin (later Sir Sidney), the keeper of prints and drawings at the British Museum, to make her feelings felt. He said 'If our figure leaves this museum, it will be over my dead body.' It is still there.

The living Greeks delighted her as much as the ancient ones did: 'On the lovely beach beyond Phalaron native riders, stripped, would come down to water their horses in groups of eight or ten, looking for all the world like the Parthenon frieze, glorious in pose and a marvel of colour, their red-bronze limbs against the blue sea.' One morning, lying on a grassy ledge where she had taken herself off to sleep, she was woken early by a goatherd playing his pipes. 'I watched his beautiful movements, so light and sure-footed, his bare shoulder and arm, bronzed and supple, his ragged clothes and his tossed hair . . .' The sight of her, in her white clothing with her hair down, gave him such a shock that he fled down the rocks and grass, his herd bounding behind him. She thought he must have taken her for a goddess or devil of the mountain.

Sleeping out gave her no fear and much pleasure. On this occasion she had an arrangement with her companions that if she rattled a stick on a petrol can (which she took with her for the purpose) they would fire their one revolver to frighten off any ill-intentioned visitor, but it was never needed. 'A sleeper who wakes but for a moment in the open, be the night starlit, moonlit or black, gains, be he never such a clod, some feeling of grandeur,' she wrote.

Whether it was the 'greeting the rising sun with joyous songs and dances', or the refreshing themselves with 'a modest bowl of goat's milk', or the 'afternoons to be spent in meditation', or the 'evenings given over to pagan ceremonies with appropriate music', or the fact that there was no water and the artesian well they dug was only partially rewarding, Kathleen decided to leave. She set off to a small island, Methena, accompanied only by Isadora's sister Elizabeth, 'a kind and unobtrusive girl'. Methena was visited by one boat a week, and the two young women made their home on a rock linked to the island by a jetty. They had a small wooden cabin which hung over the water, and there they lived like the crabs that they idly watched each day. Kathleen unnerved her friend by swimming by moonlight, and the local fishermen by swimming too far out: they would come up to her in boats and make it known that there were enormous fish that would eat her up. The two companions had three books between them, of which Kathleen couldn't quite stomach Thucydides, so she read and reread Plato and Walt Whitman. They ate bread and goat's cheese and fruit: figs – 'great juicy things' – at twelve a penny, and melons a penny each. Once a week they would go to the village café and eat a limonaki, 'a tiny lemon preserved in some kind of rich, sweet liquid. This was our dissipation.'

One of the fishermen was a boy named Anastas – she thought him a boy, he was sixteen, but he felt himself a man. He had a little green boat and a scarlet kerchief that he wore diagonally across his forehead, his black hair flying out beneath. Kathleen thought him 'the most eye-catching splash of colour', and was delighted with him, until he leapt out of the picturesque context in which she had set him by producing a dictionary (when she had seen that he was bringing something she thought it must be pomegranates or a lobster). He looked up the words to say first how clever he was, and secondly that he and Kathleen should be married.

Her enchantment with the land of her ancestors was not so great that she took him up on it, but she remembered his proposal, 'fresh and sad and pretty', for the rest of her life. When she and Elizabeth left Methena he tied his little boat to the big one, only unloosing the rope when the speed became too much. Her last memory was of him 'standing up perilously in his little green boat, waving the red handkerchief he had snatched from his forehead'.

Kathleen was now twenty-eight, an advanced age for a spinster at the time. Her combination of intelligence, independence, chastity and maternal affection won her many admirers, but she was still holding fast to the idea of the father for her son. Jocelyn had said to her in Paris, 'there is no end to your young men', and she agreed that they

did make up 'a large and exceedingly varied assortment. They were
an enchanting crowd, but I kept my goal, my star, firmly fixed. None
of these was the right, the perfect father for my son. None, I feared,
could even be trained for the role. Still, what dears they were, so new
and exciting.' She still felt as Miranda did, 'O brave new world, that
has such creatures in it!'

The Englishmen she met in Paris didn't interest her much – she
found it easier to be less judgmental of foreigners. 'The mysterious
veil of only half understanding which was spread between me and
those who spoke no English dimmed their crudities and caused fewer
recoils. My over-sensitive petals had less cause to curl up.' The half-
understood picturesque foreigners whom she would never think of
marrying gave her great pleasure. Years later she remembered the
Greek, 'rich, flashing and good looking' who had infuriated Hofbauer
by insisting on an introduction, and been refused. 'Why?' he had
demanded, 'when all I want is to bite her little finger?' Kathleen
found that an enormous joke, but Hofbauer was 'blind with fury'.

Then there was Bugatti, a fair-haired Italian sculptor, brother to
the car designer, who would sit for hours in her studio while she
worked, but who if she picked up a book would take it from her and
fling it across the room. Years later he killed himself. There was a
Dutch youth, Lou Van Telegen, who looked like a Greek god and
worked as a model. He was arrested for stealing a rich lady's jewels,
and later toured the United States as Sarah Bernhardt's leading man.
There was another Dutchman with long golden hair who wore a robe
and sandals: he ate only brown bread, fruit and nuts, and claimed
that salt was the devil. He persuaded Kathleen to try his diet and
when she became ill 'assured me that it was the bad things of my
former unregenerate self working themselves out'. Kathleen and her
contemporaries thought this very eccentric, though we can recognize
him now as simply an early Californian.

There was a German pacifist who happened to work as a military
attaché, who would thread her needle for her when she sewed, and
there was Emil Hovelacque, a Frenchman in government service who
piled thirty beautiful Persian rugs in front of his fire for her to sit
on. This one acquired and furnished a luxurious apartment for her in
Passy, such as he might for a mistress, and was terribly angry and

hurt that she would not accept it even when he was offering marriage too.

'It was odd,' she wrote, rather naively. 'My son didn't seem to mean anything at all to any of them.' 'Vraiment, ma petite, tu es difficile (Really, my dear, you are difficult),' said they, and she couldn't disagree.

When Kathleen met her star, her goal, she didn't at first recognize him. When she left the wholly unsuitable Anastas weeping on the blue waters of the Aegean she was heading to London, summoned, as she had been from Macedonia, by the ill-health of her brother Wilfrid, the sailor. By the time she got there he was quite recovered and had gone fishing in Scotland.

After months as a crab in Greece she was delighted to become a social animal in London, dancing and going to plays and concerts, and of course going out with young men. She had been on a trip to Florence (Isadora hoped that she would not be waving flirtatious lanterns across the rooftops at Gordon Craig, who was living there at the time), but it was London that appealed to her now. She took a tiny flat in Cheyne Walk, in those days more an artistic address than a smart one. Her neighbours included the sculptor Sir John Tweed, Charles Ricketts and Charles Shannon, Wilson Steer, Henry Tonks, Gaudier-Brzeska and the young Charles Wheeler, later Sir Charles and the president of the Royal Academy. The flat cost her £16 a year, and she made an arrangement with a neighbour to bring lunch each day for 4d, and clean for 2/6d a week. It was not quite so cheap as Greece, but the £72 per year would probably stretch. She started a series of portraits of 'young men of note or character', but she was not yet prepared to try to sell her work. She felt that her knack for portraiture was 'a goldmine waiting to be worked' but for the moment, in this at least, she was rather shy and ladylike.

Soon after her return Mabel Beardsley invited her to lunch. It was a party of lions, with 'no balancing lionesses: the hostess herself was only a vicarious lioness, not really a lion hunter. She was the very charming sister of a dead lion, and her luncheon party was chiefly for his close friends: but lions they were, and to me very splendid ones indeed.' She sat between Max Beerbohm and J. M. Barrie, and wished they would roar a little louder.

Away down the other end of the table was a naval officer, Captain Scott. He was not very young, perhaps forty, nor very good-looking, but he looked very healthy and alert, and I glowed rather foolishly and suddenly when I clearly saw him ask his neighbour who I was. I was nobody, and I knew the neighbour, my hostess, would be saying so. I had heard that he had just returned from a very heroic though rather sensational exploit, and for the last few months had been subjected to the torture of intrusive popularity. [The exploit was Scott's first Antarctic trip, with the *Discovery*, which had in fact taken place three years earlier.] I was introduced to him after lunch, and he wanted to know where I got my wonderful sunburn. I was of the richest brown, which made my eyes a very startling blue. I told him I had been vagabonding in Greece, and he thought how wonderful to vagabond like that. I had to leave immediately to catch a train.

This small talk was the sum of their acquaintance for the next ten months, and neither of them thought about it. Kathleen had other things on her mind: work, pleasure, young men, and a curious medical condition. For discretion's sake she called it appendicitis; in fact it was an abdominal cyst made up of the hair and nails of what she was told would, if it had developed properly, have been her twin. (There were after all two sets of twins among her siblings.) She was operated on to remove the cyst, and she half-expected to die, particularly when she was asked by the nurse if she would like to see a clergyman. No, she said, she would like to see Bernard Shaw. The nurse was horrified at the idea of this noted atheist, and reiterated the offer. It turned out that it was her brother Rosslyn come to visit her. 'Oh, of course I'll see *him*,' she said. 'I'd forgotten he was a clergyman.' Again she was told off for being too cheerful in a bad situation – a nurse woke her specially to tell her that she wasn't taking it seriously enough, and that she ought to know she might not live through her operation. All she was concerned for was that she would be left 'enough insides to make a fine baby some day'.

Max Beerbohm had his own theory about her illness; he put it down to peacock feathers. They had become friends after Mabel Beardsley's party, and particularly after Kathleen had relieved him of a loose eyelash: 'You can't think how different my whole outlook on life is since,' he wrote on 19 June 1907. And on 28 June:

My Dear Kathleen, A very delightful letter from you but I do think you are mad as a hatter, and stark staring mad, not to destroy the feathers once and for all. I am sure you won't get well, so long as you hang on to them, you foolish creature. Or at any rate I am sure other unpleasant things will happen to you as soon as you do get well. Possibly shipwreck on your way to the Rocky Mountains. And if you do get safely there, you won't catch any horses. Very likely they will catch you, and make an example of you. A furious breed. I know them. You wouldn't be ill now, but for the feathers. Your diagnosis about dancing and sculpting is all nonsense. But for the feathers you might have danced all night and sculpted all day, you might have danced sculpting and sculpted dancing, without being a penny the worse, all the fault of the feathers. Into the fire with them, this instant! Otherwise you are simply flying in the face of providence. This must be a very charming sensation for providence . . . oh well, I suppose there is no use in adjuring you to be a little sensible. How are you feeling? (Physically I mean, mentally I despair of you.) Much better, I hope? Nearly well? I do so look forward to the time when we shall have the pleasure of seeing Miss K Bruce again . . . Good night and good morning, Kathleen. Max.

And a little later: 'I cannot explain why I am borne into the consciousness of people recovering from anaesthetics, I give it up, wondering for my own part what there is in you that makes you somewhat haunt me all the time when I am quite wide awake. (I admit that this is much the less difficult of the two problems.)'

Early in July Kathleen was well enough to see him:

I did not stay long [he wrote] – tore myself away – partly because I supposed you ought to be 'kept quiet', and partly because I assumed that the American was in love with you; and partly because you may, for aught I know, be in love with him. The possible gooseberry, therefore, rolled down the stairs as soon as it could, well-pleased, however, to be clasping to its rotund surface those feathers. As soon as I reached a place where the water flowed right up to the embankment, over went the feathers – gorgeously protruding from their envelope, and exciting utmost curiosity in the breast of a costermonger who was leaning over the parapet, and who, I do trust, didn't presently dive in to clutch them and present them to his doner [lady friend].

Above: Kathleen, taken in Scarborough in the late 1890s.

Right: Kathleen (*fourth from right in front row*) at Velizy with Rodin in 1903.

Kathleen (*third from left*) in Colarossi's studio, *circa* 1902.

Edward Steichen, *Self-portrait with Brush and Palette*, 1902.

Above, left:
Edward Gordon Craig,
in Brussels, 1905.

Above, right:
Isadora Duncan,
in Brussels, 1905.

Right: Kathleen.

Above: Kathleen and Con's wedding.

Left: Kathleen and Con with Sir Clements Markham, photographed by Herbert Ponting on board the *Terra Nova* during the preparations for the Antarctic expedition, 1910.

George Bernard Shaw, 1932.

Sir James Barrie, by Harry Furniss.

Asquith in 1919, by
A. Cluysenaar.

Nansen, bronze by Kathleen Scott,
1934, from a sketch done in 1912.

Left: Kathleen and Peter
at Sandwich.

Below: Riches, bronze by
Kathleen, made in
Paris 1905/6.

Kathleen was not supposed to be well enough to write letters, but she bribed a nurse with a peach to send a letter to Beerbohm thanking him for a copy of *The Happy Hypocrite* that he had sent her. He was glad she liked it, because he 'should have supposed it rather sentimental for you. But there is a certain amount of sincerity in the sentimentalism of it; and the writing is decidedly pretty. It is the only popular thing I have written: I might be quite rich now if I had continued in that vein. But that vein left me, and I have to make the best of myself as a more or less earnest critic of things.' Happily, that vein came back.

He drew her a little picture of his new moustache ('it entirely takes away all the character from my face, and I am so refreshed!') and one of flowers, when the shops were shut and he couldn't send her any. When she was better she sculpted him, and the letters continue frequent and affectionate into the autumn of 1907: 'Don't imagine yourself too well,' he wrote in October, 'I mean don't go climbing elms for rooks' nests, or getting up at 3.30 a.m. to hunt otters, or sleeping on mountains (the Shepton Range) to test whether English shepherds are as easily frightened as Greek ones . . .'

Another admirer, a minor contender, was a tall thin fair diplomat, a little younger than her, named Coleridge Kennard. He took her one night on a tour of opium dens, of which there were many at the time, mostly in the East End by the docks. It was not very unusual for louche society to go there; Kathleen however hated it. The first den she visited was 'dark and hellish, its inhabitants evil and desperate'. The second was well-lit and clean, with blue curtains and clean pillow-cases on the berths around the wall. On the wall an inscription read in Chinese 'Whatever is, is good'. A polite and friendly Chinaman offered Kathleen a pipe and she took a tiny puff. In one of the berths she could see a young man in evening dress lying prone. She found the serenity sinister. The third was sad, dull and sordid. Everybody, men and women, lay about in various stages of coma. Kathleen got home just before dawn, sucking oranges. A more cheerful outing was to Covent Garden, where he hired a 'four-wheeler' and filled it with blue flowers for her.

Opium dens were not her only midnight forays. Upstairs from her at Cheyne Walk lived the district maternity nurse.

One night a small girl came to fetch the nurse to an urgent and difficult case; there was a drunken husband, and the family were at great enmity with the landlady, a difficult case to get neighbourly help. The nurse knocked at my door and asked me if I would consider getting up and coming to help her. I had been dancing and had not been long asleep. I leapt up and the two of us, led by the minute, frightened child, went running through the wet night. The husband was in a sodden sleep, and the woman was suffering as quietly as she could, lest he should wake. 'He's safest like that, Miss,' she said. Dexterously and beautifully the nurse worked, while I boiled kettles and did as I was instructed. I made the little girl lie down on her mattress on the floor and covered her eyes with her own scarf, so that soon, in spite of all, the mite was asleep. When the baby was born I took it and waited till the nurse was ready to attend to it. In two hours we were back home, promising to return at daybreak. From that time seldom a week went by without a summons to go and help. It was terrible to me that out of seventeen cases I only met two who did not look upon the new birth as a misfortune.

Kathleen did not advertise these outings, 'lest it should seem a shocking and disgusting enterprise for a young lady', and on one occasion she had to sneak out of the house to avoid being noticed by Kennard, who was lounging against the railings on the Embankment, gazing up at her window.

+

SEVEN

Frighteningly in Love with Captain Scott

+

1907–1908

IN THE AUTUMN of 1907 Kathleen met two men who were to make her decide about her future. In September, through the dramatist Harley Granville-Barker, she met a young lawyer and writer named Gilbert Cannan; in October she met Captain Scott again, at tea with Mabel Beardsley. Kathleen thought that a man like Scott should not be going to tea parties, but she chopped up her two hats to make a new one for the occasion anyway, and made a collar and cuffs out of a handkerchief. Here is how she recalled that meeting, twenty-five years later:

> There were a dozen or more people in the room when I arrived at the tea party, mostly men, artists, dramatists, actors and the like, many of them known to me. Sitting on a sofa in the back room, with an elderly lady, was Captain Scott. With my invariable instinct to avoid what was attracting me, I moved to the furthermost corner of the party, and allowed myself to be diverted by the gay comedy of Ernest Thesiger, and the heavy disdain of Henry James. What an unexpected setting for a simple, austere naval officer!
>
> Then all of a sudden, and I did not know how, I was sitting in a stiff uncomfortable chair with an ill-balanced cup of tea being trivially chaffed by this very well-dressed, rather ugly and celebrated explorer. He was standing over me; he was of medium height, with broad shoulders, a very small waist, and dull hair beginning to thin, but with a rare smile and with eyes of a quite unusual dark blue, almost purple. I had noticed these eyes ten months before. I noticed them again now, though by electric light. I had never seen their like. He suggested taking me home.

And that, by her own account, was it. 'Life followed up the decision it had made ten months earlier,' she said, as if it were all very clearcut. They walked home together, 'laughing and talking and jostling each other'. On 2 November he tried to telephone her but couldn't get through, so he sent a note inviting her out that night. 'Dinner and the play, dinner and no play, anything you like but do let me come and carry you off.' On the 7th he found 'such strength of mind being brought to bear to control an inclination to stroll along Cheyne Walk . . .'; on the 8th: 'Uncontrollable footsteps carried me along the Embankment to find no light – yet I knew you were there dear heart – I saw the open window and, in fancy, a sweetly tangled head of hair upon the pillow within – dear head, dear sweet face, dearest softest lips – were they smiling? Don't tell me it's all fancy – it seems so long till Friday.' On the 9th she wrote to him, an exuberant black scrawl to his neat and elegant hand: 'To know only the joy of going forward, only the joy of going forward. It's madness, and I cling to my madness and revel in it – for it is my madness, every bit, nay more than yours. Pick up the joy. I have such faith, joy and life and love.'

'She's at home and going to eat a hot pie at 7.30,' she wrote. 'What's he going to do about it? "I'd love to share the hot pie," he replied, "but have just told my mother I would dine with her – I will come after for a little if I may – I'm a real wreck though and will want such a lot of cheering." ' In this note the two shadows which were to flaw their relationship make their first appearance: his family obligations, and his need for being cheered. For now they were small shadows, but they grew.

Kathleen and Con (from his middle name, Falcon) spent ten days together before 'this innocent rock', as she saw him, had to leave London for his naval duties. Within a month of his leaving they had decided to marry.

She was sitting for the painter Charles Shannon when she made up her mind. Shannon had become a friend since she first liked his work in Glasgow in 1901; he lived and worked all his life with Charles Ricketts, and they were known collectively as The Rickyshan. His portrait of Kathleen is in the Johannesburg Municipal Gallery.

'You don't love me at all today,' Shannon said, as she sat, distracted. She told him what was on her mind, and what she had decided. He promptly went out and walked under a bus – not on purpose, and not fatally, but it made her consider. 'What a lot of upheavals and severings I saw looming ahead. Yet, quite clearly, this healthy, fresh, decent, honest, rock-like naval officer was just, just exactly, what I had been setting up in my mind as a contrast to my artistic friends, as the thing I had been looking for.'

This talk of simple austerity and rocklike innocence can give a simplistic picture of Robert Falcon Scott. He was in fact a complicated man and, rather like his bride, a self-created person. Kathleen, since the neglect of her early childhood, had made herself, almost by decision, into a happy, cheerful and energetic woman. She felt happiness to be her duty, and wore that duty so lightly that it seemed a spontaneous and natural part of herself. Scott made himself into a great leader of expeditions, an honourable officer, a British hero. His great achievement was in conquering his own weaknesses. What they had in common was willpower.

Con was the son of a naval family from Devon. He was born on 6 June 1868, and at thirteen, in 1881, he joined the naval training ship *Britannia*. Here he slept in a hammock and learnt to be a seaman – navigation, astronomy, elementary physics, geometry and trigonometry. He first went to sea at fifteen. He was bred in naval discipline, in obeying orders and surviving bureaucracy, in accepting what was and making the best of it. He was trained in obedience, toughness and in covering up feelings and delicacies. His childhood, though, had been comfortable and loving, and he had been a fairly weedy boy, given to dreaming, and happy to play in the garden with his brother and four sisters. He had a pony. His mother Hannah was religious and devoted to her children, as they were to her. His father John had escaped a service career through bad health, and the family lived modestly but securely on the proceeds of a small brewery which he had inherited from his father. Con had had time to develop a gentler side which was always to remain at odds with the navy.

The main result of this dichotomy was personal insecurity. He was never certain of himself, never sure that he would be able to do what was asked of him. A scrap of diary remains from when he was twenty-one:

It is only given to us cold slowly wrought natures to feel this dreary deadly tightening at the heart, this slow sickness that holds one for weeks. How can I bear it. I write of the future; of the hopes of being more worthy; but shall I ever be – can I alone, poor weak wretch that I am, bear up against it all. The daily round, the petty annoyance, the ill health, the sickness of heart – how can one fight against it all. No one will ever see these words, therefore I may freely write – what does it all mean?

Scott's financial situation made things more difficult for him. Naval officers in those days were assumed to have a private income with which to maintain certain standards. Through his youth, in the lower ranks, things had not been too bad for Scott, but as he came to adulthood, with the attendant extra expenses, it was often difficult for him to keep up. He was doing well in the navy, specializing in torpedoes and advancing at a respectable rate. Then in 1894, when Con was twenty-five, his mother announced to the family that they were virtually bankrupt. John Scott had sold the brewery a few years earlier, and they had all been living not on the interest, as they thought, but on the capital, and now there was none left. John took on a job as a brewery manager; one sister, Ettie, went on the stage and the other two set up as dressmakers. From Con came 'a fine manly reliable letter offering help', wrote his mother. Three years later John Scott died and the family was penniless. Hannah went to live with her daughters Kate and Monsie in rooms in Chelsea, and Con gave £70 a year, not much under half his salary, to her upkeep. His brother Archie sent £200 a year from Africa, but in 1898 Archie too died, and the family's security fell to Con. He never resented this, never said a word of complaint, and never even thought of it lightly. He loved his mother.

On top of this Con had a sense that his profession, his whole line of expertise, was in some way valueless. He terribly wanted to be able to write, 'to express myself on paper even as an ordinary gentleman should', and was aware of his deficiencies in artistic and intellectual matters. He wanted more than the navy was giving. He wanted to test himself, he was restless, he had to make further headway in the navy to earn the money to keep his family, and to keep himself up to naval standards. There must be no slipping. In 1899, about the same time that Kathleen lay tossing and turning at her uncle's great granite house at Downhill deciding that yes she would go to Paris, Con was applying to command the naval expedition to the Antarctic.

That first expedition started with hard work, frustration and delay in the setting up and organization; it continued with hard work, frustration and delay in the accomplishment, and at the end, in 1904, Scott returned to London something of a hero. 'Never has any polar expedition returned with so great a harvest of scientific results,' said Sir Clements Markham, the Royal Geographical Society president, whose inspiration had maintained the expedition from conception to completion. There was an invitation to Balmoral, a CVO, press accolades. That there was no knighthood was commented upon, and put down to rivalry and politics between the RGS, the Royal Society and the navy. There were those who held that scientific exploration was not the job of the navy, that scientists not sailors should have led the expedition, that the navy's job should have been simply to get the scientists there and back.

For Con personally, the expedition was a success. He received medals and approbations from geographical societies around the world, and he was made a member of the French Legion of Honour. He was particularly pleased by an honorary doctorate of science from Cambridge University. His immediate plan was to give lectures and to write his book of the expedition, and for this purpose he rather nervously took nine months off from the navy. He was lionized around London. 'I've had enough of notoriety to last me a lifetime,' he wrote at the height of it all. 'There's been no peace, no quiet – nothing but one mad rush.' He did, however, like meeting the sort of people with whom he had had no contact before: writers, actors, politicians, society figures. He was excited and interested by this world, but despite his status in it as a dashing explorer, he became even more aware of what he felt to be his deficiencies. James Barrie, who became a great friend of Con's and later of Kathleen's, met him at this time, and recalled arguing at length 'a comparison of the life of action (which he poohpoohed) with the loathly life of those who sit at home (which I scorned)'.

This was the not-so-simple naval officer whom Kathleen met and fell in love with. She soon began to learn his complexities. He went back to sea shortly after their meeting and began to write to her. His letters echo the sad diary from his youth. 'I seem to have a million things to say to you yet a sense of oppression of forty years wrestling with hard facts. I fight myself,' he wrote; and 'I know we stand on such a trembling insecure foothold.' He wrote of 'waves of difficulty washing all round our feet'. He was afraid that she couldn't love him, that he couldn't be good enough for her, that he was a dull old thing compared to the people she'd known, that he would come between her and her work, that she would prefer someone else, that they wouldn't have enough money. This last at least was true, and was the root of the trouble between Kathleen and Con's family.

He was by now earning about £800 a year, though he would be on half pay whenever he was not at sea. To Kathleen, quite accustomed to counting her centimes, this seemed a fortune, but Scott had his family to think of, and his family had always expected him to do his duty by marrying money. He himself had said 'half in joke . . . if I married I would look out that the young lady had lots of money.' He was paying at least £200 a year to his mother, and he drew up a potential budget for his and Kathleen's married life, covering coal, food, laundry and a servant at £45 a year. If it was poverty, it was poverty of a certain class.

Kathleen met Hannah Scott in November 1907, and even the first meeting was not without problems.

> My dear Mrs Scott, [Kathleen wrote] I wish I could have come down at once but I have things to do tomorrow which I cannot escape. May I come down before lunch on Wednesday? I have an engagement that evening with Mabel Beardsley, I shall find out from her if it would matter if I broke it and will let you know. I do hope you aren't hating me very much, I'm afraid I should if I were you . . . Con tells me such beautiful things about you, so that I hated never seeing you, Yours, Kathleen Bruce.

What the deeply religious and financially nervous Hannah Scott made of a young penniless artist who had lived alone in Paris and was on engagement-breaking terms with Aubrey Beardsley's scandalous sister can only be imagined. Con played mediator: 'You're in a fair way to capture my mother's head, she was full of you today,' he wrote to Kathleen. 'What did you say to her, do or say you little witch?' And to his mother he wrote, 'Dearest Mother, of course Kathleen loved you. She came back full of her visit to you.' Hannah didn't want her love to interfere with Kathleen's; Kathleen had never imagined that it might. 'I can't bear to be disliked and distrusted and I felt (foolishly maybe) that it amounted to that,' Kathleen wrote. 'She shall love me for I shall love her and make her.' But feelings were not too bad. On New Year's Eve 1907 Hannah wrote to her son clearing the way for him. 'You have carried the burden of the family since 1894,' she said. 'It is time now for you to think of yourself and your future. God bless and keep you.'

This helped, but it didn't solve all the panics that struck the couple. On 2 January Con wrote to Kathleen: 'Dear my dear I see so little of you don't I. I'm very gloomy about everything tonight.' On the 4th she had a grand attack of cold feet, and wrote to him:

> Dearest Con. Don't let's get married. I've been thinking a lot about it and though much of it would be beautiful, there is much also that would be very very difficult. I have always really wanted to marry for the one reason, and now that very thing seems as though it would only be an encumbrance we could scarcely cope with . . . The relief of knowing that you need not worry or uproot your sweet little mother will compensate. If we had gone and done it right away, I would have gone through with it and made it all right, but now the more I think of it the more it seems to me I'd better stop. We're horribly different, you and I, the fact is I've been hideously spoilt. I am not going to tell you to forget me or any such nonsense, but let's abandon the idea of getting married and don't let's look at any more houses. There are things about it I'm not sure I can face.

It was all rather too much for her. It may have occurred to her that twenty-eight years of independence was quite something to give up; that her baby plan was a fantasy which had never really involved anyone else in any realistic sense. The first story she wrote as a child started 'Mr — had a wife but she did not live with him', and in the face of real marriage to a real man the combination of inclination and circumstance which had moulded her orphaned independence suddenly came to the fore again.

Con replied in the tone that led Kathleen to describe him as 'a grand man; no self-pity, no suspicions, no querulousness, no recriminations. Perfect man!'

> I want to marry you very badly, [he wrote] but it is absurd to pretend I can do so without facing great difficulty and risking a great deal for others as well as for myself. If I was very young I should probably take all risks and win through. In facing poverty we should be living and believing in a better future. The old can only live in the present. My mother is 67, only a strand of life remains. She has had a hard life in many respects. I set myself to make her last years free from anxiety. I can't light-heartedly think of events that may disturb that decision ... Little girl, if you care, be patient and we'll pull things straight – have faith in me. But you must work with me, dearest, not against me. Dearest heart, I love you very much. So much that it is making me unhappy to think how little it can mean to you ... You won't have to face heroics or troubles of any sort when you decide.

They were reconciled; the marriage would go ahead, though they still did not announce it.

On 25 January 1908 Con took command of the battleship HMS *Essex*. He was thinking about another Antarctic expedition. He didn't yet know when or how it could be done, but it had to be done. The South Pole had to be reached. Honour required it, England expected it, the job had been started and everybody was thinking of it. 'So near and yet so far', was the ultimate verdict on the *Discovery* journey.

Constant throughout polar exploration at this time was the dichotomy of what it was actually for. 'For scientific research', all those involved would swear solemnly, and they meant it, but the press, hoi polloi, and perhaps the explorers' own deepest yearnings, spoke of patriotic achievement, of territorial claims, of the glory of the Empire, of the Race to the Pole. Something of a belief existed that by being the first to discover and explore McMurdo Sound, Scott had an exclusive claim to that approach to the Pole, and perhaps an exclusive right to attempt the Pole at all, but this could not be relied on. In the winter of 1907–1908 Scott's old team-mate Shackleton had made an Antarctic foray and had been forced (or had chosen – there was much dispute) to land where he had promised Scott he would not. Shackleton was still in the south. What might he do when travelling became possible again in the winter season of 1908–1909? Others, 'foreigners', were interested too. Con knew that he would have to get a move on if he were to do it at all. But, in the context of the Antarctic, getting a move on was not something a person should hold their breath over.

In March 1908 Con was in France testing sledges; frequently he was away at sea. Kathleen, out and about in London, was 'pumped and pumped and pumped' by Mabel Beardsley (who had rather possessive feelings about Con) for information on the romance. An aunt informed that she had heard that Con was 'cooling off'. Mabel 'told my fortune by cards, and said that I was going to have trouble with a fairish man because of a woman's treachery, but that all would be made happy for me with a very dark man with much wealth and good fortune. What rot!' At the end of March Kathleen called it off again. 'I won't marry you, Con, anyhow. Goodbye, dearest. I love you very very much.'

'She's frighteningly in love with him I should think,' Rosslyn Bruce wrote to his own fiancée, Rachel Gurney, 'but tells me that she never writes to him without saying let's put it off again and forget and forgive! What odd things girls really are.' Fright was the key word.

But they made up again. She wrote to him from Tenterden: 'I'm staying with Ellen Terry. She says she's met you and she'd like to marry you very much. She's the biggest, greatest, largest, loveliest person to be with, with a magnetism and affection positively over- whelming. It does one good to meet such people.' Was there a note of detrimental comparison when she continued, 'You have had bad luck. Why can't I help you?'

Soon after, she was staying with Lady Muriel Paget at Shepton Mallet, and aligning herself entirely with Scott, in her own way. 'There are seven or eight men staying here and I'm desperately in love with several, of course. But I'm being very good in spite of all the coercion. It is fun. Balfour and George Wyndham and Speyer . . .' This last was a city man, whom she charmed in hope of finance for the second Antarctic expedition. (There was a piece of doggerel cur- rent, about the self-made and newly-titled City men's wives: I love to see dear Lady Speyer/Climbing higher and higher and higher/I'm really quite fond/Of dear Lady Mond/And even of dear Lady Meier.)

On 2 April Scott reported a nasty accident during manoeuvres in which lives were lost. It was upsetting all round, and though he was not responsible it was still a black mark. Kathleen wrote back quickly: 'Con, dearest, I'm afraid I'm getting very very fond of you. That accident made me imagine for just one short moment what it would be like to lose you. Silly, of course, but there it is.'

'My girl, I love you, I love you,' he responded on 7 April. 'It's just ridiculous. I'm too lonely for words without you.'

✦

EIGHT

Darling I Will Be Good When We're Married

✦

1908

IN APRIL Kathleen met Gilbert Cannan again. She had been sculpting all the while, and it was as if her old wild artist's life had sent out a beautiful envoy specially to win her back from marriage and propriety.

Gilbert Cannan was the exact opposite of Scott, if such a thing could be; exactly the sort of tumultuous artistic friend from whom she felt the urge to get away, but with whom she found it very hard to break. He was a young novelist and playwright, an astonishingly handsome young man, and the very archetype of those whom the gods have cursed and first call promising. Even in his obituaries he was called promising. He was a few years younger than her, and for three months in that spring of 1908 he was quite convinced that they belonged together. He wrote every day, sometimes three times a day, to tell her so. She loved his letters, and who would not? But they disturbed her. This is the first:

14.4.08. Monday night. My dear K. Quite, quite impossible to sleep. After I left you I wandered miles and miles and miles – and miles. Exactly where I don't know, through mean streets and pompous streets, vulgar streets and streets gentle, streets where there was air and streets where there was no air, streets where the people were not asleep but all dead, and streets where there was god. NB. All these beautiful reflections are of subsequent date. The cause of the wanderings was the wonderful you, the maker of beautiful things, the creator alone and without male assistance of enough lovely babies to stock the whole world civilized and uncivilized – though I imagine that in the babies' kingdom there is no knowledge of civilization or they would surely refuse to visit civilized men and women – (I'm hopelessly lost in trying to express all the things that are whirling about in the . . . region of thoughts. Back to the beginning. You) What about you? – oh – yes. That you should have – have – have – I don't know – given me so many hours of yourself. Liked my work. Liked me. Ye Gods. It seems impossible – Do I sleep, do I dream, is babies about? There be babies about and one of them has closed a little pink dimpled hand round my crooked and rather dirty forefinger and led me clean out of myself and everything that I have ever known before like a dream. NO – everything before is the dream . . . and the reality of all the world is concentrated in you . . . Perhaps I have only dreamt it – never mind I'll hug the dream and that won't be any nuisance to you as the reality might be – but precious of persons I feel better. By the next time I see you I shall hope to have discovered whether I am standing on my head or on my heels. Goodnight. GC.

This was the first letter, and it would have been kinder of Kathleen to have told him then that it *was* a dream, that he *was* standing on his head . . . but she didn't know. If Cannan was her last fling with intellectual Bohemian romance before signing herself up to the reliable austere naval rock, and if she did it consciously, it was a cruel thing. More likely she was torn within herself. She was enchanted by his 'crooked smile and corn-coloured hair', and she was half-terrified at the prospect of marriage. She was flattered, and the neglected child in her was always willing to accept love, if only on her own terms. She didn't want to hurt him; on the contrary she wanted to help him. She compared him to 'a sweet pea, needing a good stick to twine around, otherwise strangling its sweetness in the mud; and I visualised myself as a nice, brightly painted green stick, busy propping up beautiful flowers with limp stems.'

But Gilbert Cannan was not the only beautiful flower: 'It's no use my being a green stick, I must be a bundle of green sticks; but the father of my son is not among these. He will have a stem, a sturdy hard wood stem of his own.' Cannan said himself that he found himself 'a sort of son' to 'a ridiculous number of people', and signed his letters to Kathleen 'Your Boy'. Kathleen really wanted, and had in Con, a man who had proved himself – despite, or perhaps because of, his self-doubt. Compare Cannan's letter to one from Con on 19 April: 'I am very depressed to think that I shall see so little of you, but when I can come I must be always with you. Do you understand, these are clear orders. Goodbye, take care of yourself, and you are not to go without lunch again.' Con could be poetical and romantic, but he was a grown-up, and Cannan was not.

So what did Con make of it all? He almost certainly knew that Cannan was paying court to his fiancée. This letter from Kathleen would have been in response to his objections: 'Con sweet one everything is perfectly harmonious and will be – why not – because I let you know that I'm happy when fine creatures love me and show their generosity – must I learn to be discreet and secretive . . . And if I mayn't write what I like to the man I'm going to marry a few weeks before I marry him, what may I do. Darling I will be good when we're married.'

Meanwhile she spent the evening of the 21st with Cannan: 'I see myself and yourself as one,' he wrote the next day, 'part of nature, in nature . . . Sweet, my sweet, it means freedom, light, purity, truth and love to us.' Two days later they spent the evening together again. 'The wonder of last night will be with me always,' he wrote the next day, but as he wrote it, on 24 April, she was meeting Con at Victoria Station, home from the sea. Cannan sat at home in Temple Gardens writing to her: 'If "you and me" is absurd then life is only a silly, silly game played by the gods.' And he had his own thoughts on Scott.

> It is as though I had three pebbles to drop into the well of truth. Each sinks far far down and the rings spread over the water so that I cannot see. Then bubbles rise; beautiful bubbles that look silvery truth, but at the surface they are no more and again there are three pebbles in my hand, and until you come to throw one away there will be three – which? . . . Without you it's all nothing . . . 'Without you' are words so ghastly sinister and forbidding that they come to the lips fascinating by the tenor of their sound – 'With you' is incredible and makes to swoon – ever, ever, GC

And later the same day:

> Dear, have my letters today been mad and monstrous? I am sorry. It has been a ghastly day – great joy and often black despair, misery like that which made Meredith write *Modern Love* when his first wife

left him – but you haven't left me. Dear, it was only after you had flung the first stone and we knew that each knew, that the thing grew, flamed up in us and merged the two of us. What can you be but mine, or I but yours? I must see you tomorrow . . . oh! mine, mine, mine, mine!

He did see her on the 25th: all three of the pebbles met, very civilized, very grown-up. It must have been worst for Con. Kathleen at least had the comfort of being the object of desire, and Cannan was wondering if a ménage à trois might not be a good idea. Con just wanted to marry the woman he loved, who was, for whatever good or bad reasons, leading him a dance.

'Dear You,' wrote Cannan to Kathleen the next day, 'I'm so glad that RS came up this morning. He's a dear clean thing and, 'cept that he don't see things, and never will, "right". He could laugh although he was being hurt all the time. You laughed too and I laughed and laughing all together it seems perfectly ridiculous that you can't have both of us since you are so rapacious that the love of the one you love isn't enough for you. All the same whether you take me as husband in body as well as in spirit or only as a friend I can't leave you again . . . It's a queer tangle. It really is gigantically funny.' He compared her choice with that of a child who chooses a penny over a sixpence because the penny is 'comfortably large', and he says he won't kiss her again, or only her hand, 'unless you say'.

Within two days Kathleen told Cannan that she had chosen the penny, and he let her know what he thought of that: 'Dear. You're quite wrong. But you can't help the wrongness. You mustn't leave me.' And again the same day: 'My dear, dear, dear. You shall not do this wicked thing . . .' The letters continue: 'Dear Light o' the sun, I've been ridiculously happy ever since I left you standing there . . . You belong to me, and no blazing folly that you choose to commit can alter that'; 'Dear God-in-me, you are a wicked, wicked blasphemous woman, but I love you. The wild audacity with which you can fling the biggest thing over your shoulder and put out your tongue at life forces an admiration almost shuddering from me.'

She was not writing to Con. He charged her with it on 5 May: 'Why? Why? Why? I conjure up all sorts of horrible reasons. Tell me they aren't true.' And on the 8th he offered to withdraw: 'You know if you wish things different I shall have only a silent memory of what has been. I am to be trusted altogether in such a case. I have this rather desperate thought because another mail has come and no letter.'

On 9 May she summoned Cannan but he wouldn't visit her; on 11 May he wrote that he was obsessed with her Macedonian experiences – she had given him her notebooks to read – and that he had a bad headache. Con was not cheerful that day either: 'I'm sad tonight. It is difficult to know what to do and all the time I'm conscious of bringing unhappiness to you. It is I who make you cry. Disappointment in me, I think, though your sweet generosity wouldn't admit it. Kathleen dearest don't let your happiness be troubled.'

But her happiness was troubled. After years of living untroubled by her effect on men she was learning at close quarters that being loved is not always easy.

Cannan was quite serious when he suggested a ménage à trois. He was close friends with James and Mary Barrie, whose curious relationship with Sylvia Llewellyn Davies is well chronicled, and later he and his young girlfriend Gwen Wilson lived with a second man, Henry Mond. But a ménage à trois was not what Kathleen had in mind as the family for her son, and Cannan was not the father for her son. He knew it himself; though he specially loved her baby statues, though he referred again and again to babies they might have, and likened their love to a baby waiting to be born, he accepted that a 'volcanic father and equally volcanic and vagabond mother' would not prove the best parents. Con would win on that card, if nothing else, but still Kathleen was being to Cannan a 'sweet contradiction, false woman and true woman . . . – Oh! madness, to abuse you is only to caress you with words . . .'

And madness was the problem. Cannan spent the last thirty years of his life in a lunatic asylum, quite separated from reality by schizophrenia. Before that he knew many other sorrows. He filled his novels and plays with unflattering portraits of his friends and contemporaries, and lost their friendships. He had an affair with Mary Barrie, consummated within weeks of Kathleen and Con's wedding, and though he offered to share her with Barrie he was required by honour, circumstance and a nasty divorce case to marry her. She was fifteen

years older than him, but it seemed for a while as if things would
work out well for them. However, that marriage began to fail and he
met Gwen Wilson, with whom he fell in immediate love rather as
he had done with Kathleen (Gwen had also been a student at the
Slade, and was a friend of Augustus John).

Again Cannan offered to share, again it was not acceptable to Mary.
Cannan's mental stability began to rock again, and he spent a period
in a nursing home before obtaining a judicial separation from Mary
and moving Gwen into his studio. Three years into that relationship
Henry Mond, son of Sir Alfred, the first Lord Melchett, fell off his
motorcycle near their studio in Elm Park Gardens, and in the fashion
of the times, could not be moved. Gwen brought him in, he stayed,
and Cannan finally had his ménage à trois. But it was not at his
instigation.

In 1919 Cannan went to the United States on a trip, and while he
was away, in January 1920, Henry and Gwen married without telling
him. They promised to look after him and took him with them on
their honeymoon trip through Europe to Africa; in Rhodesia he left
them, travelled on on his own, and finally went mad. Kathleen was
told years later that Mond paid his asylum fees. One of his delusions
was that he was Captain Scott, the famous explorer.

THE REAL Captain Scott wrote to his mother in May: 'Now, my
dear, I must tell you I want to marry Kathleen Bruce – but she and
I are agreed that under no circumstances must your comfort suffer.
Now all I ask of you is to get to know the girl I love and to break
up this horrid condition of strain in which we have been living . . . I
do so want to make for a happier state of affairs all round.'

In the midst of all this Muriel Paget, a distant cousin, mentioned
to Kathleen that her husband Arty very much wanted to go on a
walking tour of Italy. Muriel was not free, but perhaps Kathleen
might like to go? Whether she knew of Kathleen's entanglements is
unknown, but her suggestion was timely. Kathleen was human enough
to wonder whether Cannan could live without her, and practical
enough to realize that he would have to get used to it. Con was afraid
the trip was an excuse, and said so. 'My dear, my dear,' she wrote,

'you mustn't think if I meant to do things like that that I should do it in so cowardly a way – no no dear. Darling I'm so sorry I hurt you, so so sorry dear one.' In her 1932 autobiography, she remembered him saying just 'Write to me often, and don't stay too long', and that pleasing her, but it wasn't so simple. She did write to him, of 'gentian and baby goats and waterfalls making rainbows and swallow-tailed butterflies and yellow violets and white white mountains and green and purple valleys and joy in your vagabond's heart'. And she wrote: 'Dear dear dear Con, you must stop loving a little vagabond – I've got it in my blood, dearest – How I love it. The freedom and irresponsibility of it is very precious to me.'

> Knock a few conventional shackles off me, [Con wrote] and you'll find as great a vagabond as you – but perhaps that won't do. I shall never fit into my round hole. The part of a machine has got to fit – yet how I hate it sometimes . . . I love the open air, the trees, the fields and seas – the open places of life and thought. Darling you are the spirit of all these to me though we have loved each other in crowded places. I want you to be with me when the sun shines free of fog . . . Be patient with all this foolishness.

While in Italy Kathleen saw Isadora in Venice, and wrote to Con about that, which produced another attack of non-artistic inferiority:

> Do you realize you will have to change me, infuse something of the joyous pure spirit within you? A year or two hence it would have been too late, I should have been too set to admit the principle of change . . . All this because you have met Isadora Duncan, and I see you half worshipful, wholly and beautifully alive, and I love you for it. Here is the antithesis of all that's worldly and conventional. I know this, I say to myself over and over, I love this – but oh the grinding effects of a mechanical existence – in the end I am half fearful. Shall I satisfy you?

Later, Kathleen sent him a picture of Isadora, while he was at sea. He sent it back, saying that it was not to do with his life, and better that he should not have it.

'Sweetheart, what I know and you do not,' he wrote to her, apropos money but equally relevant to many aspects of their relationship, 'is our Service with its machine-like accuracy and limitations.' Kathleen responded with sympathy and reassurance and the odd pinprick of bathos, apropos both their relationship and his work. 'Here am I a little ass of a girl who's never done a thing in her life allowing a real man to talk to her of superiority,' she wrote. 'My sense of humour can't be doing with it.' And: 'You shall go to the Pole. Oh dear me what's the use of having energy and enterprise if a little thing like that can't be done. It's got to be done so hurry up and don't leave a stone unturned.'

One morning as Arty Paget was sitting on a rock in the middle of a stream shaving, Kathleen called to him, 'You know that lovely naval officer, Captain Scott? I'm going to marry him. Say you're glad!' Arty cut himself, and so it was official.

'What's making us half unhappy?' wrote Con from his new ship, HMS *Bulwark*, on 25 June. 'It's just simply lack of money. I see it all. My people's attitude, delighted with you personally, ready to love you, yet vaguely disappointed because their minds have nursed a thought of worldly things and in me lay their women's hopes. Don't blame them.' Kathleen, who had never had or expected or been much concerned with money, was remarkably patient with these rather shameless bourgeois shenanigans. 'All's bound to come right, and if it doesn't, why then it's probably far better that it shouldn't. I shall be happy whatever things happen and that is true!'

In July they found a house: eight rooms with a garden studio for Kathleen to sculpt in, in a Georgian terrace on Buckingham Palace Road, for £50 a year. Victoria Coach Station stands on the site now. 'Oh, dearie, don't marry me if you'd rather not,' she wrote; and, 'Oh my dear, how lovely we are going to make everything! You and me. You and me. You and me. I've always been just me before. Now it's you and me and it's good.' 'Love me more and more, because I need it,' she wrote. He wrote to his mother: 'Try to be kind to Kathleen. She has lots of friends and people who love her but she has never had a home.'

Letters began to fly. Kathleen wrote to Rosslyn: 'Man child woolly bird I've gone and been and done it now – I've gone and been and decided to marry Capt South Pole Scott. Do you think that's a good scheme? Speks we'll do it about August or September – seems rather a hurry, but there's nothing much to wait for – and my trousseau won't take long cos there ain't agoin' to be no trousseau – and we're going to be very poor but that's a sensation I'm accustomed to . . . We're going to have a darling little place in town if anyone asks what we'd like for a wedding present, if they have exquisite taste, tell them furniture, if not tell them cheques, or postal orders!! . . . I haven't told the family yet, but I'm going to soon . . . Will they all say "quite time too!" Be a good lad and write to me by return, and don't talk nonsense, but just tell me what you think of it – eh?'

Max Beerbohm sent congratulations on Independence Day, remarking how inappropriate a day it was. He promised them 'some hideous presents'. Later Gilbert Cannan wrote: 'Kathleen, dear, I don't know the date of your marriage and I'm going to France at the end of next week. I do wish you and Con all the widest and most vivid happiness – and make a splendid baby – But you will – I know, I know. In the little house I see you next a great woman striding to her purpose. So? Ever yours, and Con's.'

James Barrie was rather upset because he learnt of the engagement through a third party. Kathleen wrote quickly to Con: 'We must not hurt so sensitive and dear a person. Please write quite by return of post. He is at Black Lake Cottage, Farnham. As nice a letter as ever you can think of.' Con wrote to Barrie, and then to Kathleen saying he couldn't really cope with all the letter-writing because he was so busy and he had to get up at 3.30 in the morning. Later, when Cannan and Mary Barrie were breaking Barrie's heart, Kathleen, in a perhaps idealistic attempt at comfort, sent Cannan's note of congratulation to Barrie. She wrote on the bottom: 'You must love this boy too, because I do. He is one of the very fine natures.'

Con wrote to Rosslyn, courtesies and 'we don't know where to be married but your aunt has suggested Hampton Court and it sounds delightful – no to be more honest – from male man's point of view it seems as pleasant a place as can be chosen for a trying ceremony.'

Rosslyn wrote to his bride-to-be Rachel Gurney: 'You cannot imagine how catching her indifference to the ceremony part is. I suppose someone will wake her up to caring about it before the day, but I've heard nothing about invitations or anything.'

Kathleen was never very interested in clothes. She couldn't bear herself 'dressed up', and James Lees-Milne later described her as the worst-dressed woman he knew, with a 'sort of aggressive no-taste'. But when she thought there wasn't going to be no trousseau she was reckoning without her well-dressed fiancé, 'who has to think a little of what the navy considers *comme il faut*', as Rosslyn put it. 'She won't let him give her any jewellery not even a ring nor will she submit to the usual veil and orange blossom,' he wrote to Rachel. 'Kiddie [Kathleen] is a quaint child . . . she has offered to give me a pearl necklace Nellie [a Downhill Bruce cousin, wife of the 4th baronet] sent her.'

Con had to have words with her. 'The serious consideration', he wrote, 'is that when we are married you mustn't only look nice (which you can't help) but you must look as though there wasn't any poverty at all . . . You've admired my clothes and just think of my feelings when I am so to speak "expensively" dressed whilst your costume shows a saving spirit . . . Kathleen dearest I am dreadfully sensitive to appearances.' She promised to get a smart frock so that he could see 'what a fright I look'.

Despite the main parties' reluctance to have any fuss, the wedding, on 2 September 1908, was traditional, proper, splendid and reported in all the papers. The headline on the front page of the *Daily Mirror* read 'Famous Explorer Married', and the story followed in detail. 'The wedding took place by permission of the King in the Chapel Royal, Hampton Court Palace.' (This was thanks to Kathleen's aunt Zoe Thompson, widow of the Archbishop of York, who was living at Hampton Court in a grace and favour apartment.) The bride 'was given away by her brother Lieut. Wilfrid Bruce, R.N., of HMS *Arrogant*. She wore a dress of white satin trimmed with Limerick lace and a bodice of chiffon with a wreath of natural myrtle and a tulle veil.'

The best man was Captain Henry Campbell, so tall and handsome that when Kathleen saw him she whispered to Con, 'Could I marry him instead?' Rosslyn took the service, and scarlet-clad choristers sang. Despite the sunshine there were three nicely timed claps of thunder, seen by the naval element in the congregation as a salute from heaven. Rodin and his wife were among the 150 guests, and the King sent a telegram. 'Huge crowds gathered', continued the *Daily Mirror*, 'as Captain and Mrs Scott left by motor car for London and then France. The bride was wearing a tailor-made costume of blue serge and wore a large brown hat with blue wings.' *The Times*'s report of the wedding ended, 'The marriage will make no difference to Capt. Scott's future plans with regard to Antarctic exploration.'

Kathleen had made the sartorial effort – she even made the dress – but she didn't enjoy the ceremony. It was a lovely day and she wished she could have been outside. She was glad to head for France, to be alone with Con (Max Beerbohm had recommended hotels to them) but the honeymoon was brief, spent 'as confusedly and insecurely as most honeymoons', in Kathleen's words.

Kathleen had engaged a couple to 'do' for them at their house in Buckingham Palace Road, and they were to have the house ready on the newlyweds' return. Kathleen suggested a shoulder of lamb to be waiting for their dinner, because it was the only joint of meat she had ever heard of, and she knew they ought to have one. She had finally admitted to Rosslyn that she liked the idea of having a home after all this time, and was rather proud of being well-organized about all this. She was determined everything should be 'very snug and conventional'. But when she and Con arrived at their new home the cupboard was bare and the servants were drunk. Kathleen was terribly upset. She shrieked, and kicked the couple out. Con wondered what they'd stolen, admired the new chintzes, took his wife's arm and suggested a nice restaurant. Thus the volcanic vagabond and the not-so-simple innocent rock settled down to married life.

ALMOST WITHOUT REALIZING, Kathleen had become the innocent rock in the relationship. If ever an Englishman had a black dog in his soul – the 'dread thundercloud', Kathleen called it – it was Con at this time, and it was Kathleen to whom he showed it. 'You are the only woman to whom I can tell things,' he had written back in May 1908. His family relied on him to be strong; his men relied on him to be their captain, and he relied on Kathleen. She had joy, certainty, vitality, definite intentions, work she loved – all things that Con wanted, and that she wanted him to have.

'My funny little life is devoid of cares or worries or misfortunes,' she wrote to him. Her only obligations were to sculpt, to get pregnant, and, after all, to play gaily-painted green stick to her new husband. Con's obligations were to go back to sea, and wait. Come the spring of 1909 he would learn whether or not Shackleton had made it to the Pole: if he had not then Scott had no choice but to do it himself. For now he could do nothing definite.

Con went back to sea, captain of HMS *Bulwark*; Kathleen went dancing, gadded about town, and sold her first sculpture, a mask, for 18 guineas. 'There's something so astonishingly fine about your work,' Con wrote, 'such truth and vigour, that you must go on. The development of such work mustn't be lost.' He wasn't sure she should sell her work though. It was quite natural at the time for a man to assume that he would support his family, and to take such pride in doing so that he might actively not want his wife to earn, but for Con it was slightly more than that. He wanted 'no thought of sordid gain' to contaminate her art. But Kathleen longed to sell now – it was a tiny independence for her, and she had no pride about contributing or otherwise to the family coffers. 'I couldn't do things I don't like doing,' she wrote. 'But I love making money – not because I don't want to spend yours. It's because I want us not to think about it.'

'Dearest friend,' she wrote. 'Isn't it lovely to be alive? There's an electric light bill come which shows that we spend 2s a week. That's not much, is it? I wish we could be quite the nicest people in the world. It is lovely to be alive. I emit little shrieks from time to time, now there's no one to hear.' But she missed him. 'Life's so thrilling just at the moment. I wish you were here to share it. May circles of blessing play around you, dear, to keep off the black blight.'

His letters were a mixed joy. He reported the comings and goings of naval life, exercises, duties and pleasures, his frustration with functions: 'full stomachs, torpid brains'. Even though he half despised them, he liked her to know what important things he was doing and which important people were confiding in him. He was involved with frustrating arguments over the merits of the scientific research made during the *Discovery* trip. More pleasant argument was between him and Kathleen over Barrie's latest play: they assured each other that they must be open with each other even when – or especially when – they disagreed. They argued about 'the sex question': 'It's the women, I believe, who keep it in so foremost a place,' he said. 'Of course it's the women who keep up the interest in the sex problem,' she retorted. 'It's their life whether they will or no. They can't get rid of it, however intellectual or well educated they are.' She was rather shocked to find herself 'exactly like all the other women . . . dependent on one man's moods and comments, especially when they are so utterly illogical.'

Con was rather pleased. 'Burst out always,' he wrote. 'Upbraid me. Argue with me. You're the dearest darling of a wife as well as the most intelligent that man ever had.' And, 'Don't allow yourself to be changed. Don't ever strike a note that doesn't spring from your dear natural self because you've an irritable man to please. It is you who must sway the man bringing him better and clearer ideas and (as you have done) showing him where his happiness lies.' She agreed with him that she could be rather over-enthusiastic, but resented being called 'narrowly' so. 'I am just as capable of overdoing it about Haldane, Beethoven, Socrates, Euripides, Anatole France, Muriel

Paget, Mahomet or Leonardo da Vinci. So don't call me narrowly anything.' The word touched a nerve with the vagabond in her. But he pleased her with information, as she had asked Rosslyn to when he went to Oxford. 'A good deal of interesting talk on the sex discussion at the British Association,' Con reports, of a conversation with Hodgson, the marine biologist. 'He says much was highly technical, hingeing on chromosomes. There was much to prove the absence of influence on the embryo by the physical or mental condition of the mother. Hereditary tendencies were considered to play a very large part and then (this is much supported by stock-breeders) the dates with reference to the periodical tribulations of the female. All this would have interested you greatly.' Kathleen would certainly have had something to say about that; she believed strongly in the benefits to a foetus of a cheerful and healthy mother.

But there was also the old vein in Con's letters, the black blight: how wonderful she was, how unworthy he was. 'I've a personality myself, a small mean thing beside yours . . .' he wrote. 'I'm obstinate, despondent, pigheaded, dejected, there's something growing bigger inside that keeps shouting the greatness of you. Girl I could whip myself . . . I'm a clod, a clown, a blockhead.' 'You're so exalted, I somehow can't reach up.' And 'I'm very lonely tonight and I want you so badly. Why can't I look up and see you? I'm impatient. It's being caged here; breakfast, lunch and dinner, all alone in this palatial prison. I get up and walk, then return to sit and wonder about you again. Pity me,' even.

She did, and she tried to cheer him up. 'Dearest you are the nicest husband I've ever had so what's to be done about it. I went to a ball last night, I danced every single dance . . . and I loved it, and it apparently loved me.' 'I flirted with a sailor, just because he was a sailor,' she wrote. She tried being sad too, but it sat unnaturally on her, and she kept breaking into jokes: 'I never used to know anything about loneliness. Sir have you robbed me of my self-sufficiency?' The little house was empty without him; she wanted him to come home and 'strew about a few pipes and some ash'. And she loved him 'desperately, deeply, violently and wholly'.

'There never was, there never could be, anything so beautiful, such a treasure as you,' he wrote.

'Of course I'm not any of the beautiful things you say I am,' she replied, 'but you make me want to be.'

'Tell me more and more of better things,' he wrote.

'Con dear are you still and always an unhappy man?' she wrote. 'Oh what's the matter Con? What is the matter?'

Challenge made Con Scott happy; work fired the discipline which was a faith to him. He liked nothing so much as something to be achieved – 'That fine conception which is realised when . . . men . . . by days and weeks of hard physical labour succeed in solving some problem of the great unknown.' Apsley Cherry-Garrard, the young 'adaptable helper' who went on the second expedition with Scott, summed it up: 'Indefinite conditions always tried Scott most: positive disasters put him in more cheerful spirits than most. In the big gale coming south when the ship nearly sank, and when we lost one of the treasured motors [motor sledges] through the sea ice, his was one of the few cheerful faces I saw. Even when this ship ran aground off Cape Evans he was not despondent.' Tooling around marking time in a series of naval mundanities, wondering whether Shackleton was reaching the South Pole at that very moment, and being separated from his new wife were none of them things to fill Con's heart with joy.

On 4 January 1909 Kathleen wrote: 'My very very dear love, I'm getting so excited and frightened. I'm just going out to post a letter to my doctor. I feel as tho' that will clinch matters . . .' Was she frightened that she might be, or that she mightn't be, or of the fact of being, after all these years of treasuring the idea in her heart? Anyway, she was. Her child was due in the autumn.

'My love my dear love my very dear love throw up your hat and shout and sing triumphantly for it seems we are in a fair way to achieve my aim.' Our end, surely, Con pointed out, not just hers, and though he didn't throw his hat in the air: 'not from want of inclination – only I think a growing sedateness of demeanour, proper parental dignity, prevented me', he did roll the nearest officer on to the floor. And she told him not to worry, because 'we are agreed it is not wise to make life into Hell by anticipating things that may never happen.'

'I did like your philosophy,' he had written soon after the wedding. 'It's true and oh so good for me to reflect on the exaggeration of evils and all the pains we suffer from anticipation.' There could be no painful anticipation here. Kathleen was 'living in a state of exaltation almost amounting to delirium. The sublimation of my existence was now assured. I knew my son would be born in the autumn.' She called the bulge Griselda to start with, perhaps not to tempt fate. 'I have christened her, given her godparents, estimated her wardrobe, designed her tiny trousseau, educated her and soon shall have married her. Oh dear, oh dear, it's too wonderful.' Kathleen lived on fruit and nuts, walked and danced and swam, and studied 'all that I could find'. 'Not for a moment did I fear that the gods would interfere with this gloria in excelsis,' she wrote with hindsight. 'It would be safely born and it would be a boy.'

Three weeks after Kathleen's announcement Con learned that he would be back in London in April, taking on a desk job at the Admiralty for nine months, with a pay rise and a chance to live at home. In March they travelled together to Norway to test out the caterpillar-tracked motor-sledges which Con intended to use in the Antarctic. He wasn't certain that they would be of great use, but he knew that they had to be tried out in the South by someone. Cherry-Garrard said of him later, he was 'always keen to sift even the most unlikely theories if by any means they could be shaped to the desired end'. In Norway Kathleen met for the first time Fridtjof Nansen, the universally respected Norwegian explorer, politician, diplomat, writer and nationalist who became a true friend both to her and to Con. Con knew him already – Nansen had given him useful advice before the *Discovery* trip.

And then later in March the news came from the South. Shackleton had made a superb journey, but he had not reached the Pole. In April 1909 came news from the North. The American Robert Peary, after six attempts, had become the first man to lead a party to the North Pole. This claim was later discredited, but for the moment, territorial claims or no territorial claims, the eyes of the exploring world turned South. The way ahead was clear, the dread thunder-cloud dispersed, and Con knew what he had to do.

James Barrie said that all polar explorers came back vowing that nothing in heaven or earth would tempt them to go near the polar regions again; and at the end of six months they were on their knees to whoever might be able to get them there. Nansen said that the hardest part of any expedition was before departure. Con worked all day at the Admiralty, and in the evenings worked on the expedition – budgeting and finance, motor-sledge design, personnel, routes, livestock, diets, supplies . . . Kathleen sculpted during the day and in the evenings sat pregnant on the sofa, her presence a comfort to him as he devised the expedition which would take him away from her. Early on she took a trip to Paris, and loved it. Con was less pleased, he saw it as a 'glimpse of old-time freedom' and wondered if things were really working between them. He remembered that she had said 'I will love you', as if it were a decision rather than true heartfelt knowledge. 'I want someone to anchor to,' he wrote, 'someone sweet and sound and sure, like yourself. Part of me is wanting this with heart and soul, part is bitterly critical and sceptical of the possible realization of such a dream.' She continued to reassure him.

Why did he not feel sure of her, even when she was married to him and carrying his child? It was a wicked temperamental combination, and an unusual one for the time: the woman who loves her freedoms and her friends as well as her husband, and the man who despite his many attractions ('I have never known anybody, man or woman, who could be so attractive when he chose,' Cherry-Garrard wrote) does not quite believe that he is lovable. And what frightened him in her was the very independence he loved her for.

In the summer she went to Studland to stay with Herbert Alexander. A relative wrote to Rosslyn: 'Kathleen is a nightmare to me, she will do such independent things . . . now she is camping out in Dorset.' Here she received the news of Rosslyn and his wife Rachel Gurney's first child being born. 'Bravo to you,' she wrote to her brother on 3 August:

'Isn't that splendid. Do be a dear and write and tell me all about it. Was she very ill, poor precious, and how much did the new thing weigh, and was everyone there in time, and is she very happy. We're camping, Mr Alexander, Wunchi [a girlfriend from the Slade days] and I, and Con comes tomorrow. Give mother Rachel my dearest love, tell her I am a wee bit jealous that hers is a boy and mine is a girl. You'll have to help us get funds for Con's expedition soon, you know lots of rich people. We must have £40,000 by Xmas. Hurrah to you and Bravo. I go home in about a fortnight unless Griselda arrives too early and sudden-like.

She stayed on at Studland, eating wild raspberries and mushrooms, sleeping on the beach, and swimming by moonlight in the calm water. 'It all seems to do her a world of good,' Con wrote to his sister Etty Ellison McCartney.

Thirty years later, when she thought that she had always thought her child would be a boy, Kathleen remembered floating on her back and gazing at the moon, thinking 'My son will love the nights, and he will love the sea.' On 14 September 1909 he was born – not Griselda at all, but Peter.

> Very large, very healthy, quite perfect was my boy baby; and then a very strange thing happened to me. I fell for the first time gloriously, passionately, wildly in love with my husband. I did not know I had not been so before but I knew it now. He became my god; the father of my son and my god. Until now he had been a probationer, a means to an end. Now my aim, my desire, had been abundantly accomplished. I worshipped the two of them as one, father and son, and gave myself up in happy abandonment to that worship. Now my determined, my masterful virginity, sustained through such strong vicissitudes, seemed not, as I had sometimes feared, mere selfish prudery, but the purposeful and inevitable highway to this culminating joy and peace.

He was named Peter Markham after Peter Pan and Sir Clements Markham, and James Barrie and Sir Clements were to be his god-parents. Con was no more religious than Kathleen in any traditional sense, but as with the wedding there were things considered *comme il faut* and relatives, Con's mother in particular, whom there was no point in upsetting.

THE DAY BEFORE Peter's birth Con's other baby saw the light. The Antarctic Expedition was announced on 13 September (after a courteous exchange with Shackleton, to avoid any further stepping on toes), and Scott declared what the nation wanted to hear: 'The main object of the expedition is to reach the South Pole and secure for the British Empire the honour of that achievement.' He knew perfectly well that whatever his personal priorities, the South Pole was a more glamorous aim than scientific research, and the glamour was what would raise the cash. 'People whose knowledge is derived from the sensational press count success in degrees of latitude,' he told the Royal Institution in May 1910. And to the public, in an article in the *Strand* magazine at the same time, he wrote of exploring 'the entire unknown region of King Edward's Land'; 'the nature and extent of the Great Ice Barrier formation', the higher regions of Victoria Land, the search for radium-bearing pitchblende, meteorology, marine biology . . . 'I admit that the main object of the expedition is to reach the South Pole,' he put, 'but this is largely a matter of sentiment.'

The British press and the public, more than anyone more directly involved, decided that Scott's expedition was to win the South Pole for Britain, and it was from the public that the money had to come. Con needed only the £40,000 that Kathleen mentioned to Rosslyn, but he had no single main sponsor. Every penny had to come in dribs and drabs.

Two months into Kathleen's culminating joy and peace her husband resigned from his Admiralty post, went on half pay and set off around Britain in search of money. Though everyone was very keen for Britain to win this Polar race, no one specially wanted to pay for it. Con travelled the land, talking, holding meetings, courting millionaires, trying to inspire the public. He hated it, and wrote wearily optimistic letters home: 'between £20 and £30 since I went to Wolverhampton'; '£40 today – nothing from Wales'; 'Very poor day yesterday . . . but d'Anson has offered me £30 a year for four years, a really fine subscription.' Kathleen's charming of Sir Edgar Speyer bore fruit: he gave £1000 and agreed to be treasurer of the fund. 'Hear hear,' said *The Times*. In the midst of this Peter caught whooping cough.

Con drummed up £10,000 before the government relented and made him a grant of £20,000. In June 1910 his position was made official, and he went back on full pay as the commander of the National Antarctic Expedition.

Though people were reluctant to give Con money, they were keen to offer themselves. Eight thousand volunteers came forward, including Kathleen's brother Wilfrid, 'broad, beaming, always with a weather

eye for the girls'. He was taken on at a shilling a month, a token
wage. Sixty-three more were chosen; officers, crew, scientists and a
photographer. They included Dr Edward Wilson, known as Uncle
Bill, Scott's old friend and scientific colleague from the *Discovery*; and
a little, ugly and extremely tough fellow called Henry Bowers, known
as Birdie because of his enormous nose. He had been a navigator on
the Irrawaddy and a hunter of gun-runners in the Persian Gulf, and
Cherry-Garrard said he 'never knew a man who treated difficulties
with such scorn'. There was Lieutenant Edward 'Teddy' Evans, later
the First World War hero Lord Mountevans of the *Broke*, who contributed the money he had already raised for an expedition of his own
on condition that he be made second in command, and Petty Officer
Edgar Evans, a huge Welsh seaman with a taste for drink. Captain L.
E. G. Oates of the 6th Inniskilling Dragoons, a Boer War veteran
with a limp to prove it, laconic and dry, paid £1000 to join up and
took charge of the ponies. Cherry-Garrard also offered £1000 to be
allowed to join. When he was turned down (he was only twenty-four,
and had no specialist skills) he insisted the expedition keep the money.
Such gentlemanly action convinced Con that Cherry was just the kind
of man they wanted.

This is Kathleen's story, not Con's: his story has been told so often,
so well and in such detail that it would be foolish to attempt to tell
it again here. Suffice to say that the arrangements were made, the
men engaged, the internal politics solved, the wrangles untangled,
the potential rivals placated, the money raised (almost), the dogs
and the ponies found, and the ship, the *Terra Nova*, purchased.

Throughout, Kathleen was there, giving, as Sir Clements Markham
put it, 'signal help to her husband in all his work connected with the
expedition'. She is recalled seated at Con's feet with a South Polar
map spread out between them; making drawings from his sketches;
charming potential sponsors at every possible opportunity; encourag-
ing her husband in word and deed. On Valentine's Day 1910 Con
wrote to her: 'I was lying abed thinking last night, and all you've
done and are doing for me spread itself out . . . when things look bad,
when I'm tiresome or petulant, don't think your care is wasted. When
I'm away on the snows it will be bad to remember that I've grieved
you, but it would be infinitely worse if I thought that you didn't

know that I understood your sacrifices. My dear, my dear, my heart is very full of you . . .'
And finally everything was ready.

In the course of time, [she wrote] there followed the heart-searchings so well known to those who serve their Empire far away from England. Con must join his ship in Australia for his second Antarctic expedition.

Should I travel to Sydney with him, leaving my nine months son behind? I should; I did. But looking back over my life I can think of nothing that hurt more hideously than unlocking the sturdy fingers that clung around mine as I left the laughing, tawny-haired baby-Hercules for four months – four months of enchanting change and growth that I would be shut out from and would never come again. He would not know me when I came back. He would look to someone else, maybe, for protection from me. Well! I had known; I had chosen, and joy never left me for long. In agonies and ecstasies of reciprocated love I followed my husband.

Despite her expectations, she had turned out to love her husband just as much as her son.

TEN

✦

Going South

✦

1910

ON 16 JULY 1910 Kathleen and Con left Britain together on board HMS *Saxon*, bound for Cape Town. With them were Ory Wilson and Hilda Evans, wives of Uncle Bill and Teddy. The *Terra Nova* had already left, but Scott had remained behind to carry on fund-raising, and was alarmed when the *Saxon* arrived in Cape Town on 2 August to find that the *Terra Nova* was not there waiting for them.

He had enough on his mind already; despite all the work, and he would be gone at least two years, the expedition had still not raised enough money to pay wages beyond New Zealand, and he had to raise another £8,000 from South Africa, Australia and New Zealand to make up the deficit. He had nightmares until the 15th when the ship turned up, safe if not entirely sound. She was overladen, and leaky, but it was not the end of the world. Scott was happy to take command of her – certainly happier than the interim captain, Teddy Evans, who now had to step down again, and than Bill Wilson, who was put on wife duty accompanying Kathleen, Ory and Hilda by liner, RMS *Corinthic*, to New Zealand.

When Con left, Kathleen began to keep a diary. She always had done, intermittently, but this was to be proper and regular. Where Con was going was as far as a person could go from Britain. It took months just to get to New Zealand. For half of each year the explorers would be iced in, with no possibility of any contact. It could take a year for letters to reach them, and a year for a reply to get back. By the time they had got to their initial stopping point on McMurdo Sound they would only have time to settle themselves and make a few trial sledging runs before the Antarctic winter set in and the sun disappeared, not to rise again until late in 1911. They would head for the Pole during the Antarctic summer of the British winter 1911–12, hoping to get back before winter reappeared in the British spring of 1912. Then there would be another winter before they would be able to leave – assuming they didn't decide to stay on for another season. Kathleen decided that for these years she would keep a full and detailed account of her life and their son's to give Con when he returned, to supplement the letters she would write him. On the opening page of her diary for 1910 she wrote: 'Don't lose this book if you can help it, it is fun looking back on.'

They would not actually say goodbye until New Zealand. Kathleen was not at her best during the trip there. She was a bad sailor; she missed Con and didn't want to admit it, and she didn't like being treated as a mere wife. Thirty years as an independent woman had not trained her for the role of overlooked appendage. 'Being treated as an outsider as regards expedition affairs' she felt was particularly unfair. Con, the expedition's leader, didn't treat her that way, so why should anyone else? Wilson, who had been well into the swing of the all-male life on the *Terra Nova* (a favourite game on board was 'Furl Topgallant Sails', where they all ripped each other's clothes off), to her annoyance lumped her in with women in general. 'I gather he thinks women aren't much use, and expect he is judging from long experience, so I bear him no malice,' she wrote in her diary.

She quite understood him being irritated with women in general, she often felt it herself. 'My hatred of women is becoming a monomania and must be curbed,' she wrote; but her dislike was not so much for women themselves as for the follies that contemporary women indulged: 'the vapours', whimsical fey femininity, wilful impracticality. As Michèle Roberts put it: 'In a world which frightens girls by equating femininity with constriction, self-sacrifice and lack of potency, who can blame a female hero for choosing transcendence [and] denial of solidarity with "ordinary" women . . .?' Kathleen hated the weakness of women in putting up with, let alone making the best of, the nonsense of Victorian feminine ideals. Suffragettes, on the other hand, she found graceless. There were many individual women whom she liked. Women she didn't like she had no patience with. Mrs Wilson and Mrs Evans were among the latter.

Kathleen felt that the wives of the expedition should be chosen as

carefully as the men themselves – 'better still, have none'. Wilson
may have thought that the same should go for wives of expedition
leaders, when the *Terra Nova* reached Melbourne on 10 October 1910
and Kathleen insisted on being taken out in heavy seas on a wet
evening to greet the ship. 'Bill was furious and protested that the
other women were cold and hungry, but I knew my man would expect
me . . . I heard my good man's voice and was sure there was no danger,
so insisted, getting more and more unpopular . . . we at last got close
to the beautiful *Terra Nova* with our beautiful husbands on board.
They came and looked down into our faces with lanterns.'

'It was for them on board, Capt Scott and Lieutenant Evans, to say
whether I should risk drowning their wives now,' reported Wilson,
'and as they seemed in favour of it I went in and they soon dropped
down the side of the ship into our launch, and I went on board with
the mails.' Kathleen went on board too, delighted to get away from
Wilson and the wives. Wilson hoped that in future 'it will never fall
to my lot to have more than one wife at a time to look after, at any
rate in a motor launch, in a running sea, at night time.'

In Melbourne there were parties, horseraces (Captain Oates wore
'an indescribable hat') and a visit to a timber yard where the wood
was boiled in sugar. Kathleen was always interested in such practical
details. During the stopover in South Africa she had been taken down
a gold mine, where she had been fascinated by the processes, delighted
by the muscularity of the naked torsos and by the singing by candle-
light, and horrified by the number of men, black and white, obviously
sick with phthisis ('breathing at a horrible rate, coughing that cough')
who had no choice but to continue working.

Also in Melbourne was a telegram from the Norwegian explorer
Roald Amundsen, sent from Madeira on 9 September 1910. 'Beg
leave inform you proceeding Antarctic. Amundsen.'

Amundsen was a brilliant and respected explorer. He was also, as
everyone knew and he had said, going to the North Pole. His sudden
about-turn revived all the argument about territorial rights, explorers'
courtesies, British supremacy and so on. In fact Amundsen had decided
to head South as soon as Peary had (ostensibly) achieved the North,
he just hadn't told anyone – not the public, not Scott, not his financial
backers, not his crew, and not Nansen, who had lent him his ship,

the *Fram*, for the Arctic trip. Amundsen knew Scott's plans, which were entirely public. Whether he was under any obligation to make his plans public, knowing that if he didn't Scott would continue at his leisurely pace, is a matter of debate. 'The Pole was only a side issue' for the British expedition, he said, but he knew it wasn't, even though Scott might have preferred it if it had been. And anyway, Amundsen had, some felt, a prior claim on the South, having been there before Scott's first journey, though he had not landed. Still, and at best, Amundsen's secrecy was underhand.

It was a blow, and Scott took it. He emphasized again the scientific side of his expedition, concentrated on getting the money still required, and said that if he had an address he'd send Amundsen a good-luck telegram. Having done so much preparatory work his attitude now was stoical. 'None can foretell our luck,' he said a few days later in Sydney. 'We may get through, we may not. We may have accidents to some of the transports, to the sledges, or to the animals. We may lose our lives. We may be wiped out. It is all a question that lies with providence and luck.'

On 22 October he and Kathleen sailed from Wellington, New Zealand. She was sick for the five-day journey, and Con nursed her. On the next leg, to Lyttleton by steamer, she must have been feeling better. She immediately found out all about the other passengers: 'Captain Shannon, Captain Maitland and 3rd ADC Captain Hamilton who loves a Miss Elgar with pretty red hair. Captain Shannon loves Miss Boyle but there's no money.'

In Lyttleton the Scotts stayed with Joseph Kinsey, the expedition's New Zealand agent. The *Terra Nova* was unloaded and completely repacked with food and forage, scientific equipment, 15 ponies, 35 dogs to haul the sledges, 32 tons of pony fodder, three motor-sledges, 460 tons of coal, collapsible huts, an acetylene plant, 5 tons of dog food, an ice-house with 162 carcasses of mutton, 35,000 cigars, a guinea pig, a fantail pigeon, three rabbits and a cat who had his own little hammock with blankets and a pillow. Kathleen sat on a crate and sewed on name-tags. There were balls, including one with powder and patches, and a visit to a sheep show. Kathleen and Con had a happy fortnight at the Kinseys', on a cliff above the sea, with distant snow-capped mountains to look out at: 'working and thinking with bare toes and my hair down and the sun and my Con and all the expedition going well. It was good and at night we slept in the garden and the gods be blest.'

Others were less peaceable. Petty Officer Evans (not to be confused with Teddy Evans) got drunk and had to be shipped out of town temporarily. Mrs Teddy Evans was on edge, and made rather more of her fears than everybody else. On one occasion she sulked and refused to go to a reception because her invitation had arrived a day later than the Scotts'. Kathleen felt she was being a bad influence on her husband, 'working him up to insurrection'. He went to Scott, 'excited by vague and wild grievances, the only reasonable one concerning [Petty Officer] Evans', and taking him to task over supposed short-comings. Kathleen felt that Mrs Evans was childish and no help to anybody at a time which was strained enough anyway. Mrs Evans probably felt that Kathleen was heartless and bossy. Ory Wilson put her word in, and there was a ruckus. Captain Oates described it in terms both dramatic and ironic: 'Mrs Scott and Mrs Evans had a magnificent battle, they tell me it was a draw after 15 rounds. Mrs Wilson flung herself into the fight after the 10th round and there was more blood and hair flying about the hotel than you see in a Chicago slaughterhouse in a month, the husbands got a bit of the backwash and there is a certain amount of coolness which I hope they won't bring into the hut with them, however it won't hurt me even if they do.' No doubt there were high words, but blood and hair flying would be very out of character.

November 26 was Con and Kathleen's last day alone together: 'a good merry day', she called it. They went walking over the hills, and crept off after dark to sleep at the Kinseys' empty house rather than the more boring one where they were meant to be staying. On the 28th they met up with Evans and went with him to Port Chalmers, whence the *Terra Nova* would finally leave. 'A nice little journey, we were happy and good all the way.'

The 29th was the day of departure. 'Evans' tantrums spoiled the day,' she wrote. 'He told me a string of lies and hot air.' But they made it up enough for her to give him letters to give to Con at Christmas and on his birthday. Kathleen, Ory and Hilda went out on board the *Terra Nova* as she drew away, surrounded by tugs and cheering crowds. Then a tug, the *Plucky*, came to take them off.

'I didn't say goodbye to my man because I didn't want anyone to see him sad,' Kathleen wrote. 'On the bridge of the tug Mrs Evans looked ghastly white and said she wanted to have hysterics but instead we took photos of the departing ship. Mrs Wilson was plucky and good . . . I mustered them all for tea in the stern and we all chatted gaily except Mrs Wilson who sat looking somewhat sphinx-like.'

Teddy Evans described the feelings on board the *Terra Nova*:

Personally I had a heart like lead, but, with everyone else on board, bent on doing my duty and following Captain Scott to the end. There was work to be done, however, and the crew were glad of the orders which sent them from one rope to another and gave them the chance to hide their feelings, for there is an awful feeling of loneliness at this point in the lives of those who sign on the ships of the South Pole trade.

So Con was gone. She never saw him again. Nor did Ory Wilson see her Bill, nor the families of Captain Oates, Petty Officer Evans or Birdie Bowers see their husbands, sons and brothers.

Back on shore she left the other wives to their own devices and went to visit a babies' home. It didn't cheer her up. They were all very ill-looking.

ELEVEN

◆

At Opposite Ends of the Earth

◆

1910–11

Dec 2 1910

Dearest Mummy [Kathleen wrote to Hannah Scott],

At last they are off, all in the best of spirits, and exceedingly glad
to see the last of ports and stopping places . . . I am sending you some
papers about the departure and about the bishop's service and sermon
at Lyttleton. I don't allow myself any photographs of him yet, just
surround myself with the Boodle's [Peter's] who must be my only love
for a while . . .

I haven't begun to realize that he's really gone yet, and I don't
want to.

Peter seems slow getting his teeth but if he's perfectly well of
course it doesn't matter . . .

It will be very nice to get home again . . .

Kathleen was alone again, yet she was not alone. Her husband
gone, she was landed instead with his family, and with the obligation
to behave herself. Her letter is dutiful, but soon she rebels. In her
autobiography, she wrote:

Poor little Kathleen! My babe at one end of the earth, my lover just
off to the other, and I to stay primly at Admiralty House in Sydney
for a week, until my P. and O. should convey me back to England.
At night I wrapped myself in a rug and slept on the zinc of the
balcony, and lay hour after hour under the stars, watching the light
of the ships in the harbour and taking the vagrant decision that I
could not remain there and behave nicely for a week.

'I was altogether the good-mannered nice little wife of a junior officer,' she reassured Con in her diary, but 'I cannot be a tame cat to a sick woman [her hostess, Lady Poore] for so long with no outlet.'

So she set off vagabonding with an 'intelligent and adventurous' (and discreet) South African whom she had met on the ship coming out, and spent the waiting period trekking through the Blue Mountains, 'out in the sun making love to wallabies', waking up at dawn to find the forest warbling, and getting terribly lost. 'It's the first time I had been anything approaching happy since Con left. Con said "Do anything you like but don't get talked about." I shall not be talked about this time anyhow.'

'I journeyed home as countless sad wives have journeyed before,' she wrote in her autobiography, but that was not entirely accurate. When her P. and O. arrived 'one look at the passengers was enough. Ye gods what a crew. I instantly determined to get in an additional stock of geology books.' In fact the journey was not uneventful. Her married state did not prevent a fellow passenger, Mr Wesche, from falling in love with her before they even got to Ceylon, but Kathleen was more interested in 'the play of the back muscles of my rickshaw driver' which 'caused me much pleasure'. (She always liked short hair, because it let her see the muscles at the back of the neck. The muscles of the body said as much to her about a person as the face.)

At Kandy she walked round the lake with Mr Wesche and 'explained to him very carefully and finally how very distasteful it is to me to have him make love to me. He was very nice about it and there should be no further difficulty.' She saw nutmegs with red jackets, and watched rubber milk turning glutinous on her finger; she sketched coconut palms and banyan roots. On 5 January she got up early and 'went to see the Temple of the Tooth', where she found 'ridiculous frescoes of tortures, 1817', leeches, and an Indian magician who hung weights from his eyes and made a snake and a mongoose fight. Also there was smallpox, so the passengers were not unhappy that it was time for the ship to sail again.

At dinner that night one Captain Blair said: 'It seems rather absurd for me to drink this soup because I'm going to drown myself directly' – and he did. The ship searched for an hour but they couldn't find him.

On 16 January the ship docked at Port Said. Kathleen had written to Rose Campbell, Con's sister: 'I feel I oughtn't to waste this opportunity of seeing something of Egypt which I have always longed to see . . .' Peter or the Pyramids? 'What if even now through my absence a harm had already been done to him?' She was torn, but decided that if she rushed around she could see everything quickly and be back in Britain by 11 February. Of course it was not satisfactory. 'It seemed most impertinent to attempt to see these things in one day. Each wall merited a week's study.' But she headed straight to Cairo, booked into Shepheard's Hotel and set off in search of first Ricketts and Shannon, and second the Pyramids by moonlight. Not finding the RickyShan, and too impatient to hold off the magnificent sight, she had to make do with her 'bored and unintelligent' ship acquaintances. Two of them went back to sleep in the car. Kathleen could hardly believe their philistinism.

She visited the tombs by donkey, then, tired of donkeys (though she liked camels, because 'they fold up like a telescope for you to get on and then unfold again when you are ready') she arranged to hire a boat. It cost £5 a day all in for four passengers, which included six cabins, a saloon, a cook, a servant and the captain. The crew 'made Fantasia' for them, singing and dancing. A four-year-old made Fantasia: 'It was curious seeing this mite dancing dances that the Parisienne cocottes would emulate, in the dim light, surrounded by some 20 eager Arab faces, to the weirdest music.' When Kathleen did her exercises on deck in the morning the crew thought she must be praying, bending and stretching to some private Mecca of her own. The party felt very luxurious until, setting off up the Nile, they came across another 'jellaby' which had a grand piano on deck.

She finally caught up with the RickyShan, and went with them to Luxor and to Karnak, where she visited the lion-headed goddess who eats babies. Back in Cairo she got news of Peter's teeth from Henley, and learnt that 'mummies' hair grows after their death. How odd!' On her penultimate day circumstances and a friendly archaeologist, a Mr Quibbell, allowed her a great treat.

Sunday 19th: At the end of lunch he told me quite casually that that morning he had come upon a 2nd dynasty tomb, about 3600, probably the earliest ever found. He said he had left the sarcophagus untouched as he thought I might like to help him uncover it. I was of course most awfully excited. Together we descended a shaft, rather a climb, and there was the sarcophagus, a large wooden box, much eaten by white ants. We had to prop up the sides with sods before he dared lift off the lid. We found three mummies inside, greatly decayed and indeed little left but bones. They had been buried in a contracted position. One set of bones was to be sent to a professor at the museum at Manchester. He numbered each set of bones. I helped him. As I was lifting out one of the heads he said 'I suppose you know how to prevent the teeth falling out of the lower jaw?' As though I'd been at it all my life! It was a great burial place and there were many tombs of varying dates up till comparatively recent times. We hoped to find jewels or papyrus in our tomb, but there were neither. Mr Bruce sat at the top of the hole, smoking and regarding us as harmless lunatics. I did enjoy myself.

That night at dinner she sat opposite a German princess 'who was much prettier than princesses generally are and didn't look a bit bored'. On 30 January she returned to the boat, to find the passengers this time 'all millionaires and cardsharpers'.

Kathleen allowed herself one more visit before returning to her baby. Set down by the ship in Marseilles, she went to Paris to see Isadora, only to find she'd just gone to New York for two months. Elizabeth was there, however, Isadora's sister with whom Kathleen had lived as a crab in Greece, and also Edward Steichen. 'It was interesting to see him again but no more,' wrote Kathleen in her diary, very properly. They went to Isadora's huge studio next to Rodin's, and had tea with Ted Gordon Craig. In Versailles Kathleen found her friend's babies: Deirdre, whom she had helped to deliver, and Patrick, Isadora's son by the American sewing-machine million-aire Paris Singer, to whom she turned after finally breaking up with Craig. 'A perfect duck but much too fragile,' said Kathleen of Patrick, as she did of any baby less fat and bouncing than her baby Hercules. She took a sentimental journey round her old haunts, and bought some chocolate from the old lady from whom she had always bought chocolate. The old lady said Kathleen had grown very thin. Con thought so too, and had written to his sister about it before he set off. The determination to behave well that the couple shared took its toll in different ways. Con, the determinedly responsible leader, suffered terrible indigestion; Kathleen, the resolutely cheerful wife, grew thin.

Early the next morning, 7 February, Kathleen reached Dover. She was met by Brand, the good servant who had replaced the terrible couple. The house in Buckingham Palace Road was spotless. Kathleen had a glass of hot milk and then raced off to Henley, where Hannah Scott and her daughters were living, to find her son. 'He was in splendid health, a little lumpy and dull I thought and with long hair which I immediately cropped.' The 'long, enforced separation from Con' was not so bad now she was back with Peter – 'the only authentic thing in my life'.

KATHLEEN'S LIFE as the London wife of an absentee Antarcticist settled down, in a way. The proper pastimes of teas with her son, lunches with other Antarctic wives and waiting for letters from the far South shared a timetable with sculpting and more unlikely habits.

Peter's tea normally took place in St James's Park, and Kathleen would join him, his nurse and the ducks for bread and jam and milk. Kathleen had very specific ideas on upbringing. She was horrified once when out at tea to find the host's child was allowed to eat new scones and cakes. The child was (of course) 'the poorest puniest spottiest creature beside Peter', and also 'couldn't be reconciled to Peter having no shoes, and finally brought one enormous shoe of her nurse's. It really is tragic.' Kathleen's lack of interest in civilized notions of dress extended to dressing Peter: 'My Peter was about in the drawing room after his bath with no clothes on. He must like the freedom of movement for he rushes about and shrieks with the merriest laughter.' She thought it was rather nice for him to be naked; other respectable folk were rather alarmed. Charles Wheeler remembers him tricycling around Chelsea 'scantily clad', Sybil Colefax couldn't get over it and even now the rumour persists that he was always half-naked. Of course by Victorian standards, which still largely prevailed, he was. Kathleen also put Peter to bed herself, which most respectable mothers of her class didn't find necessary.

Lunches with Antarctic wives took second place to lunches with Antarctic explorers, or with the old men who backed up the younger men who were out there. There was a great deal of internecine politicking, and Kathleen on the whole worked to calm it down. Sir Clements Markham wrote a letter to the *Daily Mail*; Shackleton wrote a reply to which Sir Clements responded with a eulogy of Con which Kathleen had to persuade him not to send. Douglas Mawson was trying to put together another expedition, and she talked to him about aeroplanes, and introduced him to people who could help, and thought him a bit of an ass for running away in mid-conversation at a lecture when he saw Shackleton approaching. Kathleen felt the right thing to do would be to shake hands with Shackleton, talk to him if need be and change the subject if he started to be rude.

There was more money to be raised, still, and she overcame her distaste for speech-making in order to raise it. She felt very strongly that she herself was not at all glorious and should not be lionized, and quite regularly sent journalists off with fleas in their ears, but when money was at stake she had to be canny. Her domestic finances were not that much better than the expedition's: she overdrew her bank account for the first time in her life, which made her feel sick, and despite considerable disinclination for it took in a paying guest during the coronation in June.

She did see other expedition relatives – Cherry-Garrard's mother, 'a very charming lady, very sweet and gentle and very intelligent, and a very nice pretty young girl her daughter, Mildred' became particular friends. Ory Wilson was missing her husband badly, and thought that she might go to New Zealand on the off chance of the explorers coming back after one year, and then if they didn't she would just stay there, with various friends, until they did. Kathleen thought this would be awful.

She didn't wait for letters though. She knew when she could expect to hear anything, and until then she did her best – a pretty good best – not to think about it. The time was nearing by her birthday, 27 March. She decided to give a party, 'a great party like the ones we used to have'. She filled her studio with daffodils and fifty-two guests who stayed till 2 a.m.; and there also came a telephone message from a news agency: 'Ship sighted all well'. 'A nice birthday message. Curiously enough I had reporters here not knowing about the cable, but come about my statue of Florence Nightingale. I was so excited.'

The next day the cables themselves came from New Zealand: 'A state of frenzy all day. Mr Pennell's message was such a muddle that no one could make head or tail of it. I was of course bombarded with reporters . . . I told them we still wanted money!!! and nought else.' As the messages were unravelled it turned out that a party of Scott's men had met Amundsen and visited his camp on the Bay of Whales, sixty miles nearer to the Pole than their own Camp Evans at McMurdo Sound. Like it or not, the race was on.

Con wrote to Kathleen of the journey so far: of the terrible storm on the way down from New Zealand, when the deck cargo came loose, and sacks of coal flung about like battering rams in the pitch and swell, and the men struggled to tie it down again without being swept overboard. Two ponies died then, and tons of coal were lost. Then came the pack ice, which started sooner than expected and held them longer. For 370 miles they were pushing aside, breaking through or dodging ice floes, some so obstinate 'one would almost believe [them] possessed of an evil spirit'. The *Terra Nova* seemed to Con 'like a living thing fighting a great fight'. Once they were stuck dead for five days, another time for four-and-a-half. 'To wait idly is the worst of conditions,' he wrote. But they were not dispirited.

Christmas in the pack was cheerful: 'We had the most splendid dinner, with soup, stewed penguin, plum pudding and mince pies, asparagus, champagne, and liqueurs, and afterwards everyone sang. I may say at once that there is very little talent' – though Herbert Ponting, the photographer, 'sang rather nicely to a banjo' – 'but the absence of talent doesn't deter our merry party at all. Everyone has to sing his turn, and the choruses are deafening. On Christmas night it was kept up till one a.m. and no work is done without a chanty . . . the merchant service sailors have quite a repertoire and invariably call on it when getting up anchor or hoisting sails. Often as not they are sung in a flat and throaty style, but the effect when a number of men break into the choruses is generally inspiriting.'

They were through the pack on New Year's Eve 1910; there was another gale, and Con fervently hoped that the New Year would bring better luck. At 4 a.m. on 3 January 'we were nearly up to Cape

Royds. I have never seen a fairer scene than met our eyes as we steamed up the Sound. The sky was quite clear and the sun brilliant, the blue shadows were sharply marked on the distant mountains, and the great fields of snow on land and sea seemed to flash in the bright light.' Kathleen had been in Ceylon then, seeing off her inappropriate suitor.

The night after her birthday Kathleen went to the theatre and arranged for Sir Edgar Speyer and Lady Wemyss to sit for her. 'First nights seem businesslike,' she observed. She had begun to exploit the 'goldmine' of portraiture. Work could help to fill the gap of Con's absence. She liked to talk to people as they sat for her: she liked to sculpt her friends, and often became friends with those she sculpted.

When she sculpted Charles Rolls that spring, this could not happen. Rolls had been a dashing young man, the owner of the fourth motor car in Britain, and in 1904 he had founded Rolls-Royce. In June 1910 he had flown the English Channel, circled and flown straight back again, without touching French soil. A month later he had been killed in a flying accident over Bournemouth. Kathleen noticed a plane over Bournemouth as she and Con set sail for New Zealand, and it could well have been his. His portrait, to be erected at Dover, was her first commission for a public monument, and she was working on the statuette which precedes the big work. She didn't really know how to make a big statue. She asked John Tweed for advice; he 'gave me a book and I must work it out for myself'.

To South Lodge to get Charlie Rolls' clothes: Lady Llangattock [Rolls's mother] was away but had wired that I was to go to his bedroom and get all I wanted. It was horribly grim. I came away with his coat, trousers, leggings and cap – the cap has bloodstains on it.

20th: Having got Rolls' clothes I was now in despair over who to put into them . . . *faute de mieux* I had Hal Bailey, it was dreadful and I couldn't stand it, and gave it up and went with May Playfair to play golf at Ranelagh. I'm too bad at golf, but so is May.

21st: In despair for want of a model. Mark and Rosie Kerr came to lunch. Got in a footman to wear C. S. Rolls clothes but he looked too appalling, I was also so scared that he soon wanted an excuse to hurry away. At 5.30 Mr Basil Blogg, a clerk in the Lord Chamberlain's office

and a nice lad of 23, came to pose. He was splendid, and once rigged
up in Rolls' clothes looked quite like enough to be very useful. He
stayed till 10.30 so we worked by gaslight.

    24th: A press photographer came to take my finished statuette of
Mr Rolls – it is a great relief to get that satisfactorily completed. I
began it altogether afresh on Thursday (today is Monday). Four days
was a very short time for a monument's sketch.'

Lord and Lady Llangattock both wept when they saw the statuette,
and in the end Kathleen made 'forty beautiful pounds' from sales
of casts.

The day before she finished it, 23 April, the Antarctic sun had
gone down on Con and his comrades, safely tucked up for the winter
in their hut ('really a home of considerable size', Con wrote, with a
roof weighing six tons and coated in seaweed solution) at Cape Evans.
They had laid stores for the Pole journey at depots on their route
south, they had tried out their methods of transport, their scientific
research was underway, and they were very comfortable and on the
whole pleased with each other. But ten of their nineteen ponies were
dead, one of the motor-sledges had gone through the ice, and they
knew that Amundsen's dogs were much, much better trained than
their own. Men, sleds and dogs had fallen down crevasses; Bowers,
Cherry, Thomas Crean, three ponies and four sleds had floated off on
an ice floe one night, and awoken to find themselves being circled by
killer whales.

Fortune was not smiling on them, nor would it, but even so news
was received at home with delight. Antarctic wives and mothers
would send each other copies of letters, and complain to each other
of only receiving postcards.

Kathleen saw a lot of Con's family, and did try to behave well. 'I
shall come down and we will have a perfect Antarctic orgy,' she wrote.
When she went vagabonding she limited it to Kent, and took her
girlfriend Wunchi with her, and actually slept indoors at hotels and
inns. A new pastime of hers, however, worried them. She had been
taken to an air show, which delighted her, by Arty Paget, and she
frequently spent afternoons at airfields, chatting with flyers, learning
about engines and, occasionally, going up herself. (Later she recalled
that she had probably been the second woman in Britain to fly,

and that she had flown with Mr Sopwith, with dual controls.) This was considered rather too independent, and might well have broken the rule of not getting talked about. Her picture appeared in *The Aeroplane* – without her name, to her relief. Later she had to take the editor to lunch to request that he stop printing stories about her as if she were a celebrity. The Scotts deputed Gerald Ellison McCartney, Con's brother-in-law, to express their disapproval, which worked not a whit, because she happened to know that he too went flying, and didn't tell his wife. He was rather embarrassed; Kathleen was amused.

Going flying, golf lessons, and looking for a coastguard's cottage to rent became her pastimes. She found one; a tiny place on the beach at Sandwich in Kent, and she rented it from the Admiralty and took Peter there when they wanted to get away from things. She went out a lot, to dinners: 'I thought there might be Expeditiony useful people but there weren't. Lady Stanley who I disliked cordially talked awful rot.' And to the theatre: 'I am really not fit to go out to plays, I sobbed loudly all through it. I'm too beastly emotional. Dunno what to do about it.' She had lunch with her admirer Mr Wesche: 'He has kept coming to say goodbye "last time" – "never see me again" and so on, but I expect this really may be the last'; she visited Shannon to see the things he brought back from Egypt. She 'called on Lady Lucy hoping to get Sir Henry to take farther steps – you know he wrote about money wanted for us in Toby's Diary in *Punch*, but it only raised a guinea!' She went to the first night of Bernard Shaw's *Fanny's New Play*: 'all his critics come in under the thinnest disguises: Gilbert Cannan as Gilbert Gunn and so on . . . talked to Shaw afterwards and he was awfully hilarious.' One evening she went to a show, then to a fancy dress dance till three, and then drove straight on to Hendon airfield to see a flying race take off at dawn, then home for breakfast with Peter. No wonder she didn't want to wait around in New Zealand like Mrs Wilson. And then 'first night in for about a fortnight – a joy – but only in contrast.'

Loving Peter was her main joy. She was exceptionally proud of him, and of his love for her. But as it comforted her in Con's absence, so it suffered from something of the same stress: the stress which is always present when total love comes to an independent woman.

When she came back from her vagabonding in Kent she brought him primroses, and he took one 'to bath and bed' with him. Once he cried when she had to go out, 'which was foolish of him but rather sweet'. She spent a weekend in Paris with Isadora, and missed him terribly. She sat in Isadora's bed with her two children; Isadora danced for her while she lay on a divan; Hener Skene, now Isadora's pianist, played for them while they did exercises in the garden.

When she got home 'the angel boy was so pleased to see me, and called me so often and made me fetch your photo, saying "Dada too!" and then he kissed us both in turns and made me too.' One afternoon when Sir Clements Markham came to tea 'Peter was particularly entrancing and pleased the old man because he fell an awful cropper and didn't cry. He's really rather a plucky little beggar. He always comes and buries his head in my lap for a moment when he picks himself up after a spill, but soon trots off again saying "betty now!"' The little boy was taking after his parents: sensitive but tough.

Her baby love was not exclusively for her own son. She chronicled every baby she ever met, and compared them to Peter. A couple she knew were divorcing: the mother ran away with an Italian and the father disowned the three-year-old son, and Kathleen wished she could have him as neither of them did. When an old friend, Gladys Bailey, turned up, pregnant and unmarried, Kathleen took her on.

> The man responsible is a man I know and rather like. He evidently doesn't love her a bit, and doesn't intend to marry her. He could quite well, he lives in a house the rent of which is £600 a year, but he knows lots of people far nicer than she and it would not help his career to marry her. I don't know what to do about it. I have told her if she will go on with it and not have any disgusting and horrible operations, I will see her through – I believe you would tell me not to, but one must live up to one's own views and to me it seems only playing the game to look after her.

For the sake of children she would do a lot, but she had a great impatience with parents. Another young girl came to her in distress when her parents died; Kathleen tried to sympathize, but 'knew' that the girl must really feel relief at their passing. In the Victorian fashion, when her parents had died she had had to put them away from her, and she could not now, particularly when stiff-upper-lipped against her husband's absence, let any sign of what she would have thought of as sentiment infect her. She had learnt the habits of that kind of strength early in life, and now she had other people to be strong for too. A gaily painted stick she would continue to be.

Self-analysis was not part of her scheme of things, but she knew something of her own nature. She met Una Troubridge, the lesbian novelist Radclyffe Hall's lover, then a young sculptress of twenty-four. She found her 'a solemn lesson in egoism. She rather reminds me of myself [crossed out] what I should be if ever I let myself get out of hand. She told one everything she had ever done and thought herself quite wonderful, but she is a human little thing with an engaging laugh and I think I like her. She is very young, in that she tells one all the people she knows!! What a dreadful thing to want to be known in terms of people one knows! She's got a baby girl and wants to be great friends. She's only twenty-four poor mite (Kathleen was now thirty-three).

The summer of 1911 was very hot. 'No wonder the House of Commons is disgracing itself,' she wrote, of the 'formidable consti-tutional disturbances' taking place, and the Prime Minister Asquith's threat to create hundreds of 'ignoble peers'. On top of that, measles had broken out at Sandwich so Kathleen and Peter could not go to their coastguard cottage for relief. They spent a week with Con's sister at Rye, from which she absconded one night for a dinner in London given by Gordon Craig. He was now 'respectably married' – not to Isadora, though; she was married to Singer. Ellen Terry was there, being 'perfectly delicious'; and so were Mary and Gilbert Cannan, 'both looking so well and happy. She looks ever so much younger and less made up. I believe perhaps it may be a success. They are quite certainly still very pleased with each other. She was very nice and sweet indeed.' Another guest was Henry Nevinson, the journalist who had been in Macedonia. 'He didn't know I was married, and couldn't get over the appropriateness of our union – what do you think?'

At the end of July a summons came from Isadora, who was on holiday with her two children on the northern French coast. Kathleen and Peter went to Boulogne, where they were swept up again into

Isadora's world of dramas. Isadora and Deirdre 'came in a big motorcar to meet us, both dressed in Poiret gowns looking perfectly beautiful'; then 'for several days we motored violently in a 40hp Napier by day and by night.' Various members of Isadora's family joined them; there was a row with Patrick's nurse; they ran into a couple of Kathleen's aviator friends, one of whom Isadora set her cap at: 'the charming way he warded off Isadora's advances was delightful'. Paris Singer arrived and fascinated Kathleen with talk of pathology.

> Then the usual domestic tragedies began. Isadora and Paris are more married than the most married people I ever knew. He was tired and thought to have peace and she would tell him all about how the nurse was, how she'd dismissed the governess, how the chauffeur had sent in a huge bill and not got insured and so on and so on. How natural that she should, how natural that it bored him. Finally their nerves gave out, and he dined elsewhere and she came to me saying she would go to Paris at 6 the next morning. Now Paris is six hours from here and the heat excessive (hottest known since '72 or something) however I didn't worry feeling sure that feeling better after a good dinner all would be well with both of them – unhappily both were too proud to open the door between their rooms and so they didn't meet. How easily and how stupidly these things happen.

Isadora bolted to Paris. Kathleen decided she and Peter should go home, but Singer persuaded them not to. It was the children who swung it – she didn't like to leave them with the horrid nurse. Singer had planned a cruise by yacht to Sweden and St Petersburg, dropping Kathleen and Peter off in Dover on the way. Singer, Kathleen, Elizabeth Duncan and the children decided to go and live on the yacht anyway, until Isadora came back, which she did a few days later. 'Everybody felt the idiocy of the thing, but nobody said a word.'

On August 10 they set out to sea as planned. 'No sooner out of the harbour than Patrick began to yell. It was quite rough. Peter was on my knee. "No like it, get down, get down", then "Sick, feel sick", and then he was – very – and then so was I, and so was nurse, and so was Elizabeth, and Patrick's nurse, and the maid. Still we went on and on, all the while Patrick yelling and howling, and Isadora grey with terror.' They didn't make it to St Petersburg.

Kathleen, two nurses and the two boys moved into the Palace Hotel at Ostende ('the most magnificent place') while Isadora and Singer headed off again with Deirdre on the beautiful cruise he had planned. The nurse – 'a beastly rough horrid old hag' – left, amid awful scenes, and Kathleen settled happily into sorting out the miserable, sickly, nervous, fiendish-tempered Patrick. 'He has been shockingly brought up, but if Isadora leaves me time I intend to make a fine fellow of him.' Kathleen was remembered by a young friend of Peter's as hardly ever saying 'don't'; Isadora too believed that 'continual don'ts . . . make children's lives a misery'. As with their attitudes towards sex, the ideal was similar and the practice very different. Kathleen was disciplined without being negative; Isadora was undisciplined.

A few days of respite followed, broken only by Peter spearing his foot on a broken shell, and Patrick screaming. Then Isadora came back and, insisting on leaving the babies behind, swept Kathleen off in order to 'motor wildly all over the place'. Patrick, who had shown some improvement, was now sick again. 'Isadora wouldn't let me attend to Patrick, she would take me hither and thither, motoring – I got angry and determined to go to Sandwich.' Isadora let her go, after making her promise to come back, and saw her off at the port 'giving us roses and everything else she could think of to shower on us, including a private cabin on the ship'. That was 23 August, the day the sun came up again in Antarctica. The explorers toasted it in champagne, though they could not see it through the heavy snow whirling in the 70mph wind.

Safe back at her 'absurd' cottage, hidden among sand dunes and unreachable by road, Kathleen strung up a hammock on the beach and thought she could happily live there forever, in peace and quiet. Then she started to miss Con.

> I rather need a man down here, but hesitate to ask one because I am afraid I should make love to one if I had one. [Make love did not mean quite the same then as it does now. She was making love to wallabies in Australia, after all.] One has so much time here, and I am so overflowing with vitality; so though it seems rather a waste to impart one's pleasure to no one, maybe I'd better not. One wants someone to help one see the sunset and the moonshine and to swim

– but there! I am very happy alone, and maybe Peter is gaining by my undivided contemplation. He is very good to contemplate. I am amazed by his very existence – still! It is wonderful to make a creature like that. Tomorrow will be our wedding day, we shall have been married 3 years. I bet anything you won't remember it. What fun we've had one way and another since, haven't we? What a lot we've crowded in. It's curious to me to think how unwittingly in a way I've got my heart's desire, at least what I used to think my heart's desire. I used to say I wanted a baby but not a husband, and I've got it, but with a difference, one hasn't got one's husband in the body, but one has got him so very firm in the spirit that it spoils everything!! One can't think of loving anybody else, and yet one's whole being is crying out 'You are young, you are healthy, go out and love!' – I think decidedly I had better get back to work . . .

     . . . As a punishment for what I wrote yesterday I was ill today – it came on in the night when I was sleeping out on the beach – horrid. Tonight I went for a long walk along the beach, along to where you and I once went . . . you won't remember, right along to where the river flows into the sea – and I saw the very tuft of grass on the sand that we'd sat down upon, primarily to light your pipe. That was a long time ago. It was more beautiful today than then, for there was an exquisite sunset, and over the marshes the moon was rising, and not a sound but my own toes in the sand. I have been here ten days now. It does not pall. I wonder if you will be here with me next year – you should love it as I do . . .

     Have just had the most wonderful bathe by moonlight, all all by myself . . . It was so beautiful, only one wanted someone to come back and tell how lovely it is, so I have to write it all to you, on the chance that in half a year you may (or may not) cast a careless eye on it.

Con too was rejoicing in nature and solitude. 'We are all adventurers here, I suppose, and wild doings in wild countries appeal to us as nothing else could do. It is good to know that there remain wild corners of this dreadfully civilised world.' As she sat on their tuft of grass, he was writing in his journal:

The weather still remains fine, the temperature down in the minus thirties. All going well and everyone in splendid spirits. Last night Bowers lectured on polar clothing . . . My whole time has been occupied in making detailed plans for the Southern journey. These are finished at last, I'm glad to say . . . I have tried to take every reasonable possibility of misfortune into consideration, and so to organise the parties as to be prepared to meet them. I fear to be too sanguine, yet taking everything into consideration I feel that our chances ought to be good.

TWELVE

•

Daddy Won't Come Back

•

1911–12

September 20, 1911

Rather a horrid day today. I woke up having had a bad dream about you, and then Peter came very close to me and said emphatically 'Daddy won't come back', as though in answer to my silly thoughts. By the time you read this you will probably be comfortably lounging in an armchair on a P&O near Colombo or something and will say contentedly 'silly little maid' and you'll be quite right.

Con was chirpy that day: halfway through 'a remarkably pleasant and instructive little spring journey' which involved marching 175 miles in ten days, temperatures from −15° to −40°, and 'many frost-bites'. The 20th he spent happily measuring glacier movement with Bowers and a theodolite.

Two days after the bad dream Gladys Bailey, the girl 'in the worst of plights', came to stay. Kathleen had been visiting her regularly, finding her sad, sick and hysterical. She had had her child, and it had been taken from her. She had been ill, and could still scarcely walk. The coastguards carried her to the cottage, and Peter took a great fancy to her, he 'always called her and went to fetch her, and looked so perplexed when she cried. He was very touching, and though he helped her a lot, it rather hurt her too, she did so wish she could keep hers.' A few weeks earlier the father, 'quite a nice simple creature, an eye specialist', had been staying at the cottage too. He had passed his time playing golf, walking on the beach and reciting 'The Pied Piper of Hamelin'.

It was getting colder, and Kathleen and Peter packed up to go back to town. In the South, it was getting warmer, and on 1 November

Con set off for the final long trek to the South Pole. They had the whole summer, and expected to be back at Cape Evans around the middle of March. 'The future is in the lap of the gods,' he wrote in his diary. 'I can think of nothing left undone to deserve success.'

The two motor-sledges had gone in advance, and now the men, each on foot leading a pony and a sledge, started out. It was planned that only four men would be required to go the full 1766 miles to the Pole (though in the end five went), and no one knew who would be chosen.

The night before they set out Scott wrote to Kathleen, congratulating her on being 'the antithesis of a pathetic grass widow. Bless you.' The fact that she was 'sturdily independent and determined to make the most of the life you possess' gave him comfort.

For Kathleen the antithesis of grass-widowhood was starting up again – all the things which took her mind off his absence and the danger that she never mentioned. On her first night back in London she was summoned to hold the hand of another friend on the verge of giving birth. Relatives came to call. Her old admirer Lou Van Telegen was appearing at the Colosseum with Sarah Bernhardt. Shannon and she went to lectures. She organized some casts of a head she had done of Gordon Craig – 'he is just becoming very famous and I thought I might sell some heads'. 'Rather an awful type' 'made love' to her passionately one weekend. 'He's fairly intelligent but so ugly that it didn't amuse me much.' He was not the only one to try. 'I cannot take it at all,' she said crossly, wondering how they could be so vulgar.

The exception was Fridtjof Nansen, the big rugged Norwegian. She was initially shy when she met him after a lecture he gave, but soon after, on the day before he was due to leave the country, she invited him to lunch. He stayed till 5.30. 'I think we are very great friends,' she wrote, after talking about their children, childbirth in general, sociology, exploration and how he had 'only crossed Greenland at first [he walked] by accident to get away because he was overworked and unhappy,' about Scott and about Amundsen. Nansen thought the ideal solution would be for them to meet up and go on together, and was glad that Amundsen had not told him his plans because it would have put him in a very difficult position. He thought he would probably not have lent Amundsen the *Fram* if he had known his true intentions, and his support and admiration for Scott were such that he had written to Queen Maud (of Norway), who was staying at Sandringham, to arrange for Herbert Ponting's Antarctic films to be shown there.

The next day Nansen wrote Kathleen a letter. 'It is nice to know there is a woman so like what one has dreamt of but never met,' it said. 'I am inclined to think explorers are rather a comprehending race,' she wrote in her diary, before settling down to a full day's work. His admiration was acceptable – even inspiring – to her, where that of others wasn't, for the simple reason that he was clearly an honourable man. The attraction, for her, of a man who could understand through first-hand experience what her husband was doing, who was intelligent, knowledgeable, admiring of her but not vulgar in his expression of it, is not hard to gauge. Plus one evening when they went to the theatre they left by the wrong door and got lost, and Nansen navigated them home by the stars.

Seventy years later a biographer of Amundsen claimed that Kathleen and Nansen had an affair at this stage. A television programme was made based on this book, and because this may be the only reference to Kathleen that many readers have come across, it is worth pointing out that they didn't.

The evidence offered for her adultery was that Nansen sent her a telegram asking her to book a hotel room in Berlin (he did, but there is no evidence that she booked a room, or that they shared one); that she marked in her diary when her periods were due and when they came (she did this all her life); and that he wrote nostalgically of looking at a sofa on which she had lain.

Nansen's letters to her (hers to him have not survived) are deeply romantic, so much so that when, late in life, she had some of her letters from important figures bound, she kept some of his out 'while he was still alive'. Although she felt that anyone reading the letters would see that theirs had not been 'an affair *à outrance*', she didn't want people to think worse of him for addressing her so lovingly while she was married. Were they modern letters, it would not be unreasonable to assume that some sexual connection went with them. But they are not modern letters, they are letters between romantic idealists, and Victorians to boot. They are full of phrases like 'your lips, which I have never touched' and 'shall it ever be?'; of 'and then you showed me pictures, we were sitting together, you were close to me, and I felt you touching my arm and oh, I cannot say what I felt then.' If they had slept together, he would have had some more intimate memory to recall than the touch of her arm when looking at pictures. And throughout the letters Nansen expresses heartfelt concern for Con. 'I wish you to love your husband as much as you do and would not for my life do any harm there.'

One letter – one of the ones that Kathleen kept back – makes it clear: ' "There's only one thing you want to avoid", you say,' Nansen wrote, ' "even at the cost of losing it all." I wonder what it can be. Or do I know? Is it passion you are afraid of? . . . You, your splendid husband and baby are above everything in this world, and will remain so, and still that does not prevent the possibility of a friendship that may make life richer.'

As Kathleen wrote to her second husband many years later: 'I was going to remain a completely faithful wife, only I was not going readily to throw aside such a divine friendship.'

Meanwhile the money for the expedition was running out; there was only enough to cover expenses till the end of October, and more had to be got. A man from the *Daily Mirror* said he could raise £4,000 for the expedition by using a picture of Peter writing a begging letter. 'My dear I do humbly beg your pardon if I have done wrong, but I said "No!" Not only can I not bear my [son] being bandied about in the halfpenny press, but also I doubt greatly that any sum approaching £4000 could be got.' A cinematograph company she had hired to film Peter for Con had already, without her permission, sold pictures of him, and strangers had started to recognize him in the park, which she hated. To make up for it she addressed envelopes endlessly, wrote to Lloyd George, and organized a first-night party at the Colosseum, where Herbert Ponting's films of the expedition were to be shown. Peter delighted the guests by crying out 'That's my Daddy!'

Friends, and relative strangers, poured out their troubles to her – their failing marriages, their unwanted children, their love for someone impossible. It constantly surprised her that they should, and they always did. Her sympathy was often tinged with a realistic impatience with human folly. 'Constant interruptions from my poor girl . . . She even sobbed down the telephone so I asked her to lunch, poor mite she is terribly unhappy and quite hysterical. She shrieked so loud. I don't know what to do for her. I want to give her back her self respect. It's hard. She wants to go back to this man after all this ugliness and knowing that he doesn't want her much. Bad isn't it? You were right when you recommended me not to mix myself up in it, it's rather sordid and endless, and one can't help much.' Then in the margin she remembers 'of course you weren't here and didn't recommend anything, but you would have done if you had been, being wise.'

Isadora was irritating her too: 'She is now living in a large house belonging to Paris Singer . . . she is having a turkish bath built and plans to live over here. My feelings before I was married would have been altogether unmixed about it, I would of course have been enchanted. Now – well I wonder if you will understand a wee bit how I feel.' The problems of others no longer helped her to keep her mind off her own loneliness. She began to need all her optimism for herself and Peter.

'The more I see of life,' she wrote, 'the more extraordinarily fortunate my lot – or my temperament – seems to be. Lucky dogs, you and I!' And then she went off to post her diary to her husband. Early October was the last date for sending parcels. 'It's the record of a very happy year, and thanks to you for giving me such a nice Peter.'

As the winter set in she grew less cheerful. 'November 20th: I wonder what your diary records today. I am horribly depressed and you know that doesn't often happen to me. I have been entirely unable to make myself do anything or read anything all day . . . November 21: Had a rotten night, behaved in a ridiculous way I haven't done for ages, with the result that I had a fearful headache all day.' (Probably she cried.) The next day she felt better, worked until the light went and then went to see the films again at the Colosseum. 'They are ripping, and bringing in thousands.' At Sandwich and at Buckingham Palace Road she planted hundreds of daffodil bulbs in case he should be back in the spring.

Con was then twenty days into his southern journey, on his way to the Pole. That Monday, 20 November, his diary deals with the health of the remaining ponies. They had struck a very bad surface the day before with 'confused' sastrugi (waves in the frozen snow, caused by wind) which had tired out the animals. The explorers were marching by night, making fifteen miles, and sleeping during the day, because that seemed to suit the animals better. Even so, the ponies were not doing well – but it was not expected now that they should. Their main use from now on would be as meat, deposited for the return journey. The weather was bright and clear, with temperatures between −14° by night and +4° by day. As the journey went on the weather became worse: 'Our luck in weather is preposterous,' he wrote on 3 December. An unseasonal blizzard delayed them for four days, then it took them eleven hours to struggle five miles through the soft wet snow.

On 14 December Amundsen reached the Pole, though Con didn't know it – he was struggling up the Beardmore Glacier after a night of indigestion, cramp, raw and blistered lips, and soggy clothes. 'The eyes of the party are improving, I am glad to say,' he observed. But, 'We are just starting our march with no very hopeful outlook.'

'Today, about, you should be turning,' wrote Kathleen on 22 December, before going to lunch with a depressed friend at the Admiralty. 'I bet you won't though.' She was right – on the 21st Con, still on the glacier, wrote her a note: 'So here we are practically on the summit and up to date in the provision line. We ought to get through.'

Kathleen spent Christmas at Henley with Con's family, wondering how on earth someone like him could be related to people like them. Hannah thought it sad that Peter did not know the divine meaning of Christmas Day. Kathleen told her that he knew there was a little baby in history born in a stable who grew up to be a very wonderful man, and that was more than most babies of two knew. 'It's hard for the passing away generations. Let us hope Peter will be lenient with us when our turn comes.'

Con spent Christmas Day marching seventeen miles into a facing wind, pulling 190lb on his sledge, and watching one of his men being fished out of a fifty-foot crevasse (he was too far off to help). They celebrated with pony hoosh, plum duff, cocoa, four pieces each of caramel and crystallized ginger, and a hoosh of chocolate, biscuit and raisins. Con couldn't finish his pudding. 'I am so replete I can hardly write,' he said in his diary.

That was the last jollity. On 16 January, after seventy-seven days and almost eight hundred miles, Scott, Bowers, Wilson, Petty Officer Evans and Oates reached the South Pole. They knew where they were without reckoning because Amundsen's flag was there to welcome them. They reckoned anyway and, estimating the Norwegians to be seven miles out, went to what they calculated to be the right place.

Until the last moments their hopes of getting there before Amundsen had been high. Without news, and without seeing any sign of the Norwegians, they had been able to believe in their chances. It was no good reminding themselves now that the 'race' was only a secondary goal.

'All the daydreams must go; it will be a wearisome return,' Con wrote. 'Great God! This is an awful place.' The heart went out of them, but only for a while. When Con wrote 'The worst has happened, or nearly the worst' he was already set firm on the next goal – getting his party back alive. With the pipe-dream of the Pole no longer either inspiring them or obscuring their vision, Con had only this one thing in mind.

They took photographs, made measurements, built a cairn and planted their 'poor slighted Union Jacks'. Nigh on eight hundred miles of man-hauling were ahead of them, and there was no reason now to hope that they would have better luck than they had had on the way out. Indeed the seeds of their bad luck were already laid: they had no time to spare for bad weather; the food supply was recurrently tight, partly because there were five of them instead of the four initially (and generously) planned for, but mainly because it was taking them longer than they had expected to get from one depot to the next; and Evans had a wound on his hand which would not heal.

On the day of her husband's disappointment Kathleen was in Berlin visiting her cousin Benjie. She skated, went flying and to concerts and met a lady who had inherited a large income 'of which she is forced to spend every penny each year . . . she lives in a palace with marble floors and on the day I met her she wore (in the day) a white velvet frock covered with pearls.' She went dancing, and found the German officers 'all spotty and poor-looking creatures'. Charlie Rolls's sister was there, and some American friends, and a painter, Harrington Mann, whom Kathleen had arranged should paint one of the Americans. Nansen was giving some lectures; she went to an art gallery with him and modelled his head. (This is the trip on which they were alleged to have consummated their 'affair'.) 'He really is an adorable person,' she wrote for Con, 'and I will tell you all the lovely times we had together when you get back. He thinks you are marvellous, and me still more!' Nansen was a link to Con as well as a pleasure in his own right.

Back in London her sister Elma, now widowed with seven children, came to stay. Kathleen went to lunch with the First Sea Lord and someone asked her if she was panicking. 'Not a scrap!' she replied, and went out dancing till 2.30 in the morning. On 12 February she had dinner with the RickyShan and Somerset Maugham, resisted going on to a dance and wondered if Con would be pleased with her. Perhaps he would have been. As it was he had very much more serious things on his mind.

The party was 'in a very critical situation'. Approaching a depot, with one meal's worth of food left, they lost their way and had to camp not knowing where they were. 'We are cheerful with an effort. It's a tight place, but luckily we've been well fed up to the present. Pray god we have fine weather tomorrow.' They didn't. The weather, which ever since the pack ice had over and over again presented unforeseeable difficulties, did not smile on them now. They marched anyway, through fog and broken ice. Almost by accident they found the depot, and another three days' worth of food. 'We mustn't get into a hole like this again,' Con wrote. Evans was very weak with his bad hand, and Wilson and Bowers both had snow blindness.

On 15 February Kathleen went to lunch with the Prime Minister, Mr Asquith, who was 'extraordinarily pleasant'. Con was again running short of food: Wilson's leg was troubling him and Evans had just revealed a badly frost-bitten foot which no one had known about. They were not making good time.

The next day Peter had a temperature and no appetite; Kathleen worried. Con worried more. 'Evans has nearly broken down in brain, we think,' he wrote. The sick man stopped the march twice 'on some trivial excuse', which was hugely time-consuming and thus dangerous. He had been one of the physically strongest and most reliable of the party. He would never have stopped had he been in his right mind and full strength. The weather was still against them. 'After lunch we were enveloped in a snow sheet . . . It is anxious work with the sick man. But it's no use meeting troubles half way, and our sleep is all too short to write more.'

On the 17th Kathleen was offered an exhibition, and heard of the death of a young aviator friend. She had once refused to fly with him, because flying led to notoriety. He had had seven sisters, 'so a fellow must do something definite,' he had once said to Kathleen. She wrote it down for Con, thinking perhaps of his family of womenfolk.

In the South it was 'a terrible day'. Evans kept falling over; his speech was slow and he had taken his gloves off despite his frostbite. By the time they got him into a tent he was comatose. He died soon after midnight.

Con was miserable, but he could not let that undermine his responsibility for those remaining. 'It is a terrible thing to lose a companion this way,' he wrote, 'but calm reflection shows that there could not have been a better end to the terrible anxieties of the past week.' The damage was done, however. Even though they had not been able to get him to safety, Evans's sickness had delayed them.

On 18 February Peter's temperature was 101° and a *Daily Mirror* reporter doorstepped Kathleen. She had to ring the editor to tell him not to quote her. 'Very taken up with you all evening, I wonder if anything special is happening to you. Something odd happened to the clocks between 9 and 10pm.' Con, Bowers, Wilson and Oates made it to the next depot, and ate pony meat.

On the 19th she was 'still rather taken up by you and a wee bit depressed. As you ought about now to be returning to ship I see no reason for depression. I wonder.' The polar party made only four and a half miles that day, over a very bad surface. 'I wonder what is in store for us,' Con wrote, 'with some alarm at the lateness of the season.'

On the 20th she felt rotten, and had to go out and meet some people who wanted to put on three matinees to raise money for the Expedition. She knew she should think about it in case it was a good idea, but she couldn't help taking against the whole notion. She wanted to talk to Con about it. Instead she went to the House of Commons to hear Bonar Law speak. She thought him puny and vulgar.

Con and his comrades made seven miles and reached the camp called Desolation to find that there was no pony meat there. It was $-15°$ at suppertime, and the going was terrible. 'Pray God we get better travelling as we are not so fit as we were,' he wrote, 'and the season is advancing apace.'

On the 21st the Prime Minister came to call: Kathleen was in bed with her period. 'I have never dressed in a shorter time,' she wrote, 'and he never guessed. He really is amazing to find time to come when all these political crises are on (you know there's an appalling threatening of a universal coal strike, etc).' She was delighted that Asquith was being friendly. 'I am sure he may be impossible in some respects but to me he is absolutely delightful.'

'Heavy toiling all day,' wrote Con, 'inspiring gloomiest thoughts at times . . . We never won a march of 8 miles with greater difficulty, but we can't go on like this.'

And so it went on. For Kathleen, distraction, and a cheerful resistance to making any show of concern: a dull dinner party and three interesting hours talking aviation with, among others, Mr Sopwith, by firelight. For Con, just the merciless dragging of optimism over the Antarctic wastes, and the growing realization that 'There is little doubt that we are in for a rotten critical time going home.'

Kathleen had no particular reason to worry at this stage. If the polar party got back to McMurdo Sound in good time, it would be just feasible they all might leave for New Zealand before winter set in. But then a message would come saying so. No message at this stage would probably mean that the polar party had made it back to the base camp, but not in time to get a message out, so they were settling down to winter it out. It had remained undecided anyway whether or not they would stay another year. In October 1911 Wilson had written to Hannah Scott: 'We may not be back before March, and when we arrive the ship may have gone North again. I know it will disappoint you sadly when the ship, if she has to, reaches New Zealand without either the person or the news you are hoping she will bring . . . but there's a good day coming which will be none the worse because deferred. We are a very happy party here and a second year will quickly pass and all will be well.' The early spring of 1912 was a tense time for all the relations because they were hoping for good news, not because they feared bad.

On 2 March Captain Oates revealed to his comrades that his feet were badly frostbitten. It was a serious blow. They needed to make up time, but they couldn't. Their oil supply was short, their rations were short because of the poor time they had been making. Temperatures were going down as far as −43°. It took them an hour and a half to get their foot-gear on. They needed all the physical strength they had, and it was depleting fast.

The memory of how Evans's decline had slowed them was in everybody's mind. 'We still talk of what we will do together at home,' Con wrote, but the optimism was fading. On 10 March Oates asked Wilson if he 'had a chance'. Wilson had to say that he didn't know. 'In point of fact he has none,' Con wrote. 'Apart from him, if he went under now, I doubt whether we could get through.'

On 9 March the polar party reached the depot on Mount Hooper, where they had hoped — but did not necessarily expect — to find extra supplies. Seventy-two miles on, Cherry-Garrard had deposited those supplies at One Ton Depot. He was caught for four days in a blizzard there, and had to choose between going on, against orders, in hope of finding Scott's party, or returning to the Hut, leaving the supplies at One Ton where he knew Scott's party was eventually to arrive. He had no reason to suppose that the others were in any great need. The extra supplies were to have been an extra security, not a relied-on necessity. The blizzard meant his own (and the dogs') rations were short too. His companion Dmitri was falling sick. He returned to the Hut. No blame rests on him, but for the rest of his long life Cherry-Garrard never got over the idea that he might have been able to save his friends.

On 11 March Oates 'practically asked for advice. Nothing could be said but to urge him to march as long as he could.' Gentlemanly behaviour notwithstanding, Scott made Wilson hand out the opium from the medicine cabinet; 'the means of ending our troubles, so that any one of us may know how to do so.'

Oates's hands got frostbite, too. 'The surface remains awful, the

cold intense, and our physical condition running down. God help us!'
'Long time getting supper in dark.' 'Truly awful outside the tent.
Must fight it out to the last biscuit, but can't reduce rations.'

On 14 March Oates couldn't go on, and asked them to leave him,
in his sleeping bag. They couldn't do it. They all went on, and made
a few miles.

'Should this be found I want these facts recorded,' Con wrote on
what he thought was probably 16 March. 'He slept through the night
before last, hoping not to wake; but he woke in the morning –
yesterday. It was blowing a blizzard. He said "I am just going outside
and may be some time." He went out into the blizzard and we have
not seen him since.'

Scott, Wilson and Bowers knew now, if they had not known before,
that they had no chance of a safe return. 'We all hope to meet the
end with a similar spirit,' Con wrote, 'and assuredly the end is not far.'

It was about two weeks. They kept on marching. 'My companions
are unendingly cheerful,' he wrote. About the 21st they were laid up
by a blizzard, eleven miles from the One Ton depot, where food and
oil awaited them. Every day they were as ready as they could be to
start out, every day the blizzard blew. They had determined not
to take the opium, to 'die in their tracks', but the weather would
not even let them leave the tent.

Even now, Scott filled his time usefully. For a week they sat in the
tent and as they waited to die they wrote letters. Con wrote to Ory
Wilson, Birdie's mother, Sir James Barrie, Sir Edgar Speyer and others
connected with the expedition, to his own mother and to Kathleen.
He told her to 'make the boy interested in natural history', to make
him a strenuous man, and to keep him in the open air ('I know you
will'). He wrote: 'What lots and lots I could tell you of this journey.
How much better has it been than lounging at home in too great
comfort. What tales you would have for the boy. But what a price
to pay.'

On 29 March Con wrote his last entry:

I do not think we can hope for any better things now. We shall stick
it out to the end, but we are getting weaker, of course, and the end
cannot be far.

It seems a pity but I do not think I can write more.
R. Scott.

Last entry. For God's sake look after our people.

There was an instruction that the diaries should be given to his wife. 'Wife' was crossed out, and 'widow' written in its place.

THIRTEEN

✦

Living in Ignorance

✦

1912–13

KATHLEEN knew none of this.

On 6 March 'the rumours began, that you had got to the Pole, and reporters began to flock and telephones to ring.' She ignored it all, because there was no solid news. The next day 'came the clash and turmoil. Cables right and left to say "Amundsen arrived Hobart states Scott has reached the Pole." Thank all the gods I was not taken in, and whilst the posters shrieked "Scott at South Pole – Brilliant Victory" etc I was certain there was something wrong.' Reporters tried to trick interviews from her by claiming to have 'definite and startling news'. She knew that Amundsen could only know Scott had got to the Pole if he had got there after him, in which case chances are he would have returned after him, in which case why was there no news from Scott? And the cables were not from Amundsen himself – why not?

The next day was if anything worse. Messages of congratulation continued to pour in even after Kathleen learned that it had been Amundsen, not Con, who had got to the Pole. Con's sister Etty came to tea and they took the phone off the hook. 'I don't know whether I have ever found my own company less entertaining,' Kathleen wrote, and then, in a firmer hand, with her pen refilled: 'And yet "God's in his heaven, all's well with the world", and let us never look backward.'

On 8 March the public learned that it was Amundsen who had reached the Pole. 'My friends are afraid of me,' Kathleen wrote: 'I worked badly and my head racked. I am not going to recount what I have been feeling, even if I could it would not make pleasant reading. It's better only to record the gay things of life – and through it all I have hope and confidence – I know out of it all great good will come.' Nansen wired a message that his thoughts were with her.

She wired back 'Hurrah for Norway in spite of all' – she wanted to send a cable to Amundsen too but was discouraged from doing so. Peter asked her if Amundsen were a good man; she said yes, she thought he was. Then Peter said 'Amundsen and Daddy both got to the Pole. Daddy's stopped working now.'

'Ever in the back of my mind drums "is my man unhappy, will he be unhappy" – I try to give myself no leisure, for that way surely leads to madness.'

It was very easy for her to avoid leisure. Her life anyway was a whirl of work and visitors. It was a rare day when she hadn't people to lunch, people to tea, and dinner, theatre or a party in the evening. In the mornings she took Peter swimming, and worked. Now she made sure that there were no gaps at all in her schedule, and beneath all the activity, she waited. The public furore died down, she continued to address her diary to Con and she suffered terrible headaches. (Years later when she went to a doctor about her headaches he asked her if she ever cried, and she said no, not really. It was a matter of pride for her not to. The doctor said she ought to, it would help.) Her release now was dancing: 'I went to a dance at the Savoy – yes I did, and it did me a world of good – one's mental feelings vanished away and one's blood circulated happily.' On her birthday, 27 March, she had a party – 110 people, till two in the morning. She did it on principle, expecting news hourly and remembering her last birthday, when the telephone message had come: 'Ship sighted, all well'.

This year's message came on 31 March: Central News rang 'to say you were staying another year and that on 3 January you had been 150 miles from the Pole. I didn't enjoy the rest of the night very much . . . it is difficult to bear the thought of your disappointment . . . Also it's hard to think of you out so late in the season, but there I suppose you know your job and wouldn't take too awful risks.'

The next day – April Fool's Day – letters arrived from the husband she did not know was dead, and reading them dismissed her headache and filled her with inspiration. She was glad he was staying an extra year, it would have been a waste if he hadn't, a 'thousand pities', she decided. She went to Sandwich, entertained Duncan Grant to lunch ('he is a curious ingenious painter of 27, a rather beautiful face but ill and poor and somewhat dishevelled and surprised'), she went to see Pavlova dance and laughed when Peter's nurse decided to leave because Kathleen wasn't having another baby. Hugh Walpole, then twenty-eight and a successful novelist, told her about his virginity.

Her work was going very well. She sculpted Asquith, Nansen, Gustav Hamel, Sir Matthew Nathan, and Compton Mackenzie, who told her that he thought menstruation was 'due to tides affecting earliest forms of life in the sea', which 'gave her furiously to think'. She sculpted babies for a hospital, limbs for nurses to practise bandaging on, 'bishops in nitches' for the chapel at Winchester College. (This rather upset her, because the bishops were to replace some carvings by Grinling Gibbons which had been taken down and sold.)

In April her statue of Charles Rolls was unveiled with many speeches at Dover. She had loved doing the big sculpture; it felt like real work, clambering up and down scaffolding with masses of clay and a huge armature. She wished that Con had been there for the ceremony, and hoped that when one day a monument was erected to Peter she wouldn't weep and sob in front of the cinematographers as Lady Llangattock did here. The Walker Gallery in Liverpool wanted to exhibit her work, and Nansen wrote saying the King and Queen of Norway (Queen Maud in particular was very taken with Kathleen) wanted her to sculpt them, and their little boy.

She was making £300 a year, as she reported to Con when a letter came in May telling her he was signing over all his money to the expedition. Kathleen wrote to Hannah Scott to tell her:

You must be very proud and happy, and all I pray is that I make Peter into as fine a fellow as you have made Con – I can't desire more. His letter to me is the most amazing document of sacrifice and unpretentiousness I ever read and makes me feel more and more (if that be possible) our extraordinary good fortune in being associated with a man of such calibre. He has done a thing that is magnificent and at the same time an immense relief to me. He has put all the moneys from whatsoever source (book, cinematograph, articles, photographs, lectures, stamps, newspaper news, etc) all with no qualifications into the Antarctic Fund, and he is to cease to have an Antarctic salary – this I think is splendid! He once said he believed one did one's best work when there was no question of financial gain. I believe he was right, and it gives me great pleasure to think he won't make anything at all out of it. He is so happy, the dear, to find that he is still as strong and fit as the youngest of them and can't be outstript. He is not worrying about Amundsen, and though the odds have been horribly against him his spirits – I can see – are high. Now that he has a little leisure he has more time to appreciate the good things he possesses ... Apparently Bowers is the great marvel, and Oates and Atkinson, also Cherry-Garrard and of course first and foremost as ever is the faithful Bill [Wilson]. I have as you know known many men of many nations, but I think I have never met a man one can so wholly admire as your son. He astounds me.

As too often with Hannah Scott, Kathleen's enthusiasm outweighs her tact here. Hannah, widow of a feckless bankrupt, had no inclination to admire her son for giving up money, however nobly, and no desire to be reminded that her daughter-in-law had known 'many men of many nations'.

Male admiration never stopped coming Kathleen's way. It irritated her when it was inappropriate, but it flattered her and she liked that. Her particular thing here was truth. She liked men, and saw no reason why she shouldn't be friends with them. Being married, and being desired, were in her mind no reason to curtail a true friendship. Nansen was the prime example of this. Sir Matthew Nathan was a long-lasting admirer; he annoyed Kathleen by saying he cared so much for her he couldn't see her any more, which she felt was foolish, but in the end to her relief he stopped seeing her 'as a woman'. An 'appalling bounder' called Leonard Avery made such 'monstrous suggestions' to her during a weekend away that she stayed in bed until he left. 'Upon my word,' she wrote, 'he is more than even I can bear.'

Asquith was beginning to be a friend. One thing Kathleen and he had in common was a disapproval of women's suffrage. He felt at this stage that most women didn't want the vote, and that women's interests were not being harmed by the absence of women in parliament. Kathleen would certainly have encouraged him in this view. Asquith described to her one morning how a suffragette had thrown a hatchet at him, which for her exactly proved the folly of suffragettes. 'The more I hear of them, the more hostile I become,' she reported, after hearing Ramsay MacDonald make 'an impassioned speech, moving and eloquent without a word of reason or good sense from beginning to end' on the subject. She believed, quite simply, that most women were either too uninterested or too silly to deserve a vote, and those who were not could make their political views known perfectly well through men. If she wanted to influence parliament, she spoke to the Prime Minister. It seems curious that so independent a woman should be so against this manifestation of female emancipation; in fact her very individualism informed her hostility. She was not given to forming alliances and associating herself with groups. She didn't see herself a woman, one among many, all being denied the vote. She saw herself as Kathleen, doing what she wanted. It is not sisterly, in feminist terms, but neither is it quite as illogical as it first seems.

Bonar Law, the leader of the opposition, she found unimpressive, not a gentleman, 'though obviously a thorough dear, very gentle and Scotch'. She introduced Peter to him ('so as not to bias his political tendencies'), and he told her that Winston Churchill did everything for advertisement. 'I suggested does one really want advertisement when one is in Churchill's place?' and he agreed, no.

Meeting her hero Augustus John she found 'a day's work in itself'; Marconi often called, and explained his inventions to her which was 'thrilling', but despite all the high society she found her Italian hairdresser 'so much more intelligent than most of my friends – he talks about you and your work and Post-Impressionism and the Balkans, and knows four languages equally.'

In the summer she went to Sandwich, and, like the year before, had time to think and to miss her husband, wondering, as she had the year before, whether he would be there with her next year. She wrote to Hannah: 'how splendid to hear how fit and strong and alive he is', but soon after she was making plans about whom to leave Peter with should both she and Con die. She chose Sydney Holland (later Lord Knutsford, the hospital administrator and reformer, known as the Prince of Beggars) and his family, rather than any relatives. Con's family she thought too female (or that was her excuse) and her own she did not consider.

News came while she was at Sandwich of the death of a *Terra Nova* hand, Robert Brissenden, who drowned off New Zealand. Kathleen was called upon to tell his wife, who lived nearby. 'Con, dear, it was just terrible. We told her mother as best we could and told her to tell her daughter, but she daren't, and so eventually I had to. It was most terrible. She was a dear quiet little woman with a fine boy of seven. I don't suppose anybody could have felt her blow more poignantly than I, but I doubt if my sympathy was any help. It seemed so terrible to descend on her gay neat little house, drop a bomb like that and depart. I wrote to her too when I got home but it all seems so paltry in the face of her sorrow.' Another neighbour was Mabel Beardsley, who was dying of cancer but nobody had told her. Kathleen left her now-shadowed haven for Scotland, to a British Association conference where she was fascinated by speeches on neurons, algae, her husband and the origins of life.

She had already decided to go and meet Con in New Zealand the following spring. She wasn't sure she was a good wife – 'I'm quite a good mother and quite a good sculptor but beyond that I seem rather a failure' – and she didn't know if he expected her, but for her there was no question. Some of the explorers – Teddy Evans, Meares, Ponting the photographer – had returned after the first year, and seeing them whetted her appetite. She edited those of Con's journals that had been sent back, sorted out finances (which she hated), continued when necessary to placate potential outbursts of rivalry and Amundsen-bashing and to deal with the press. Amundsen was coming to London to give a lecture, which caused all the Expedition-connected people to wonder at length whether they should attend, whether they should shake hands with Amundsen, whether they should accept invitations from the Norwegian embassy. Feelings ran high. Sir Clements Markham ('the old dear', as Kathleen called him) simply left the country, saying that he didn't know how anyone who met Amundsen would have the impertinence to speak to Scott when he returned. Kathleen went to the lecture, tactfully incognito, and found it 'plucky, modest, but dull, and of a dullness!!'.

In September she sent her husband a box of 'silly things', including sponges and the news that she was coming to meet him, via the United States, where she would go riding in the Grand Canyon. At Christmas she was working on a statuette of him in uniform – 'I'm obsessed with it and want to finish it before I leave' – and drank to

his 'joyful and triumphant return'. On 4 January, having wept and
fled from Peter at Henley, she set off from Liverpool for New York,
seen off with flowers and a note from Marconi allowing her to send
unlimited Marconigrams without paying.

The journey, of course, she loved. New York thrilled her. Hofbauer,
her friend from Paris, met her from the boat, and on her first night
she checked into the Colony Club, had tea at the Plaza, dined at the
Ritz, went on to the Winter Garden and Martin's ('a sort of Maxim's
where people dance more or less improperly'). At Martin's she bumped
into the explorer Peary in the lift: it turned out there was a dinner
for Amundsen going on upstairs. The next day she devoured the
museums, and was amused to find works by Steichen. Nearly as many
people came to call on her as did in London; her London friends had
alerted their New York friends. One had a chauffeur who enquired if
she wasn't the Mrs Scott who went flying; she said, well yes, she did
fly sometimes. The chauffeur then apologized, saying if he'd known
it was her he would have put on his new carburettor and driven her
at 90 mph. Even so he drove fast enough to lose his cap.

Kathleen had an extraordinary knack for attracting favours. Her
train journey went via New Orleans and El Paso; in both these places
she was met, and she soon had under her belt an invitation to go out
riding and camping with a party of cowboys near 'Tuconne', and a
letter allowing her to ride on the engine throughout the entire Mexican railway system – which of course she did, 'rushing through the
prairies of Mexico at 120 kilometres an hour on a giant engine,
throwing off with the cowcatcher any cattle that were too slow getting
off the line . . . since my first flight in an aeroplane I have never been
so thrilled.' She wanted to ride on the cowcatcher but the driver
thought she would probably be killed by a flying cow. That night
she borrowed a revolver from the hotelkeeper and climbed a small
mountain; the next day she galloped through orange groves and left
the horse on the platform just in time to catch the train.

The next four days she rode with the cowboys of the Diamond Box
Ranch, eating stewed corn off tin plates and sleeping outside under
an eiderdown of Con's, with the horse stamping round her head and
the cowboys snoring. One of them, Frank Wild, hung a lantern in a
tree for her. The cowboys were 'such darlings: Tim, Walt, Mack and

Win . . . tall lean powerful fellows . . . full of jokes and amusing gallantry. They all wore the usual cowboy kit, wide-brimmed hats, leather chaps with fringes, belts with guns in them and coloured hankies round their necks.' She wore divided skirts that she had brought specially in order to be able to ride astride on the Mexican saddles. After roping and branding a calf, Wild cut off its ear as a trophy for Kathleen. She cooked cornbread for them, and felt absolute pride when they said 'Say, woman, that's bully bread'; and she and Mack discussed Byron around the campfire. 'Why don't you just stay right here with us and make your old man come and fetch you?' they said to her. 'Sunshine, exercise, health, mountains, so many horses! so many men!' She was absolutely in her element. The next day she spent at an observatory, discussing gravity and magnetism and going up 160 feet in a swinging basket.

AS SOON AS the weather allowed a party had set out from Cape Evans to look for 'the Owner'. On 12 November 1912 they had found him, Wilson and Bowers, dead and frozen in a tent so well pitched it had withstood the whole long winter. They were in their sleeping bags; Bowers and Wilson neatly tucked up and Scott with his arm outstretched across Wilson's body. He had died last.

Atkinson, Wright and Tryggve Gran read the burial service, sang 'Onward Christian Soldiers' and let down the tent over the dead. They built a snow cairn and made a cross of skis to put on top of it. Then they marched on until they found Oates's body, and erected a cross to him. Atkinson took charge of the diaries, and they turned back to Cape Evans.

The bodies are no longer there: the movement of the ice will have brought them gradually north. In about 1985 their cairn will have broken off as an iceberg, sending them out into the Antarctic seas like a frozen Viking burial.

FOURTEEN

◆

'Got My Wireless'

◆

1913–14

NEWS OF THE DEATHS of the polar party reached London on 11 January 1913. A memorial service was held for Scott and his companions at St Paul's Cathedral in London on Valentine's Day. The King was there, though he officially only went to Royal funerals and memorials, and they sang 'Rock of Ages'.

Kathleen, at sea somewhere between California and Tahiti, knew nothing. Wireless, still an embryonic form of communication, was not strong enough to reach her ship. The *Evening Standard* correspondent at the memorial service spared a thought for 'one who is still ignorant of the frightful tragedy, that hapless woman, still on the high seas, flushed with hope and expectation, eager to join her husband and to share in the triumphs of his return. It made one feel that the service was rather unreal.'

On 19 February she heard.

Got my wireless. I was sitting on deck after breakfast not feeling very well [she had her period]. The captain came and said he wanted to speak to me in his room. It didn't occur to me in the slightest what he wanted but I went. Poor old chap's hands were trembling when he said 'I've got some news for you but I don't see how I can tell you.' I said 'The Expedition?' and he said 'Yes'. 'Well,' I said, 'Let's have it' and he showed me the message which ran 'Captain Scott and six others perished in blizzard after reaching S Pole Jan. 18th.' I remember I said without the least truth 'Oh well, never mind, I expected that – thanks very much – I'll go and think about it' and I went downstairs.

She went straight to her Spanish lesson, for an hour and a half. Then she went to lunch and discussed Australian politics – she had asked the captain not to tell the passengers, though the officers already knew. Later she read a book, *The Sinking of the Titanic*. She wanted to keep her mind off the subject until she was sure she could control herself. It was too hot to stay in the cabin, so she spent the whole day on deck.

> My god is godly, [she wrote] I need not touch him to know that. Let me maintain my high, adoring exaltation, and not let the contamination of sorrow touch me. Within I shall be exultant. My god is glorious and could never become less so. Loneliness is a fear that I have never known. Had he died before I had known his gloriousness, or before he had been the father of my son, I might have felt a loss. Now I have felt none for myself. Won't anybody understand that? – probably nobody. So I must go on and on with this tedious business of discretion. Must even the greatest visions of the heart be blurred by discretions?

What did she mean by this? She was speaking a language all but forgotten two World Wars later, the language of patriotic idealism and mystical romanticism. Patriotism was the default state of mind for British society at that time; the very high and pure romantic standards were specifically hers. Her god, it seems clear, was Con. It was better to have loved and lost, she was saying, then never to have loved: the real loss would have been if they had never loved and never had Peter. This is not to say that her grief was not absolute at his loss, it was, but the joy she took from his life, his achievement and what he still was to her was bigger than her grief. Or if it wasn't yet, she knew it would be, and she would not indulge self-pity in the meantime. The 'discretion' was the social face she would have to put on when she got back to London: the face of conventional widowhood she would wear to cover the intense importance to her of her private reaction.

Con carried with him to the Pole a letter from her, a torn piece of paper written in pencil:

> I left off just where I was going to tell you a very difficult thing. Look you – when you are away South I want you to be sure that if there be a risk to take or leave, you will take it, or if there is a danger for you or another man to face, it will be you who face it, just as much as before you met Doodles [Peter] and me. Because man dear *we can do*

without you please know for sure we can. God knows I love you more than I thought could be possible, but I want you to realise that it won't [crossed out] wouldn't be your physical life that would profit me and Doodles most. If there's anything you think worth doing at the cost of your life – Do it. We shall only be glad. Do you understand me? How awful if you don't.

He did. They were from the same school. Without deep religious conviction, they nevertheless had a sense of honour that was more important than life. To the late twentieth century it seems almost unbelievable, but that doesn't make it any the less true. Read by facile or cynical eyes, or quoted out of context, that letter could be misinterpreted. But when she says, 'We can do without you please know for sure that we can', she is not saying, 'we don't care if you live or die', she is saying, 'please don't add worrying about us to the many worries and duties that you have and will have – do what you are there to do.'

Her self-control, too, is extraordinary to later generations. She didn't cry or shout or see a therapist or join a support group. She didn't sue anyone. She didn't express her pain or admit her anger. She sat on a coral beach at Raratonga in pouring rain, watching the breakers rolling in over the reef, accompanied by a young South American chosen specifically because he spoke no language she could understand, and anyway didn't know what had happened.

There was no privacy on the ship. She would have liked to have headed for the hills; as it was she played deck golf and 'read violently'.

Anything to get the awful haunting picture out of my head. It is good I do not believe firmly in life after death, or surely surely I would have gone overboard today, and left Peter to Sydney Holland. But I'm afraid my Con has gone altogether except in the great stirring influence he must have left on everyone who had knowledge of him. Certainly I couldn't have faced this with complete self-control but for his teaching. Ever since I knew him I have worked striven and strained that he might applaud ever so little, though one will never have the applause, perhaps it has become so much a habit one will go on. I've always recognised how much he has been my god and my conscience, but now it grows more evident. He has been my motive power all this while, I feel as though even now it will not give out.

So she sat on board ship, marooned with only the fact of his death but no detail, living by his example of self-control, waiting for more news, waiting to find out what had actually happened, and how, and thinking about him.

All these long weary days with no more news, always only his pain – his mental agony – boring into my brain. I sleep (or don't) on the top deck and the nights are beautiful with the moon, and all the different aspects of it come to me one by one. How one hopes his brain soon got numbed and the horror of his responsibility left him, for I think never was there a man with such sense of responsibility and duty, and the agony of leaving his job undone, losing the other lives and leaving me uncared for must have been unspeakable.

Then there came 'the strangest nights'. 'At about 11 or 12 the wireless messages began and would go on till about 3 a.m. I sat in the wireless room watching the moving pencil of the operator. It was like planchette – a few words would come and then stop at the most critical moment. A ridiculous thing happened. Messages of condolence (lovely messages) kept coming through, coming and coming without ceasing, thus blocking the line and preventing me getting press news. Without knowing it my kind friends (and so kind some of them) were baulking my news and keeping me absolutely in ignorance except of the main fact.' The third officer, Murray Johnstone, 'like a big dog sat by me and was sorry'. In fact he had his eye on her in case she looked like going overboard, not knowing that she did not believe you could reach the dead that way.

And a message from beyond the grave did come through on the planchette: Con's appeal to the country. 'For my own sake,' he had written, half starved, half frozen, hours from death:

I do not regret this journey, which has shown that Englishmen can endure great hardships, help one another, and meet death with as great a fortitude as ever in the past. We took risks, we knew we took them; things have come out against us, and therefore we have no cause for complaint, but bow to the will of providence, determined still to do our best to the last . . . Had we lived, I should have had a tale to tell of the hardihood, endurance and courage of my companions which would have stirred the heart of every Englishman. These rough notes and our dead bodies must tell the tale . . .

Kathleen rallied: 'That was a glorious courageous note and a great inspiration to me – if he in his weak agony-wracked condition could face it with such sublime fortitude how dare I possibly whine. I will not. I regret nothing but his suffering.'

That was the way of it. After her arrival in New Zealand, when Atkinson gave her Con's diaries, she copied out excerpts from them into hers, and from his letters: instructions to put a strong bold face to the world and to face it sturdily; declarations of love, sorrow and no regrets. 'You must know that quite the worst aspect of this situation is the thought that I shall not see you again,' he wrote, and she wrote, 'Any more magnificent invigorating document I have never read, and one would be a poor creature indeed if one could not face one's world with such words to inspire one . . . much was written after eight days without food and temperature –40. A wonderful record of valiant clear-headed courage. Indeed indeed he had left a goodly heritage. My Peter has now a great birthright and we must be proud and happy and make our gratitude drown our pain at the thought of his terrible mental suffering.'

Pride, happiness and gratitude – such were the combined requirements of the Victorian ethos and the personal insistence on joy of this most determined woman. When, many years later, Peter's wife told him that she had imagined him 'a dark-eyed tragic little boy living under the perpetual shadow' of his father's death, he told her that his mother 'could never have tolerated any kind of continuing tragedy. She was one of the gayest people I have ever known.' Con's death only steeled her determination for joy.

At the same time as Kathleen learnt of her tragedy, Isadora had hers. In January 1913 she had been touring Russia with Hener Skene; on her return she went to Versailles to rest. There a car carrying Patrick and Deirdre accidentally rolled into the Seine, and they were drowned. Isadora's grief was strangely like Kathleen's. 'They feared the shock would make me insane,' Isadora wrote later, 'but I was at that time lifted to a state of exaltation. I saw everyone around me weep, but I did not weep. Looking back, it is difficult for me to understand my strange state of mind . . . I knew that death does not really exist – that those two little cold images of wax were not my children, but merely their cast-off garments . . . that the souls of my children lived in radiance, but lived forever . . .' No communication between Kathleen and Isadora from this time is recorded, though each must have known of the other's bereavement.

THERE WAS GREAT FALLOUT from the end of the Expedition. It was still £30,000 in debt, and so many funds were set up that nobody knew which to give to. When, at Barrie's suggestion, the funds were amalgamated into one under the auspices of the King and Queen, the £30,000 was raised in a few days, and the final total was £74,509. It went to the widows, orphans and bereaved mothers, and the residue went to set up the Scott Polar Research Institute in Cambridge. Kathleen received £8,500, plus £100 a year, plus her Admiralty pension of £200 per year. Peter was to receive £25 a year until he was eighteen, plus £3,500 held in trust until he was twenty-five.

The press made a meal of it. Colonel Lawrence of Arabia once compared press attention to having a tin can tied to your tail, and Kathleen learnt the truth of that now. Everybody who knew anything about Con's death, and plenty who didn't, had an opinion and an urge to make it public. The judgments on Con were positive, the headlines heroic and poetic: 'The Great Disappointment: What Captain Scott and his Party found at the South Pole', and 'A Nation's Tribute to its Heroic Sons Dead in the White Wastes of the Far South'. The comment was similar: 'The calamity has its consolations in that it has proved once more the inherent heroism of British men of action. Like other great deeds it will brace the moral nerve of the nation.'

The *Daily Mirror* produced a special supplement, and the *Illustrated London News* gave the story their cover two weeks running. On 15 February 1913 it ran ten pages, including pictures of Kathleen, Peter, Bowers, Oates and Evans, the wardroom of the *Terra Nova*, two full-page portraits of Con, a group shot in Polar gear with sledges, drawings by Wilson, a copy of a letter in Con's handwriting, a picture of Con with Peter, an artist's impression (on a double-page spread) of an Antarctic blizzard: 'weather of the kind that "wrecked" Captain Scott'. The cover of the 22 February issue was a picture of the memorial service, and flagged a Photogravure Supplement and a 'Coloured Portrait of Master Peter Scott' – full page, naked, sitting by the sea looking angelic, entitled 'PETER'.

'Because of the Antarctic story I was, even as a small child, regarded as "fair game" by the press photographers and reporters,' Peter wrote in his autobiography in 1957. 'My mother made great and, on the whole, successful attempts to protect me' but even so he was frequently recognized on the street. Kathleen thought it vulgar, irrelevant, intrusive and worse. The attention to and judgments on her husband she knew were unavoidable, but not Peter.

It is probably fair to say that Con had greater celebrity in death than he would have had had he survived. Reaching the Pole second was not nearly so great an achievement in the eyes of the country as dying so noble, British and well-documented a death. Within two years men all over Europe were suffering and dying in the First World War, and many young Englishmen having to face that wrote to Kathleen about the inspiration of her husband's example. Her cousin Colonel Percy Bruce wrote to Rosslyn: 'It just shows how one can face death . . . How splendid it all is. I can't help feeling a little proud of myself for being of the same flesh and blood even [though he wasn't, he was a cousin by marriage]. This is indeed a case of death where is thy sting.'

It was announced that Kathleen was to be accorded the rank, style and precedence that would have been hers had Con lived to be made a Knight Commander of the Order of the Bath, as the King had intended. She was surprised, almost offended, when people congratulated her on becoming Lady Scott rather than on the glory of her husband's death. And it *was* glorious, both to her personal world-scheme and to that of the time. Scott and his companions died doing what they were meant to do, to the best of their ability, and as well-equipped as the knowledge of their time allowed. They had not shirked. Kathleen was proud of her husband, and it was her proud face that she wore in public and in private.

She made such a good job of it that Bernard Shaw, by now a friend and one who really should have known better, wrote in a letter that she did not seem to feel her loss at all. But it was not stingless, of course it wasn't. The stress of the aftermath of the expedition was considerable, and Kathleen's way of dealing with it was to work, to have terrible headaches, and finally to bolt.

The diary intended for Con she gave up in New Zealand, filling the pages instead with pictures of Peter, barefoot and healthy in his baggy cotton rompers. She worked on a massive bronze of her husband which now stands in Waterloo Place in London (a white marble version is at Wellington, New Zealand), and statues of Captain Smith of the *Titanic* and of Asquith. She saw friends, went to Sandwich, and she suffered what she called violent heads. Barrie in particular was a good friend at this time. One of the letters Con wrote as he waited to die was to Barrie, wanting to make up for an unknown breach between them, and asking Barrie to help Kathleen, his godson Peter and the other dependants. Kathleen and Barrie were both glad of the opportunity to do something they knew Con wanted.

Kathleen knew Barrie well; knew that when he was very small his beloved brother had died, and of the complexities which that had added to his relations with his mother; knew perhaps that Peter Pan was a symbol of a love of boyhood which though undoubtedly not improper was very intense. Perhaps she was aware of the way in which Barrie's affection had taken over the Llewellyn Davies family, five boys and their mother Sylvia, after the death of their father. Sylvia had died in 1910, and her boys were now growing up. Barrie's favourite, Michael, the youngest, had just started at Eton. Perhaps Barrie needed a new small boy to love.

After Peter saw a performance of *Peter Pan*, Barrie asked him what was his favourite bit: 'Tearing up the programme and dropping the bits on the heads of the people below,' Peter replied. Barrie was very pleased with that; careless charming heartlessness was the aspect of boyhood that delighted him. He wrote to Kathleen (April 11 1913): 'I know a hundred things he [Scott] would like me to do for Peter, and I want out of love for his father to do them all. And I want to be such a friend to you as he wished.' Rather as she kept her admirers as friends, Kathleen kept Barrie as a friend for Peter but did not take him as a father figure. Barrie was good with Peter as he always was with boys; he would come round wearing a white beard to amuse him, and throw up postage stamps to stick to the ceiling. In return Peter made him a model of a walrus. In 1917 Barrie offered to become Peter's legal guardian in the case of Kathleen's death: 'If you have sufficient faith in me it is my earnest wish . . . Experience teaches me that the one drawback in my tending my boys is that I have no female influence for them; the loss to them is very great and I must tell you this bluntly, as I think its value increases as the boy grows into a man.' Kathleen, no doubt partly for that reason, in the end preferred Sir Sydney Holland and his jolly family.

Besides knowing that their being friends would have pleased Con, Kathleen and Barrie liked each other, and gave each other some comfort in their mourning. He told her that Shaw had bought a motorcycle: 'He is so happy and excited, my dear I wish you could tell me something I could buy that would make me happy or excited for one minute!' He told her too about 'his favourite boy, and how he writes to him every day and how he adores him.' This was Michael Llewellyn Davies.

They were not, however, such good friends as the news editor of the *Daily Chronicle* was led to believe. He wrote to Kathleen on 9 May 1914:

> The News Editor of the Daily Chronicle presents his compliments to Lady Scott and would be obliged if she would affirm or deny a report which has been forwarded to the News Editor this afternoon, that she was married to Sir J. M. Barrie six weeks ago. The News Editor hesitates to trouble Lady Scott in this matter, but on account of the many rumours which have been in circulation lately, begs to suggest to her ladyship that an official statement from her, in regard to the matter, would be of service.

Far from settling down with Barrie, she spent more of this period on the run. In August of 1913 she had bolted, to Andorra with Arty Paget, leaving Peter behind. She hated to leave him except 'on duty', but she felt this trip to be duty because 'I very certainly must have more rest if I am to preserve my reason.' Early in 1914 she bolted again, to North Africa. Eighteen years later she remembered this trip as 'one of the loveliest loftiest experiences of my life . . . I had escaped from the eulogy and sympathy and notoriety of the Antarctic disaster, alone at last and at rest.' She went into the Sahara on camel-back, dressed in flowing trousers, a red cummerbund, a turban and a burnous like an Arab boy. She got a third of the way to Timbuctoo before turning back, promising to return the next year and go the whole way. But the war came, and put a stop to vagabonding.

THE LAST DAYS before the war Kathleen spent in briny idyll at
Sandwich with Peter, who was growing up as Con would have wanted,
much in the open air, and interested in nature. Peter remembered 'a
paddling and bathing beach, with shells and sandhoppers and wading
birds and glass balls washed up from the fishermen's nets. The striped
curtains in the cottage smelled of damp and the rush mats were full
of sand and there was an earth closet at the bottom of the garden.'
Dennis Lillie, the biologist on the *Terra Nova* expedition, came to
stay, and Julian Huxley, and they showed Peter who was who in the
rockpools and the fishing nets. A day out visiting John Masefield
involved catching a minnow and learning all about badgers – Kathleen
was as interested as Peter. There were lizards and moths and seabirds,
and all his life Peter remembered seeing his first wild geese here. The
beach was tangled with barbed wire and riven with trenches, for
invasion was expected any moment, and forty Brent geese flew in low
over the sea, astounding and delighting a small boy.

In July 1914 Peter found two toads at Sandwich and came to his
mother in tears. As she dried his eyes, he whispered, 'It's just because
my beautiful toads are so sweet.' When his father wrote in that
freezing tent: 'Make the boy interested in natural history. It is better
than games. They encourage it at some schools', he was completely
in line with the boy's own inclination. Kathleen regularly took Peter
to the zoo where he cradled a baby crocodile and stroked a wolf. She
took him to the Science Museum too: 'and the fellow says "This is
interesting, it's the range-finder used by Captain Scott, you'll have
heard of him." Peter in calm and even tones replied, "Yes, I've heard
of him, that's very interesting," and except that he squeezed my finger

showed not the tiniest trace of recognition. I adored him for it.'

They were at Sandwich when the war broke out. Peter said 'Mummy isn't it a little fantastic that grown-up people should shoot each other? I do hope they've all made babies before they die, to keep on their lives.' Peter recalls hiding from an air raid in the cupboard under the stairs at Sandwich with Madame Rambert the dancer, who prayed continuously for their deliverance, and later taught him to do cartwheels, which impressed him more.

Kathleen involved herself in war work. In France as in Macedonia, it was just what she needed – activity to hold the shadows at bay; achievements to cheer her up. Her first job was transporting cars and ambulances to France, and helping at a hospital set up with the French army at a château belonging to the Duc de Pontiève, which she had located. She was busy organizing people, raising volunteers among her friends, demanding (and getting) money, writing her diary in the rain sitting on the running board of a car, demanding (and getting) an interview with Tuillerand, the French war minister, to discuss the possibility of mobile surgeries at the Front. 'Rather remarkable, he received one as though he had nothing else in the wide world to do. A large quiet empty palace, ushered straight up to a large quiet empty room, Tuillerand all alone, not a sign of a typewriter, not a whisk of a secretary, nor telephone nor stenographers, just an apparently lonely gentleman longing for someone to come and visit him.'

Kathleen's companion on this trip was Violet Asquith, the Prime Minister's daughter, who was cut up about Rupert Brooke's recent death. 'She talked about the coalition all morning, Rupert Brooke all afternoon and her father all evening. We read Rupert's poems, she read them aloud to me. I do very much indeed like Violet.'

She took a poignant mixed pleasure in tending to the 'French Tommies, bless their adorable courageous hearts'. Her job one day in January 1915

was to go through all their pockets and string their clothes and boots together and label them for fumigation. So pathetic and characteristic were the contents of their poor dirty pockets – oh so dirty – mud and blood and dust – and such a smell, but I love doing personal familiar things like that, I can't bear them to be mere numbers, I always feel ashamed when I have to refer to them as numbers. Some there were who had wives and babies they hadn't seen since August. One red-haired fellow hit in the jaw and delirious had a three-year-old boy.

Back in London she found a less dashing position: she sat at a bench at the Vickers factory in Erith and made electrical coils. It was the first time that middle-class women had done dirty jobs for the public good, and it affected her. Sculpture was suspended, and she grew proud of her productivity, made friends with her fellow workers and on one occasion took forty of them in a charabanc to see *Peter Pan*. Some of the younger girls rather fell in love with her, and left her devoted notes. She thought it unbearably sad that the war had so deprived these young women of young men that they needed to write thus to a member of their own sex.

The world around her started the cycle of the moods of war: mafficking enthusiasm, business as usual, the gradual realization of tragedy, the growing cynicism and determination. 'The excitement of the war breaking out was almost hilarious,' says her friend Geoffrey Dearmer, who was twenty-one at the time. 'Everyone was in the streets, larking about, enlisting. Kathleen took it all in her stride, she always did.' She was able to write, in 1917: 'Oh how ludicrously happy one is in this sad grim world. To everyone else it is sad and grim and to me an endless ecstasy of delight.' She would say, matter-of-factly, 'if he lives, he may come to something' of a young friend. Her curious logic and her determination for joy could make her seem hard-hearted: she believed that all mothers should be subsidized so that they could be with their children and not have to work, but she also said that 'Mother's grief is nothing.' How could she say this, she of all people? 'Mothers are finished, they've had their glory, they've made their miracles. But the boys are cut short before they've achieved their miracles.'

She had, after all, already had her tragedy. She had no man to lose or fear the loss of. What she had instead was lots of men, lots of boys. Kathleen was a youngish widow – thirty-five in 1914 – a woman with her own position and status, a title, financial independence (from her own earnings as much as her pension), work, and the child she had always wanted. As she had said in the letter that Con carried with him to the Pole, the loss of his physical presence was not a mortal blow to her. She kept him guarded in her heart; his presence there was massive, quite enough to keep anyone else out, but his absence did not warp her day-to-day life.

The war seemed to send everyone if not sex mad, then love mad, passionate friendship mad, waste-no-time mad. Kathleen's version had two branches: old men and young men. With the old – Herbert Asquith, George Bernard Shaw, Barrie, Nansen, politicians and writers – she would talk endlessly. (These were not, apart from Nansen, romantic friendships. Lord Grey, the foreign secretary, fifty-two in 1914, became slightly too warm on one occasion and she wrote 'I will *not* be made love to by people that age.') With the young she went dancing, three or four nights a week and even in her lunch hour. The level at which she ran her social life was extraordinary: after a foxtrot for lunch and her full day's work she would go dancing again before going home to see Peter, then a dinner out, perhaps the theatre, supper, perhaps some more dancing, and back home to talk till the small hours.

The main old man was Asquith, 'the most endearing of creatures'. They had known each other for some years by now, and in 1912 she had sculpted him. His friendships with young women – his little harem, as his friends called it – were notorious. His wife Margot knew about them and accepted them, though they caused her pain. She 'not only encouraged his female friends but posted his letters to them if I found them in our front hall', she wrote, grasping the nettle. Asquith's most famous friendship was with Venetia Stanley (a friend of his daughter Violet, as Kathleen was) with whom he had a long, romantic and chaste correspondence. He also corresponded at length with Pamela McKenna, wife of Reginald – there is an argument that his friendship with her was the reason why he would not disown McKenna, which is one reason why Lloyd George finally turned against him in 1916.

In May 1915 Venetia announced her engagement to Edwin Montagu, Financial Secretary to the Treasury and a former private secretary to Asquith himself. Asquith was very upset about it, and turned more to other friends for solace. It was then that Kathleen, who was the same age as his son Raymond, became his confidante. In the midst of the turmoils of trying to run a country involved in a mad, terrible war, he used her as (in his words) 'a haven of refuge'.

He visited several times a week, just to talk things over, and they wrote to each other. His letters are gallant and slightly flirtatious, and if it seems curious that he would have had time to write, one short letter puts that in perspective: '29th Decr 1915: 1 a.m. I must before I leave my work send you a word of gratitude for your angelic kindness this evening. It made all the difference.'

'He was awfully worried,' she reports frequently. They would sit in her studio, away from the telephone 'which always seems to go incessantly when he is here, always just when he is telling me something very interesting some fatuous ass rings up to ask me how I am or something equally absurd.' Mostly they talked politics, morals and ethics. He liked her for her inability to fret or panic, and her discretion, and her 'moral virtue'. There was only ever once a suggestion of any impropriety in their friendship, and even that is hard to estimate, given the possible different meanings of the phrase 'make love'. Kathleen recorded that the PM 'wanted to make love to me or something, and wouldn't talk sensibly at all. I didn't like him. Altogether was rather tiresome and dull.'

They developed a running joke about what it was she provided:

January 15 1916
Inarticulate comforting [he wrote].
(What a good phrase!)
Here is a suggested calculus:
$x =$ No. of days
$y =$ No. of worries per day
$z =$ quantity of I.C. earned and due
$z =$ $(x \times y)$

December 28th 1915
I came back from Vickers to find the PM had been twice. He wrote later saying he had tramped the streets waiting for me, as he was 'in great need of me'. I did wish I hadn't been out. However he came again the next evening. There is great dissension in the cabinet about conscription [Asquith was trying to introduce conscription for single men because not enough of them had volunteered for him to be able

to keep his promise not to make married men join up] and today
McKenna [Reginald, Chancellor of the Exchequer], Runciman [Presi-
dent of the Board of Trade], Grey [Foreign Secretary] and John Simon
[Home Secretary] have all resigned. He showed me the letters – Grey's
stupid and selfish, I thought – 2 sheets saying that as close friends of
his were leaving, he must too; that his eyes are bad, and he had
thought of resigning before. A childish effusion, but saying that he
had not conspired with his friend Runciman. Simon's letter was a very
dear nice letter, brokenhearted at having to abandon the PM but
convinced that forcing anyone is wrong. Runciman and McKenna were
excited and not very nice; McK saying we couldn't afford the enlarging
army and Runciman saying he couldn't spare the men from industry
– as the PM pointed out this is not the moment to discuss either
issue. The compulsion of unmarried men does not fix the size of the
army, not does it prevent the staying of those requisite for trade. The
PM was very very sad, he said he had come to me for two things, 1)
wisdom 2) sympathy. I told him I could dispense the second but not
the first, however I was awfully touched and flattered. He said I was
one of the only discreet women he'd ever met, and told me I helped
him enormously. That night he wrote me a little letter saying I
made 'all the difference'. Poor darling how he hates these
tussles.

The next day she wrote to Sir John Simon, saying she didn't believe
he was really resigning. 'Don't write and tell me I am an impertinent
young woman. I am painfully conscious that that is the case but
oh! so anxious that the neutrals should not lose further faith in
our strength.'

Asquith wrote to her: 'You did me more good than you can know
yesterday.' He quoted Macbeth: 'All our yesterdays have lighted fools
the way to dusty death.'

In the end Sir John Simon resigned and the other three did not.
Asquith told Kathleen he would ask the Allies which they would
prefer: more men or more money, as they couldn't manage both.

On 4 January 1916 Kathleen was 'drying my son's hair in front of
the fire when the PM arrived . . .' After discussing candidates for the
post of home secretary she told him she was 'haunted by the greatness
of his responsibility to the world,' and then apologized for her senten-
tiousness 'to which he replied "oh my dear, if you knew how refreshing

it is!" ' A few days later he sent her a book of poems: 'I like the PM always,' she wrote, 'but most perhaps when he is in a literary mood. His knowledge of English verse is immense.' That night she went to the Savoy and danced.

He was very aware of discretion; he reminded her always to put 'personal' on her notes to him, and after an occasion when an old schoolfriend hurtled in, having forgotten her handbag 'The Woman With The Bag' became a figure on a par with private secretaries as a threat to confidentiality. 'Do if you can with your crowd of shallops and galleons keep the coast clear,' he wrote. He would regularly wait in the other room till 'the Knights of your Tea Table – an extensive and peculiar circle' had been hurriedly got rid of. (The other drawback to their friendship was that he adored bridge and became depressed if there was none, while she thought the game an absolute waste of time.)

Once Kathleen started to think about politics she found she was fascinated by it – partly the subjects, but mainly the men who dealt with them. Another friend was Colonel House, whom she had met in New York in 1913, and who was now in Europe visiting various heads of state as the personal representative of President Wilson. The United States were not yet in the war, and what Colonel House was actually up to was a matter of some interest. Kathleen found him 'one of the most delightful and interesting men I ever met'. 'Colonel House wants to make you believe you are the only person he cares to see or talk to,' she wrote in January 1916. 'I imagine he wants to make each country he visits feel the same. He is just going to Berlin. I like him very much, but I can't forget that he is President Wilson's personal representative and that the presidential elections come on again in November. He wants to take back something to make that more sure. I can't believe, as McKenna says, that his idea is to take back each country's terms for Wilson to combine into a peace.' He complimented her so much that she hardly trusted him; she couldn't tell if he were 'rather a fraud or only American'.

She liked to do things like ask Austen Chamberlain whether he liked the Prime Minister better or worse than he used to (he replied 'Dear me, you do ask very indiscreet questions, don't you?' and then proceeded to tell her). She didn't take to Lloyd George at all until he sang Welsh songs; she teased Colonel House by not asking him any questions because the Prime Minister had already told her all the news. Almost every day she followed the minutiae of political developments: Asquith's disappointment with McKenna and underestimation of House; the King's unexpected intelligence; House's insistence to Wilson not to enter the war over the *Lusitania* because the time was not yet right; Briand calling House Monsieur Nul; the Germans telling House that they had 'vast numbers of submarines and as soon as they had fixed up with America they were going to mine and torpedo the Channel and blockade England utterly'. She was fascinated when Asquith told her how worried the King was about the Russian revolution, how he had been wondering what good he was and had drawn up a list of what the royal family had done: inspection of troops, factories, hospitals, 'every sort of thing. The press never puffed them as they should, for security reasons. What rubbish,' was her opinion. 'As if the Germans didn't know as well as the King the sites of our munitions factories.'

Working in the factory, following politics and having political friends didn't make the slightest difference to her views on the other great political topic of the time, female suffrage. Many years later she told her second son Wayland that any woman worth her salt could make her political opinions known through her husband. He pointed out that not every woman's husband was a cabinet minister, as hers was.

Her sculpture was rather on hold during the war, and she felt the lack of it. On 5 November 1915 her bronze statue of Con was unveiled by Mr Balfour in Waterloo Place. She didn't go to the ceremony, though Peter watched from the balcony of the Athenaeum. In March 1916 she set off to Carrara to carve the marble statue for New Zealand. The Prime Minister 'professed to mind [her absence] awfully'. It was snowing and the Germans were attacking Verdun. A couple of weeks later the boat she had crossed in was sunk, which gave her 'grim thoughts' but didn't stop her travelling.

And if she was going to travel, she'd make the most of it. She stopped off in Paris, seeing Hovelacque and old friends. She went to Rome, where Asquith was visiting the Pope, who told him that 'he knew he was supposed to want to make peace for his own ends, but he would much wish to explain that all he cared for was peace, no matter who made it.' Asquith then went to the front to see the 'very intelligent and very conscientious' Italian king, who had cane chairs, a trestle bed and a photo of his wife and children in his room – nothing else. 'He lives amazingly simply and the soldiers love him.'

Kathleen was most impressed by St Peter's, and 'a wonderful sight, a dense excited crowd, *Viva Asquitti, Viva Inghilterra*' by the station as Asquith set off. But the purpose of the trip was the sixteen cubic yards of fine white marble which awaited her at Carrara. 'I will carve marble, war or no war,' she declared. It seemed absurd to sculpt when all this death was happening, but equally absurd not to. Also, marble was the only thing she could sculpt – there was no metal spare for casting. One evening returning from the quarry she spotted a rather badly finished gravestone, a figure of an angel, waiting for collection. Quickly she tidied it up and honed it, and wondered what its maker would imagine had happened to it.

On 13 September 1916 Asquith wrote that he had been 'with the army in France, and under shellfire . . . at Fricourt, when I was climbing a little hill with my son Raymond . . . Everybody was in marvellous spirits . . .' A week later Raymond was killed.

20 Sept 16
. . . The war has sucked up so much of what was most loveable and full of promise, [Asquith wrote to Kathleen] that I have always been haunted by a fear that a toll would be exacted from me also. But when I saw him last – exactly a fortnight ago today – he was so radiantly strong and confident that I came away from France with an easier mind . . . Whatever pride I had in the past, and whatever hope I had for the future – by much the largest part of both was invested in him. And now all that is gone. It will take me a few days more to try to get back my bearings . . .

In November Asquith asked her to go to Paris with him and Lloyd George: 'They are going to do something new in the war and are off to envisage it with Briand,' she wrote. 'He still thinks fatigue will end the whole thing soon . . . men are not good without material and material must soon give out.' They talked at length about his own fatigue. 'He reviewed his office after nearly nine years, heartily sick of it . . . I reminded him that five or six years ago he'd said to me "I'm like a rat in a trap" and he said "Yes, and that was before the war".' When she asked him point-blank if he wanted to give up, he hummed and hawed and ended up by saying that perhaps he might just die.

Then Peter got a temperature of 103°. It was a flu, and Kathleen got it (she was delirious at times, and in bed for two weeks), and McKenna got it, and Asquith got it. 'Lloyd George finding the PM ill prepared his coup – the snake in goat's clothing,' she wrote in her diary. Well, the coup succeeded, Asquith was out and Lloyd George was in, in charge of the coalition cabinet. Asquith wrote to her on 6 December, midnight: 'I have been fighting with Beasts (like St Paul at Ephesus). The Beasts for the moment got the upper hand . . . Whether (as Browning suggests) 'God is in his heaven' is known only to a very few. Relief – if not release – is a priceless boon, but one doesn't like to leave one's task unfinished.' How well Kathleen understood those sentiments. On 20 December he wrote saying that this would be his last letter from Downing Street: he was clearing out nine years' worth of accumulations, and felt tragic.

Kathleen rounded off 1916 with her first funeral. The publisher Reginald Smith, who had published Con's book of the *Discovery* expedition, had killed himself, jumping out of a window in his pyjamas. It gave her 'the oddest feeling. It seemed a kind of insult to be burying his crumpled body – to go carrying it about in a box. The body he'd thrown out of the window because he thought it polluted water when he washed it. Surely this is a clear case of the insanity of this war having driven a sane man mad. It is the fine sensitive tender-heartedness of the man that made him mad.'

And not just him. There was a little verse current which many people identified with:

> God heard the embattled nations shout
> God save England, God save the King
> God this, God that and God the other thing
> 'Good God,' said God, 'I've got my work cut out.'

Personally, Kathleen had no need of God. She thought perhaps

when she was old and no one on earth needed her she might invent
a god to need her. That was all.

As Asquith lost his job, Kathleen got a new one. 'Pensions qua
pensions is a dull subject,' she thought, and that she was incompetent,
and that she should be with Peter, but she took it: 'being Private
Secretary to Sir Matthew Nathan at the Ministry of Pensions – hours
9.30 – 8pm with an hour for lunch and no compensations that I can
see.' Sir Matthew was the Permanent Under Secretary, and it wasn't
that she didn't like him, she frequently dined with him at Les Lauriers
and she let him come round and tidy up her desk for her. It was, as
she wrote after a year of it, that despite 'an enormous room to myself
looking on to the river I have all the while felt caged and stuffed up.
I have consistently detested the work throughout, it has bored me
unutterably, but I am divided between the feeling of utter waste of
myself as an artist and a gentleman and thankfulness at having
had the experience. Now I know something of a government office,
something of civil servants, something of the negation of life. I am
glad to have known it in order to avoid it, and have sympathy with
the poor devils who have made it their lives. I was very inefficient, I
may add.' Still, 'perhaps some 2,000 people employed in offices
robbing themselves of life give some 700,000 [people] pensions that
they may live.'

'Don't boggle at it, but get into harness at once,' advised Asquith.
So she did, and one of her friends, either Geoffrey Dearmer or Stephen
Gwynn, wrote a poem about it:

> The world is most amazing with duchess VADs
> And masquerades in khaki of uniformed MPs
> But the strangest transformation we've yet assisted at
> Was when the Lady Kathleen became a bureaucrat.
>
> As vagrant as a tinker, as vivid as the blue
> Of gentian on the uplands when spring is bursting through
> With feet that on the pavement from dancing scarce refrain
> She tempts her friends to tempt her to be herself again.
>
> We spread out flowers before her, young summer spreads the sun,
> We call the world to witness that playtime has begun.
> 'Don't go,' we plead, but firmly she snatches up her hat

Right: They had most to give (Arnold Lawrence), bronze by Kathleen Scott, 1922, now in the garden of the Scott Polar Research Institute, Cambridge.

Below right: Geoffrey Dearmer, bronze by Kathleen Scott, 1918.

Below left: Captain R.F. Scott, marble by Kathleen Scott, made at Carrara and now at Christchurch, New Zealand. A bronze of the same design, 1915, is in Wellington Place, London.

With Peter in her studio at Buckingham Palace Road, 1912. On the shelf
behind her is a photograph of Con.

Con in his den in the Hut, 1911. Behind him are pictures of Kathleen and Peter.

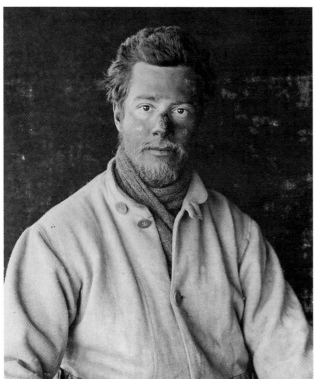

Above: Oates, Bowers, Con, Wilson and Evans at the Pole, 18 January 1912.

Left: Apsley Cherry-Garrard, 1911.

Colonel T.E. Lawrence (of Arabia).

On a train in
Ecuador, 1921.

Edward Hilton Young,
Lord Kennet, Bill.

Peter and Wayland at
the Lacket, 1924.

Kathleen, as the wife of the Minister of Health, conducts a party of ambassadors' and ministers' wives on a tour of a slum clearance scheme in Paddington, 1934.

Right: Lord and Lady Kennet in their robes for the coronation of George VI in 1936. 'A curiosity', Kathleen scribbled.

Below: Working on Sabu, 1936.

Wayland, sketched by
Peter, *circa* 1940.

Kathleen, Peter and Jane at Fritton
during the war.

Peter Scott at his lighthouse, late 1930s.

'I must,' she says, 'The bureau is waiting for its crat.'

'Twas not so bad before this, in winter and in dark
She left the world behind her with Peter in the park.
But now when spring comes flooding thro' windows and thro' doors
Pan yet may come a-piping down office corridors.

Just for a demonstration that she's alive and free
She'll maybe take the high road with some austere CB
But till the bomb explodes there and lays the building flat,
Oh what a happy bureau, with Kathleen for its crat.

Life and company outside the office made up for the despondency within. Kathleen was a frequent visitor to Cherry-Garrard's house at Lamer, where Bernard Shaw was a neighbour. She was there for Christmas 1916, and Peter dressed up as Father Christmas to take books to Shaw and his wife. At first, as with Colonel House, she wasn't sure if she really liked Shaw or was just flattered that he seemed to like her. 'He always flatters me a good deal,' she observed, after he had said that he was surprised his wife Charlotte didn't dislike her, as normally she didn't like interesting women. He told her she had the blue eye of genius, 'the Strindberg eye'. Shaw was always very keen on being portrayed, and he sat several times for Kathleen. After sculpting him and seeing him out of London they became properly fond of each other. (A radio play based on their sittings, *Imitations*, by Michael Butt, has been broadcast by the BBC.)

Once when he was sitting for her they were discussing whether a person's character and sex came through in any recognizable way in their art. Shaw had observed to Epstein, apropos being sculpted by Rodin, that 'I am a comedian as well as a philosopher; and Rodin has no sense of humour . . . accordingly, the bust has no sense of humour.' Prince Troubetskoy also sculpted him, and 'made me flatteringly like a Russian nobleman'; Epstein himself made Shaw 'a Brooklyn navvy'. Kathleen wondered whether her feminity might make her representation of him in any way feminine, and Shaw poohpoohed it heartily. 'No woman ever born had a narrower escape from being a man,' he said. 'My affection for you is the nearest I ever came to homosexuality.' Barrie, incidentally, said something similar: that she was half man half woman, but that her woman half was more of a woman than other women. She loved this, of course. It probably says something about the general view of women at the time that it was a compliment to an intelligent woman to be called masculine.

Shaw and Kathleen gossiped together; he told her all about his affair with Mrs Pat Campbell, including 'accounts of her embraces' and how after one row she had sent back a note from him unanswered, and he had sent it back again with 'Dear Stella, don't you know you are breaking my heart' written on the envelope. 'Don't ever mention her to Charlotte,' he said. He told her too about his antecedents: 'a ménage à trois, his clever energetic mother, a drunken father and a musician'. He read *Heartbreak House* aloud to her, called her Kathleen, and when they bumped into each other on the train 'descended from first class to third to play with us'.

Lamer was fun. Ricketts and Shannon came to stay, and Harley Granville-Barker. Pussy Russell Cooke was in love with Cherry, so was Peter's nurse. Pussy's brother Sidney was a bit in love with Kathleen, Kathleen was entranced by Shaw. They sang: 'Shaw amazed me. I have known him almost fifteen years [Kathleen may be exaggerating here. It is not recorded when they first met; possibly it was at Meudon in 1906, when Shaw was sitting for Rodin] and this was the first time I knew he sang. He went almost the whole way through the score of *Rheingold* on the piano and singing in a charming baritone voice.' The next night he did the same for *Die Walküre*. In summer they slept out on the lawn, where Cherry sang in his sleep. Shaw would read from his latest play, and Cherry read from his 'Antarctic book', which would much later become *The Worst Journey in the World*.

Shaw didn't at this stage tell Kathleen his own poor opinion of Con. Perhaps he hadn't yet formulated it. If he had spoken of it it is unlikely that he and Kathleen could have been friends. They argued about politics: Shaw called Asquith 'a drunken old blaggard' and Ricketts 'upheld him with sublime eloquence'. Kathleen taught Shaw to dance: 'to begin to learn to dance at the age of 61 is I think rather delicious', and at New Year 1917 they danced to the overture of *Figaro*. 'I was found to possess a senile and lumbering diable au corps which made my King David-like gambols amusing to myself and not so utterly unbearable for my unfortunate partners as might have been expected,' Shaw wrote (to Henry Salt). Granville-Barker said that standing on top of a cliff gave him a desire for suicide and Shaw agreed. Kathleen however felt nothing but exhilaration. 'Dear god everything exhilarates me. I must be on the lookout for exhilaration.'

In the summer of 1918 Kathleen had Shaw to stay at the vicarage at Streatly which she had taken for the holidays. This was something else: 'I am not good at sustained efforts of niceness,' she wrote, and sure enough the day after he arrived 'looking ill' was 'cold and wet, Shaw cross and me shy and dull, food bad and prospect hopeless'. (In 1948 Shaw wrote: 'I am quite taken aback to learn that I let her see that the Thames Valley depressed me, as it always does.') It got better – after a week or so 'Shaw took up the duties of host and behaved throughout the day in a manner reminiscent of Queen Victoria and the annual Wesleyan Conference'. However he rather sat on the other guests, and 'set up a strident noise for cheese when one Frederick Watson ['frequently extremely promising in asides'] seemed on the point of a joke'.

Kathleen was not that far off Shaw's ideal of womanhood; she was not 'tall and very goodlooking', but she was 'sympathetic, intelligent, tender and humorous ... a woman of great vitality and humanity, who begins a casual acquaintance at the point usually attained by English people after thirty years acquaintance when they are capable of reaching it at all.' Consider Lady Cicely Waynflete, the heroine of Shaw's *Captain Brassbound's Conversion*, who walked across Africa with nothing but a little dog and met six cannibal kings who all wanted to marry her, who has 'the authority of a mother' and treats men with 'a mixture of shrewdness, will-power and an attraction which does not depend on the erotic use of sex' (Michael Holroyd, Shaw's biographer). Shaw and Kathleen 'got on together to perfection'; in his words, 'she was a wonderful woman'.

Lots of people came to Streatly, including Steichen. He and Kathleen spent the evening in a punt in the moonlight. 'He remembered a great deal of the past and had banked a great deal on the future,' she observed. The actress Viola Tree came with her two 'white delicate little boys' who Kathleen feared would be killed by the treatment of Peter's nurse, who behaved as if they were as tough as Peter.

In London Kathleen introduced Shaw to Isadora, who 'made

impassioned love' to him, 'begging him to come and sit beside her and hold her hand, because "though I may not be much to look at I'm very good to feel". Shaw complied. It was all comic beyond words.' This was the only time that Shaw and Isadora met, and if the anecdote is true that she offered to bear his child, because it would be so perfect 'with your brains and my body', and he replied 'but what if it had your brains and my body?' then it must have happened then. Shaw, however, said that though the exchange took place it was not with Isadora who, he said, was 'no nonentity'.

Kathleen's affection for Isadora lingered, but exasperation was coming to the fore. When Isadora was unhappy she drank, and that Kathleen could not understand. After her children's death, Isadora had got herself pregnant by a young Italian she met on a beach and broke up with immediately after. Kathleen saw her in London in 1916, where Isadora 'had been Comte Robert de la Bas' mistress for many months – if there wasn't another man on earth I couldn't cast my eye on Robert. How lucky everybody doesn't see alike.' In 1918 Kathleen visited her with Sidney Russell Cooke at 1 a.m.: she was out, with a 'fat old freak called Angelo'. She visited her in Paris a few weeks later: at 3 p.m. she was still in bed, smoking and drinking coffee. She was 'very fat but still Isadora'. Kathleen thought it 'sad, oh so very sad'. Then Isadora told her that she'd seen Steichen and he'd given her lilies of the valley. Kathleen was feeling unusually low anyway, and didn't need Isadora playing games with her.

Kathleen had no reason for jealousy. She had her gentlemen admirers. 'You know I cherish no sentimental rubbish about remarriage,' Con had written in his last letter. 'When the right man comes to help you in life you ought to be your happy self again,' but she wasn't inclined.

Times were changing very quickly during the war. Contraception had been available to those who knew where to find it since the 1880s, but it was now that people started really to use it. Swift marriages, passionate affairs and war babies were becoming more and more common. But Kathleen did not change, she had simply reverted to the chastity she had upheld before her marriage. Why not? She still believed in the same principles.

'Of course you are not tempted,' Asquith once said to her, apropos sex. 'I imagine you have yourself very completely ruled by your head.' She explained to him that only the head had any appeal for her. He may have been teasing when he said he supposed beautifully built handsome young men didn't attract her; she said that as serious contenders they didn't. In fact she loved handsome young men, she loved to dance with them and sculpt their beautifully built muscles, but it was not physical beauty that made her fall in love, that much was true. At a dance for Canadian officers given by Lady Markham she was 'introduced to all the clever old generals and so on but I wanted to dance with the stupid young ones'. And there were her boys. Christopher and Geoffrey Dearmer, aged twenty and twenty-one, were undergraduates at Christchurch when the war broke out. Christopher enlisted that day as a private; Geoffrey a little later as an officer. They were the sons of Kathleen's old friends Mabel (the writer and illustrator – her sons addressed her as Petlambtulip) and Percy (Canon at Westminster Abbey). The boys were both devoted to Kathleen. Geoffrey wrote her poems endlessly ('riches stored up against old age' she called them), spent his leaves with her, and added to the fullness of her days by walking her to work in the mornings. In return she had Mr Heinemann and Mr Macmillan call to discuss publishing his work. Geoffrey wrote her a series of eight sonnets:

> If I had seen what hourly happiness
> In this my world your being could ordain,
> How then should I have trysted with distress
> And misery the cringing friend of pain?
> If I had seen beyond the looming years
> Your shadow, grief had haunted me in vain,
> For what are cataracts of human tears
> Beside the boundless laughter of the main?

Christopher, on the other hand, told her scandalous stories: 'He is better than Compton Mackenzie for the moment,' she wrote. 'He recounts all his experiences however sordid in every minute detail, he is very educative. If he weren't so beautiful I should dislike him, as it is I certainly don't.' One of his tales was about the farmer's wife where he was billeted, who 'having fallen madly in love with him creeps in. He is entirely cynical about it. Recounts it all to me and says it is cheaper than —. He described her and it in the most cold-blooded way.'

'He was certainly very good-looking,' Geoffrey recalls. 'Which is more than you can say for me. But she was a mad dancer, and I was a good dancer, so we went to the *thés dansants* together. And to the theatre. And we always went to see Grock the clown. He spoke no English – I don't think he spoke any language.'

The brothers both fought at Gallipoli: Geoffrey survived, had a distinguished career as a poet and with the BBC, and survives still, aged 100, in Kent. Christopher was killed.

'When Christopher was killed,' Geoffrey recalls, 'she saw my father in the street and said to him, "Isn't it sad to think that the loveliest person of all is dead?" She could say that sort of thing without sounding theatrical. She never romanced or exaggerated. Never made a thing of it.' After Christopher's death Kathleen and Geoffrey became closer, and he knew most of her friends – though not the anti-social Asquith. Shaw he remembers as 'very talkative and interesting'; Barrie as 'winsome'. Isadora, Geoffrey used to call Isador-able Drunken, and he teased her by asking if she still 'ran about'. Nansen he found 'very charming, with an accent. Kathleen was very proud to have known him.' Of the canard that Kathleen and Nansen were lovers, he laughs and says, 'They certainly didn't have an affair. Kathleen was not in the least bit dissipated. Unlike Isadora, who didn't remain either single, to put it mildly, or sober.'

The writer Stephen Gwynn, a family friend of the Dearmers who later wrote a biography of Scott, sent her poems and talked politics with her. 'I think he was in love with her,' Geoffrey says now. Gwynn was covering the Irish Convention during 1917 and kept Kathleen up-to-date through as many as three letters a day. Sidney Russell Cooke, brother of Apsley Cherry-Garrard's girlfriend Pussy, spent long evenings discussing his future. After one such, 'an unexpected madness overtook him', by which she probably means some form of romantic declaration, and she, 'old hardened woman of the world, was surprised. It made me feel rather rotten. I must try not to be so engrossedly interested in boys and their futures.'

At other times she just felt annoyed when men misunderstood and wanted too much from her, either emotionally or physically. An

American officer, Hayes Brook, was a regular companion; the next thing she knew she had made friends with his commanding officer too and he, the CO, was attempting to 'be very nice' in the car. 'How can anybody take such a serious view of me?' she wrote. 'Can't they see I'm I, not half of them?'

So was everyone in love with her? 'She would have loved you to ask that,' says Geoffrey. 'She would certainly have answered in the affirmative. She was proud of her effect on men. "I can't prevent people falling in love with me," she used to say.' What was it they saw in her? A young fellow named Jack Hills put her appeal into words: 'We sat over a log fire and he told me for an hour how wonderful I was, how vital, how he could see life coursing, dancing through me, how every gesture, every movement, was indicative of the character of me. Of course I sat back and basked . . .' Stephen Gwynn wrote what he called an Indictment of her:

> There is no consistency about her. She will argue by the hour on the personal inferiority of woman, yet in practice can seldom refrain from confuting her own argument . . . to all appearances she is fine-spun, delicately chiselled, daintily feminine, yet without warrant or necessity she will tramp ten hours carrying a knapsack on her back . . . A woman who could sit on a man's shoulder while he forded a stream should not produce a young Patagonian . . . [of] preposterous robustness . . . She has been known in difficult circumstances to behave with admired dignity. Why then fail where it is so easy to succeed? Is it so difficult to walk along a road without skipping, dancing, singing, whistling, or at the very least swaggering like a street arab, hands in pockets? . . . If her conduct is too often unladylike, I have always found her to act like a gentleman . . . I am driven to suspect that this parade of attributes which glaringly contradict each other may be a device through which she surreptitiously cancels out her faults, so that we perceive none of them. But the worst of her vice is that it carries its own infection. I have never for two days found the same reason to love her.

She was not, judging by photographs, a terribly pretty woman. She does not look daintily feminine or delicately chiselled. But that she charmed men is in no doubt. 'She had an extraordinary magnetism if she liked you at all,' her son Wayland recalls, 'and she loved being fallen in love with.' 'She was extremely good company to men she found attractive,' said her daughter-in-law, Peter's first wife, Elizabeth Jane Howard. Her second husband wrote to her many years later, 'I love you because you are gay, and I love you because you are true.'

And Kathleen herself observed: 'I am glad I am a woman, that is being born into the class I am. Nothing is expected of a woman in my class, neither brains, energy or initiative, and you have merely to display the modicum of any of these things to get fantastic kudos.' She liked to record the compliments and affections she was offered – as when Asquith told her she had the best brain of any woman he knew, and she said 'say that again', and he did. She did have that empty childhood to make up for.

It comes almost as a relief to find there were men with whom she didn't get on. Once such was Hilaire Belloc, whom she thought 'a ridiculous person . . . he says that the War Office is censoring his articles and the reason is the personal animosity of Lloyd George . . . he swanks ridiculously . . . he gets his local colour from maps at the RGS.' Another was H. G. Wells, with whom she talked about God at dinner. 'He really is (coarse little beast) exceedingly amusing . . .'

She was a contradictory woman to be close to. Hayes Brook summed up the negative aspect for her. 'He says I am a spoilt child, that I don't like him at all but am just playing . . . as though I'd seen a doll in a shop window and I just want that doll and (he contends) that's not the right doll for me, neither clever enough nor nuffin . . . I know he's exactly and amazingly right and yet I'm awfully hurt and disappointed.'

She still played green stick to droopy sweetpeas, but she kept any droopiness of her own very private. No one was to know if she was ill, for example, as she was at the beginning of 1918, 'fainting a good deal' and suffering headaches. No one was to see her low or unhappy. She was as stern with her companions as she was with herself. Sidney Russell Cooke told her 'of his terror in France, of the blue faces of the dead men. He was standing, and a shudder ran through his slip of a body as he said "Oh I am so frightened of death." I would have liked to have taken him in my arms and comforted away the horror, but I only said "Oh that's rather absurd."

He was very real. After all he is only a little kid, with all his wits. He showed me a photo of a girl he liked and didn't say more.' She talked endlessly with her friends and loved to be confided in, but 'I reveal nothing, ever.' When the air raids struck at night it was Peter who came into bed with her, and his arm she liked to feel thrown across her chest in his sleep.

She wasn't pompous about her chastity. On one occasion she was mistaken for a 'pretty lady' by a young man at the Carlton who wanted to take her somewhere quiet. She thought it tremendously funny. But she didn't approve. When Pussy Russell Cooke told her that Gladys Apse had lived with Captain Williams for three years, and had run away with a man for a fortnight when she was seventeen, Kathleen's reaction was 'Lord! These young women, they seem to think nothing of it.' Later she met the young writer Rebecca West, through Shaw. Rebecca was then halfway through her ten-year semi-secret affair with H. G. Wells, and mother of his son. Wells was married to his second wife, with whom he had an arrangement allowing for a steady mistress. He had no intention of parting from his wife, partly because if he did he would be 'obliged to attend himself to his translation business, his income tax returns, domestic bills, banking accounts', he wrote to Rebecca in the third person. Rebecca and the boy, Anthony, lived a humiliating *sub rosa* life of seaside lodgings and lying to servants.

'She is very unattractive and ugly at first,' wrote Kathleen of Rebecca, 'but inclined to be terribly friendly. She has a very spotty face and wears stays. However I warmed to her later, for she has some erudition and some wit, and I am always disarmed by candour. She believes – oh the pathos of it, really and truly confidently believes that Wells has been entirely and actively faithful to her all these five years.' If he had been faithful then he soon wasn't to be. On a trip to Moscow he had an affair with Maxim Gorky's secretary, which he told Rebecca about.

His wife knows about her and won't meet her, but Rebecca knows Amber Reeves [a former lover of Wells] and Wells' first wife does all their typing. She is a very sensual young creature and told me she likes the touch of any male quite irrespective. I am fascinated by the conversation of these exotic beings and have an inclination to lead them on until I have suddenly to retire to be sick. She did not have her child deliberately by the most intelligent man she knew. [There was a rumour that Wells and Rebecca had conducted their own experiment in eugenics.] She had been living with him months before, she says she is only 25 now. She got blood poisoning after the babe and was two years very ill. If she can make good her work it will be all right for her boy. I liked her better and better as the day went on.

Rebecca was more interesting to Kathleen than most of the exotic creatures; she was, though in a very different way, another mother without a father for her boy.

Occasionally it seems that Kathleen's chastity was harder for her now that standards of behaviour were changing. Her fascination with the romances of others was an outlet, as were her own emotional friendships and flirtations, but if anything her standard for men was even higher. Only Con had been good enough while he was alive; how much less likely that any other man could compete with the memory of him, particularly as the standards by which he had lived and which in his death he had come to personify were being threatened and dismantled day by day.

Kathleen didn't lack respectable opportunity. She and Nansen corresponded, and though their friendship gave her great pleasure she would not marry him. There was a moment in 1917 when she suddenly decided to go to New York, where Nansen was with the Norwegian Special Mission to the US, writing long, devoted, slightly lugubrious letters to her about what might have been. 'We had much delightful fun then, I often dream of it and wish it were now. Kay, how would it be to meet again, I wonder? What would we do? We were always so wise, would we be it now?' Only the fact that she couldn't get a passage to New York kept her from going. But Nansen only heard of this plan through a third party – and immediately wrote wanting to know what was going on, and was she coming after all? In the end, after the war, she couldn't give up her freedom, and he was simply too old for her.

On 6 October 1915 Gilbert Cannan came to dinner. It was, she said, 'like coming back home after a long long voyage'. The next day Christopher Dearmer was killed. 'How odd,' she wrote three days later. 'I took Christopher to myself because he was so absurdly like that Boy, then the very day the Boy comes back after eight years Christopher is shot. It seems almost a deliberate act of my gods.'

She was pleased when Cannan said that he still loved her, as much as, if not more than, before. 'I dunno,' she wrote. 'It is the jolliest thing in the world to see his grave face light up into radiance at the sight of me.' And he was 'delicious' with Peter. But she certainly didn't want the fuss and vulgarity of taking up with Cannan after all the fuss and vulgarity of his taking up with Mary Barrie in the first place. After another lapse, she saw him again in 1917; he had been in a sanatorium and had lost his looks. Kathleen wrote to him saying that whatever he did she would still think of him as a thing beloved. (Geoffrey Dearmer, perhaps with the eye of a rival, thought Cannan 'a worthless creature, a poor thing. Nothing very much. He sponged on her.')

She always had a weakness for wounded heroes. A typical admirer was Clifford Erskine Bolst, a captain in the Black Watch who wore kilts. He was 'rather a bounder but so full of life in spite of having been burned alive, wounded and gassed.' He wanted to make love to her, so she took him to the zoo with Peter instead to see the insect house. During 1917 she was much taken with a New Zealander, Colonel Freyberg, a twenty-seven-year-old with 'five wound bars: a great gash on his neck, one arm stiff, another both bones broken, a gashed tummy and a bullet through both legs – what about that for sentimental blackmail!' Freyburg was a champion swimmer and a great hero in both world wars: he won a VC and a DSO for swimming ashore at Gallipoli to set flares, and many years later Churchill described him as 'the salamander of the British Empire'. 'He made some delicious suggestions with which I longed to comply', but she didn't, 'as usual'. On another occasion Mlle Vacani, who ran a dancing club where Kathleen went all the time, introduced her to a group of blinded officers, 'a most extraordinary experience. All pity vanishes in a wonderment of admiration. They were amazing dancers.'

Kathleen's housekeeping was a little less haphazard than it had been when she fed Rodin fried eggs and pomegranates, but not much.

She would shout down the back stairs, 'Nice dinner, please, the Prime Minister's coming!' Air raids during dinner didn't bother her at all:

29 Sept 1917

We had a dinner party, oh such a funny dinner party! There were Stephen McKenna, Gilbert Cannan, Sidney Russell Cooke, Geoffrey Dearmer and me. In the middle a very bad air raid started. A strange girl came in who was going to dance later. The parlour maid came in hysterical and collapsed on the drawing room sofa. The cook panted behind, and Wink [Peter's nanny] arrived with her hair down. We fetched Pete down in his pyjamas – we were a mottled party. First we watched from the balcony then we shut shutters, lit lights and Sidney turned on the pianola. Gilbert never uttered a word. Stephen sat and made magic – 'evil magic', he said. Sidney and I sustained animated conversation, to which Pete contributed a good deal of sound information about aerial matters. More people came as the night went on, and we danced until three am.

All of which was all very well, but she missed her proper work. Rodin's memorial service in November 1917 put it into perspective for her. 'Let us remember with thanksgiving and with all honour Auguste Rodin, to whom it was given by God to make life more noble and more beautiful for his fellow men,' said the address. 'Which', Kathleen wrote, 'must stir the imagination of the humblest sculptor, and I am very humble as a sculptor, however pretentious I may be as a psychologist, a butterfly or a friend of great intellects. As a sculptor no man's flattery can deceive me. I *know*. But such thoughts make me chafe at my present occupation.'

'Oh blue-eyed owner of the skies, chuck Matthew and chase butterflies,' wrote Geoffrey Dearmer in a letter to her, and she did at the end of 1917. She gave up the pensions job with no regrets at all, only to be called back for a final stint in Paris sorting out a mess that had arisen over there. Living in Paris again she liked very much, even though every day Big Bertha, a great gun which nobody could find, bombarded the city.

On her return to London she started on her most interesting and fulfilling war work. She had been ill and despondent at the beginning of the year: neuralgia, nerves, 'ghastly head' (perhaps eyes), fatigue.

She hated it and wouldn't admit it. There was too much other suffering for her to be weak. 'What am I up to being alive anyway? To be a sculptor? Fame? No, certainly not. To rear good specimens for a future generation? To be happy and make happiness? Health and beauty I think. To make health, happiness and beauty, and enable other people to make it and feel it.' These, she said, were 'so to speak my war aims'. As the war came to an end she found a way of putting them into practice. In October 1918 she visited Ellerman's Hospital 'to fix about modelling hurt faces'.

There were all too many wounded heroes with blown away faces by 1918, and methods of rebuilding them were improving apace, as medical knowledge does in wartime. Evacuation of the wounded was fairly efficient after 1915, general anaesthesia was available using chloroform or ether, and tissues could be kept disinfected. Surgeons could mend faces, and sculptors helped them. 'Surgery calls Art to its aid,' as Sir Harold Gillies, the leading British facial plastic surgeon of the time, put it.

The scheme was that she should make models of men's faces, recreating the missing parts, and that the surgeons should then rebuild the patients' faces using the models as a basis and a record. It meant that they didn't have to experiment on the actual wounds. Surgeons imitated stages of the operation by moving putty flaps on the model as they would flesh on the face. Henry Tonks, the Slade professor with whom Kathleen had studied years before, led the way in keeping records of plastic surgery cases with diagrams and pastel drawings, and it was probably through him that she became involved.

The men would arrive from France, their wounds semi- and badly healed. 'A plaster cast of the face is made and thereon the sculptor, aided by early photographs if available, models the missing contours. With radiographs to confirm that the apparent loss is not merely displacement, the surgeon now has data for adequate diagnosis . . . Realisation [of contours] comes only by close co-operation with the sculptor,' Gillies wrote. The key was to make sure that the bone structure itself was properly rebuilt; it may have looked as if not much soft tissue was missing, but that could have been because the bone was missing too. To avoid this the wounds had to be 'reconstituted by release of overstretched tissues'; only then could the loss be diagnosed and the restoration planned.

The methods were both primitive and miraculous. Areas of skin to be grafted were mapped out with tinfoil; stitches were horsehair; molten wax and metal plates were experimented with as rebuilding materials. The best though was cartilage; it would be removed from between the patient's ribs, wrapped in sterile gauze and then shaped with a scalpel on a table 'with three raised edges to prevent disaster'. Any left over would be stored beneath the skin of the patient's abdomen: even if it wasn't needed for him, another patient could use it. ('It goes without saying that the donor must be proved free from syphilis,' Gillies points out.) When recreating a nose, the surgeon would stitch the part that should be narrow with horsehair, tie the stitch and let it become inflamed 'so that the scar tissue which ensues will take over [the stitch's] function permanently.'

The patients had already had a long convalescence from the original wound, and many were badly nourished. They might well have other wounds as well as the facial one. The operations were long, and bad wounds required several of them. In the meantime the men might well 'grow accustomed to morphia', as Gillies delicately put it. There was danger of gangrene. Some, having survived the initial wound, died during the attempts to rebuild their faces.

Kathleen leapt at the chance to be involved. Her first subject was 'a man Brooker without any mouth at all . . . These men without noses are very beautiful, like antique marbles. I have done a magnificent head of Captain Budd, got so engrossed I forgot about lunch.' She sat in on an operation, scar tissue being cut out. 'The anaesthetic and heat were rather overpowering but I stuck it out and it was very beautiful to watch. Helped hold down the man. Captain Romsey who is very nice asked me if I thought I could stand it. I replied confidently that I could, and *I did*, but I was terribly unwell when the tension was over, and the next morning very sick. This is always what happens to me in emotion – I am sick.'

Later she was able to visit the Val de Grâce hospital in Paris to see their museum of mutilated and mended faces. 'Dr Morestin is the great surgeon: they say they cast on the open wounds using boiling wax and applying it still quite hot.' (Hypolyte Morestin, a 'strange and moody octaroon', in the words of Harold Gillies, was a native of Martinique, and a surgeon of genius.) At Boulogne she drove about with Charles Auguste Valadier, and was very impressed by his 'immense' car, as well she might be. He had equipped his Rolls-Royce with a dentist's chair and drills. He had been a flamboyant society dentist in Paris, and now, 'fat and florid', he strode about 'in a Red Cross uniform, highly polished field boots and jingling spurs', according to Gillies. Though he was not medically qualified he bone-grafted fractured mandibles and repaired jaw wounds. 'He toured about until he had filled with gold all the remaining teeth in British GHQ,' Gillies wrote. 'With the generals strapped in his chair he convinced them of the need of a plastic [surgery] and jaw unit, and one was set up in . . . Wimereaux.' Kathleen visited his 'miraculous' exhibition there, and met a man with 'a cartilage rib under the skin of his forehead prior to a new nose; another nose with a little hair on the side, [the skin] having been taken from the forehead.'

'On Monday I am to make a chin for a man,' she wrote, a week before the Germans asked for an armistice. 'I feel terribly like God. The surgeon said without a smile, "Don't make it longer than you need or we shan't have enough flesh to cover it." God! It's a fantastic world.'

♦

SIXTEEN

Sculpting and Dancing

♦

1918–1922

AND THEN the war was over. Kathleen had been staying with the Austen Chamberlains at East Grinstead.

> *November 11*: Came up at about ten with the Chamberlains and George Duckworth. As we went along we thought there was an unusual amount of activity in the streets and when we arrived at the War Cabinet Austen asked his chauffeur who told him the Armistice has been signed – thus it is that our ministers of the crown learn of these trifling events . . .

She headed for Paris. The Place de la Concorde was covered with German cannon and aeroplanes and helmets. Arty Paget was there, and Hovelacque and Hofbauer, and James Barrie turned up, having been to Verdun and lost all his luggage. Kathleen and Barrie

> played together til midnight. We rang up about 4 restaurants for a table – none to be had. Then we went out and walked around all the local restaurants in his quarter and were jeered at for hoping to find a table. Finally we went to Ciro's where Philippe had seen me before sometimes and he gave us a luxurious table where we had a lovely dinner and Barrie was very dear. Then we went out arm in arm to watch the delirious crowd play Kiss in the Ring on the Grands Boulevards, mad wild scenes, girls looking like widows dancing with the rest. Finally we went back to my rooms and he told me how sometimes in the evening he wanted a woman so badly that he nearly went out in the street and offered a woman £1 to come and sit with him.

Also in Paris was Colonel House, representing President Wilson at the formation of the peace. House was deeply aware that he was 'going on one of the most important missions anyone ever undertook', but Wilson had said to him, 'I have not given you any instructions because I feel you will know what to do.' His responsibility was awesome. Between his meetings he drove with Kathleen around the Bois de Boulogne, telling her about the conferences and about the nascent scheme for a league of nations:

November 15: When he was at his farm in the summer Wilson asked him [House] to draw up his ideas about a League of Nations. He shut himself up for two days and wrote. He has not looked at it since the Armistice, but is convinced that it is good and workable. He has shown it to nobody, not even to Lord Robert [Cecil]. He seized my hand and said, 'Pray for my scheme. If it goes through it will be more important than the Magna Carta, the declaration of Independence, or anything.' I love him when he is excited like that. He said of the League of Nations, 'Oh there is no sort of any doubt, it is bound to be.'

He told her that it would work by deterrent.

In the normal course there would be no war for forty or fifty years, and people would forget that the peace was due to war-weariness, and would think it was the League that was preventing it, and so it would be prevented.

Kathleen was very taken by the idea; as it progressed her house in Buckingham Palace Road became a social centre for supporters of the scheme, and she worked to popularize and publicize it. She felt it to be typical of the ideals of youth and strength which she attached to the United States, and she argued vehemently with the 'Slay the enemy, no peace till the Germans march into our lines with a white flag' brigade. 'To be safe, England must be in the right,' House said, and she agreed. When it was all over, he told her, he wanted to do charity work. 'He had been behind the highest man so long, he would now like to be behind the lowest.' His optimism and passion delighted her, but she drew the line at religious faith. 'He uses amazing platitudes, he talks of the "spirit of God in us" and of "The other side of the River" and seems sure of it.'

Kathleen was less romantically idealistic now than she had been before the war. Her views were more cynical, more realistic. In the Coupon Election on December 14th she voted Labour, not because she liked Labour ('I hate Labour, with their Unions and their ignorance') but because of 'all the Lloyd Georgian boasting and braying, and maybe it is better that [Labour] should be allowed an outlet to stave off Bolshevism.'

The great thing after the war was getting back to work at her sculpture. It's an ill wind, and Kathleen's particular good was commissions for war memorials, regimental plaques and medals, and portraits of war heroes. 'Do you spend your days sculpting and your nights dancing? *Quelle vie!* (What a life!)' Asquith wrote to her, and indeed she did. Though she agreed with Nietzsche that one should count as wasted a day when one had not danced, she also found that 'when I am properly fed intellectually I don't need dancing'. It was less of a mania now than it had been during the frustrating years of the war.

Work was the thing. She would pick up lumps of clay when out for a walk and sculpt a couple of babies; she would make her friends sit for her – Hugo Koehler, Mr Davies the US ambassador, Stephen Gwynn, Dick Ward, Sir Cecil Smith. Geoffrey Dearmer describes the experience: 'She'd say "There's no shape in your nose, it's just a blob." As if it were my fault. "Stand there, sit there." Not a word of apology.' Pete was often in the studio with her while she worked, sketching and modelling lumps of clay. She was spoiled for choice of what to send in to the Academy in 1919. In the end she chose a marble baby, a portrait of Stephen Gwynn in bronze and a wax head of a girl.

Art altogether took her over: she went frequently to the theatre; her cousin Benjie Bruce was married to the dancer Karsavina, and through them ballet became an interest and Diaghilev a friend; she took a box for four nights running at the opera and was so overwhelmed by *Tristan and Isolde* that she nearly fainted with delight. At a party of Nancy Astor's she was entertained by 'a little American who played and sang – Cole Porter'.

In 1917 Commander Josiah Wedgwood had amused her no end over dinner because 'he wanted to get 100 charming women to have babies without husbands. How I longed to volunteer! How absurd that I, self-supporting, able-bodied, having proved my capacity, am disbarred from having babes without binding myself to some man.' The end of the war brought her maternalism very strongly to the fore, but she couldn't see any way to act upon it. Colonel House had asked Kathleen if she wanted to marry again. She said she thought not; but that she terribly wanted a baby.

Part of it was that Peter had started boarding school (where he was 'not at all good but very popular') and she missed him. 'I told him he'd have a lovely time – play football and have ever such fun – to which he replied "But Mummy what will you do? Won't you want me?" Which considering I have never said a word of my feelings to him I think is rather adorable of him.'

Other people's little children were endlessly fascinating to her; she was very jealous of Violet Bonham Carter (Asquith) when she became pregnant in 1918. Even the fact that Violet's child was a girl, which Violet said initially was 'a leaden disappointment' to her, did not douse Kathleen's enthusiasm. 'The dear busy experimenting mite . . . was busy practising beating the air with ardent adventurous little fists, so occupied with the miracle of being alive. Babies are terribly upsetting to me. I love them too much.' During a visit to a 'baby-farm' (a home) 'I had to do violence to myself not deliberately to kidnap at least one . . . I wonder if I am not permanently maiming myself by denying myself a baby.'

But what could she do? Marry, after all? She was still a long way from it: 'I wish I didn't get such very foolish enthusiasms for people I don't respect,' she wrote of Hugo Koehler, a 'ridiculously charming' American officer with 'dreadful wrists'. 'I was just as foolish about Freyberg, who now seems to me fat, dull and egoistic. I am conscious of folly.' And very strong in her was the feeling that 'I mustn't harness Pete with any but the most perfect.'

There was Colonel Stirling, whom she met when he came to see her about a silver statuette for his regiment's mess. After visiting the silver-caster they went off around Soho buying asparagus and stockings, and within weeks he brought her his Legion of Honour medal 'as an offering'. For the best part of two years he tucked fur rugs around her feet in taxis and at the theatre, and made her feel 'a brute' because she could not return his devotion. Geoffrey Dearmer, she observed, had been in love with her for five years – 'Too long'. In November 1919 she finally had things out with Nansen. 'It's quite absurd from my point of view. He's 57 and – well I am not.' She thought he should marry the woman more his own age, and his own nationality, who had been in love with him for years and had left her husband for love of him. He did, and when Kathleen finally met her she found her charming. Finally closing that avenue was a relief and, in a way, it set her free.

On 28 November 1919 Victor Campbell introduced her to a man named Edward Hilton Young. 'He has one arm,' she wrote, 'but is very clever about it. He was an amazingly gallant fighter and is an MP – a most . . .' And with that unfinished sentence her diary, normally packed, goes blank for two months. When it picks up again she is in Italy with Peter and some American officers, cruising around the artistic highspots – Florence, Padua, Milan, Genoa, Verona, Venice – in a Cadillac and having hundreds of punctures. Probably it was not meeting Hilton Young that struck her dumb, but perhaps it was. She returned to London, worked, danced, sent Peter back to school, but something is eating at her. Colonel Stirling begins to seem unctuous. He talks too much. Things are palling slightly – except Peter. 'Sculpting, society, music, men, I'd miss them all but Pete is the one thing I really love with hungry love.'

In July 1920 Hilton Young came to lunch. 'I think I adore him,' she wrote.

> He's the most exciting personality. Was a barrister, then wrote City notes, became a Naval officer in the War, commanded an armoured train in Russia – only Englishman – pushed forward 50 miles of railway, dark forests each side. 2 Russian subs. Lost arm at Zeebrugge and is now in Parliament, a Liberal Coalitionist. An altogether entrancing person. Knows the songs of all birds and is shy!

A week later she wrote: 'I grow more in love with Con every year.'

Pamela Glenconnor remembered a different version of how Kathleen and Hilton, as he was known, met: he was with a crowd of people at Kathleen's studio; Kathleen inquired of Lady Glenconnor who he was, and said 'I'm going to marry that man.'

Hilton Young was forty-one in 1920. His career was admirably described by Kathleen: he had also been president of the Union when at Trinity College, Cambridge, and editor of the *Cambridge Review*, then assistant editor to the *Economist* and financial editor of the *Morning Post*.

His war career had been distinguished. He had lost his arm early on during the famous raid led by Admiral Sir Roger Keyes, where a hulk full of concrete had been towed across the Channel and sunk, to block up the mouth of Zeebrugge, a 'nest of submarines'. Hilton had been on board HMS *Vindictive*, whose job was to draw fire, land men and fire on everything in sight. He was on deck when he was hit by a splinter of shell. 'The splinter had pulverised the bone and cut all the nerves but had missed the artery', he learnt when he took it below to the dressing station. 'That was of course very great luck', he wrote later. Learning that he was not about to die as he had thought, and feeling that 'no doubt it was of advantage that every officer that could be should be up [on deck]', he took his bandaged wound and rejoined the fray. One Bryan Adams, who was a member of one of the returning landing parties, suggested he go below. 'I must have been getting a bit queer, for I remember a violent altercation and using the most horrid language to him.' (Thirty years later Hilton's son Wayland introduced the woman he was to marry, Elizabeth Adams, Bryan's daughter. Forty years after that Wayland's son Thoby introduced the woman he was to marry: Josephine Keyes, Admiral Keyes's granddaughter.) It was downhill from there, and when he came to, a few days later, he was at Chatham and his arm had been amputated.

After that Hilton volunteered, perhaps to prove to himself that a one-armed man is still a man, for the expeditionary force of British and French volunteers which was dispatched in 1919 to fight on the side of the Whites in the Russian civil war. He commanded a fighting train on the Vologda Railway; their job, he said, was to drive slowly along until they came upon a Red train, and then shoot at it. He was awarded the DSO. When Kathleen met him he was MP for Norwich, which he remained, with one short break, until 1929, and he was about to become Financial Secretary to the Treasury.

The Youngs were a naval family; a line of runaway cabin boys and pirates which developed into admirals. The first Sir George Young had built himself a fantastic house, Formosa in Cookham, near Maidenhead. Having been at sea all his life, he only knew about boats. So he built a house with portholes, wood panelling throughout, hatches and companionways, and a copper roof because a roof is to keep rain

out, rain is water, so is the sea, and copper keeps the sea out of the
hull of a boat. Hilton was the middle of three brothers. Geoffrey,
the youngest, was a mountaineer; he lost his leg in the war and
climbed the Matterhorn carrying his best leg with him for the photograph at the top. It was said that each of the Young brothers lost
something in the war – Hilton his arm; Geoffrey his leg; and Georis
(George), the eldest, lost his head: this was because he became a
communist, and wrote some stylistically eccentric books.

That Hilton was attractive is testified to by photographs and by
an anonymous letter he received in 1925 when he was on a financial
mission to Poland:

> I have seen your charming eyes only once – and I cannot forget them!
> Napoleon must have had eyes like yours.
> The eyes of an eagle who is smiling.
> An eagle with a broken wing.
>   X
> Your friend always. Your lover as soon as you like.

Not surprising in a man of his age and with such eyes, Hilton had
a past. Before the war he had been much attracted to Virginia Woolf
(Stephen, as she was then). He knew her through her brother Thoby,
who had been his friend at Cambridge at the turn of the century,
and who had died in 1906 of typhoid fever. Hilton frequented the
drawing rooms of Bloomsbury, where his heterosexuality was much
valued, by the women at least. Virginia was at the time quite convinced that she should marry (more to the point, perhaps, so were
her friends and family) but as another suitor, Walter Lamb, put it,
she 'lived in a hornets' nest'. For example: in 1909, the year Hilton
proposed to her (in a punt, on the Cam), she had already been proposed
to by Lytton Strachey and had accepted him, feeling that his homosexuality was no bar to a friendly life together. Strachey had second
thoughts, however, and after all rejected her. At the same time Virginia
had a deeply emotional relationship with her sister Vanessa, and was
involved in a 'violent and prolonged flirtation', as Quentin Bell put
it, with Vanessa's husband Clive Bell.

Virginia was certainly pleased to be proposed to, and it was a
serious possibility. Hilton was very eligible; she visited his parents,

and at one time she was packed off on a trip by her family when it seemed possible that she might accept him. Eligibility in terms of good character and prospects was not what most impressed the Bloomsburies. Desmond MacCarthy called Hilton a sphinx without a secret; Vanessa called him 'an elephant in a china shop' and felt that it would not work, and no doubt she was right. Virginia told Hilton that she could marry no one but Lytton; Hilton's heart was not broken and there were no hard feelings.

That was before the war; he had been twenty-nine. Now he was forty-one and a different man in many ways. His general talent had focused on politics; his time was spent working rather than hanging around with clever eccentrics. One friend from before the war who also drew apart from Bloomsbury was E. M. Forster, who wrote, 'I don't think those people are little, but they belittle all who come into their power.' Hilton Young, on the other hand, Forster considered 'big'. They had become friends after Cambridge; and on Hilton's death in 1960 Forster wrote in his diary: 'As for H—. I remember something passing between us over $\frac{1}{2}$ a century ago in Malcolm's mother's drawing room. Something not erotic but affectionate and mysterious . . . He referred to it afterwards, and from that time I regarded him without fear.'

Forster would go and stay at what Hilton called his 'wretched little cot', the Lacket, near Marlborough in Wiltshire, and they would walk and talk. One night they walked from Salisbury to the Lacket, about twenty-five miles, and 'met all the worms on the road in Pewsey Vale, which come into one of his books'. In 1920 Forster had been in fear that he would not be able to write again, and had been considering taking a job.

Oct 28. Hilton Young. Tea and dinner with him a week ago. He gave me carefully and considerately, with great sensitiveness and affection, some advice . . . Summarising the artist from the egoist – he ranks himself the latter – he thought that the path to creation is to be found not by looking about one, but by peering into the lumber room of one's mind. 'It's a dark, difficult place to see in – but presently something may catch your eye that will do.' His words impressed me deeply as did their sequel. He rose and looked at the bookcase, evidently daring himself. 'And one stocks the lumber room by – ' The exact phrase I forget but the thought was familiar because it had struck me in *By Sea and Land* [Hilton's book about his war experiences]. The point is that one must think and do and frequent what is decent. What a man has lived with he will have to die with. Exactly at what in my life Hilton was hinting does not concern me, and this indicates the bigness of his personality. I am generally so worried that people might not approve, and not content until I have defined their criticism and tried to cap it with a counter-criticism. He raised the interview high above fencing. It was practical and helpful in the sense that it has sunk deep. Even if I don't and can't resume creation he had made me vaster and more happy . . . No one, in a direct talk, has helped me more, and I think my gratitude got through, he is so acute and subtle. Since, I have street-walked and entertained idleness and indecencies, but the ground beneath them seems to have worn thinner.

Hilton Young was an understanding man, and a patient one. Like many before him, he fell in love with Kathleen and determined to marry her. Like a few before, he wooed her through Peter.

Peter had a new mouse. Hilton and he decided it should be called Ovid. Kathleen wondered why.

'Dear Lady Scott, Because he has such an important and beautiful nose – Yours, Hilton Young,' written in a big left-handed half uncial.

A river party was arranged, to include Kathleen, Hilton, Peter, lizard, rabbit, snake and tortoise. 'Dear Lady Scott, . . . I think perhaps I should *like* to sit between son and tortoise, because neither can crawl up the leg of my trowsers.'

Soon he is sending Peter stories of Ovid the mouse, with original Ovid and Ovid in translation, and birdwatching notes ('I am going to find a bearded reedling here on the Broads or catch cold in the attempt') and doggerel letters are passing between them. 'It is capital of him to play with me,' Hilton wrote to Kathleen, and then told her that 'he doth bestride this narrow world like a colossus.' Kathleen of course found him to be a man of excellent taste, 'adorable' and 'delicious'.

In fact it was rather too much. One morning out walking with Stephen Gwynn she decided to get a passport, 'just in case I ever did decide to go to Peru'. (She'd never mentioned Peru before.) She was meant to be going on to tea with the Arty Pagets 'but instead of the

Pagets I thought Peru! In two hours I had secured a cabin (a beauty too), had my passport visa'd, bought a frock, got £400 from a shut bank, given Oscar, Pamela and Stephen tea – in another two hours I had sent four cables, written fourteen letters, packed my trunk and so to bed to be up good and early to catch the 8.45 next morning . . . It is only like that that I can persuade myself to leave my Pete.'

Shaw said she was a better explorer than Con, because she was always 'adventurously ready to go to the ends of the earth at half an hour's notice with no luggage but a comb with three teeth in it'. But why did she do it? Why tear herself away from work and her nice life and above all Peter? Because she felt something bigger than any vagabonding inclination threatening that nice life, and she was frightened. Going to Peru seemed to her safer than staying put and facing up to love.

She went via New York where she witnessed the election, ate at the Automat, saw Colonel House and Hovelacque and Charles Dana Gibson, inventor of the Gibson Girl. She flew from Florida to Havana in a six-man plane, rode on the bowsprit of a Caribbean ferry and (finally, after her disappointment in Mexico all those years before) on the cowcatcher of an Ecuadorian train (this in the company of a 'wild man of the woods, Col Isbelle, with Indian blood, he had shot his brother-in-law and later two cousins, wild reckless creature'). As ever, she attracted people to amuse her and who wanted to do things for her: the agency representative, the commissioner's secretary, the shipping line man, the captain's wife, the wild man of the woods. Going through the Panama Canal officials who carried portable telephones on their belts, and plugged them into sockets when they needed to, opened a dam so that she could watch the water falling eighty-five feet; in Colon one Dr Collins, whom she had met on the boat, took her round the red light district and explained the methods, prices, medical risks and racial preferences of the women.

After a while she fell sick, and returned to Europe via New York where she again spent time with House, who was despondent at the US's failure to ratify the League of Nations.

In Cherbourg she wrote, 'Lord will I ever find a man I altogether like – who do I want? No one will do. Maybe I am utterly and completely spoilt, what a grim idea . . . If God said "You may take who you like, I'll see he loves you utterly", who could I say? Just "Con again please".' So the trip worked.

She came back 'in the charge of a tortoise' as Peter wrote to Hilton Young. Geoffrey Dearmer and Colonel Stirling met her at the station. The next day she had dinner 'oh *so* happily' with Hilton, and he 'rang in [her] head all evening and longer'. So maybe it didn't work for long.

Her next escape attempt was rather more absurd. She developed a crush on Colonel Lawrence of Arabia. She was sculpting him, and thought he looked like a mild-mannered clerk. 'Don't', wrote Lawrence, 'do me as Col Lawrence (he died November 11 1918). Not as "the most romantic figure of the war". I'm tired of the limelight, and not ever going to be a public figure again. It was a war effort, imposed, involuntary.' They dressed him up in Arab robes in the drawing room – 'he took his nice little bare toes quite for granted', but Kathleen came over rather covertly and hoped that no one would come in and discover her alone with a half-robed desert hero. She found him 'a very easy responsive little soul, with a ready smile and an acute sense of humour'. The next night she sat over the fire wondering and decided to 'extinguish' HY because she couldn't extinguish Lawrence until she'd finished the statue. 'If I travel I forget them, if I'm social I forget them, if I work they clamour.'

Lawrence told her his stories and showed her his adventures on maps; he told her his history and his family, and the Arab proverb 'everyone's own louse is a gazelle'. He gave her a set of his Arab robes and a dagger. One day he stayed till seven and she was furious when Colonel Stirling and three others turned up and frightened 'the entrancing child' away. Working on the statue, with or without the model, made her think of him 'and that slightly obliterates HY'. So that worked, up to a point.

Then somebody else started telling her stories about Lawrence, including 'that L took credit for a great landing that took place when in reality he and Faisal arrived the following day saying they'd lost their way, but as they had the sea for a flank it seems that was impossible . . . that it is common knowledge that he is the Royal Mistress and that that is the reason you never hear his name mentioned in Arabia.' And a tale about a 'rather beautiful Arab boy' who wanted a passport and offered to pay for it with a slab of gold, saying 'that is the price of a night with Faisal'.

'Well well,' she wrote. 'Well well.' The next day she received a 'foolish' letter from him, which 'coinciding with yesterday's talk causes antidote to acute attack of Lawrencitis.'

After Lawrence's death she noted down a curious coincidence: she had first met him at Victoria Station, where they were seeing off the same friend. She didn't know who Lawrence was, but offered him a lift. He accepted, and when she asked where she should drop him he replied, 'It doesn't matter where I go.' Fifteen years later he visited her in London, and when leaving turned left out of the garden gate, which led nowhere of account. 'Why, where are you going?' Kathleen asked. 'Oh,' he said, 'it doesn't matter where I go.' This was a month or so before the motorcycle crash that killed him.

Really she had a lucky escape there. Wounded heroes are all very well, but Lawrence's psychological wounds made Hilton's missing arm seem almost desirable. (Though Kathleen didn't know it and would possibly not have accepted it. She felt immensely for Hilton's arm. Shaw tried to console her: 'I said that as a man with two arms is not unhappy because he has not three, neither is he unhappy if having only one he hasn't two, and she flew out at me so furiously that I discreetly shut up.')

But Lawrence was an unhappy man, and Kathleen had been through that before – with Con, and up to a point with Cannan. Lawrence wrote in 1923 (to Lionel Curtis):

I consume the day (and myself) brooding . . . galloping mentally down twenty divergent moods at once . . . I sleep less than ever . . . When my mood gets too hot and I find myself wandering beyond control I pull out my motorbike and hurl it at top speed through these unfit roads for hour after hour. My nerves are jaded and going near dead so that nothing else than hours of voluntary danger will prick them into life.

He changed his name twice to avoid the fact of who he was, and if his death wasn't suicide, his feelings and behaviour were suicidal. He told Kathleen that he was 'going to commit suicide without you knowing I have'. She told him no, it would be 'so unkind. He said "I'll make quite sure that you don't know." "But now you've said so!" "Oh yes, I'm clever enough for that. I might just get pneumonia – but I shan't do that now because I've told you." '

And as well as being homosexual, Lawrence didn't really like women very much. Nancy Astor, Shaw's wife Charlotte, and, up to a point, Kathleen were exceptions. (His mother told Kathleen after his death that he had liked her, and she felt honoured.)

It was Shaw who introduced Lawrence and Nancy Astor, in 1924. Nancy and Kathleen were not very similar, but what Lawrence liked in them both may have been: they were both non-repressive mother figures. They both had a need for male friendship and admiration combined with a fastidious attitude to sex, which was ideal for Lawrence: 'Women . . . I like some women. I don't like their sex.'

There was something similar in Lawrence's and Cannan's poetic depression/masochism. One of Lawrence's problems was that he didn't know where his fabrications began and reality ended (Shaw called him 'a born actor and up to all sorts of tricks'). Determination that it be so is part of making something true. Richard Aldington wrote of Lawrence: 'There is one achievement which nobody can deny Lawrence, and that was his capacity to convince others that he was a remarkable man.' This echoes Con's capacity to convince himself that he was brave, which in the end had the effect of making him brave; and it echoes Kathleen's own determination to be happy. 'All Kathleen's geese were swans,' as Rosslyn's daughter Verily put it (all her lice were gazelles, if you like), and she was always attracted to determined men. But Lawrence's determination was warped though not as much so of course as Cannan's, who ended up convinced that he was Captain Scott. Kathleen had probably seen enough of life by now not to fall deeply for what attracted her in that way.

Lawrencitis over, Kathleen was 'all unsettled again'. She rang Hilton and asked him to come to Kew to see the crocuses, and when he could not she became shy and confused and hung up. Then Isadora appeared and told her about Steichen's divorce, which was drawing a lot of attention in New York, and how she, Kathleen, was being cited. Kathleen thought Mrs Steichen 'rather a toad' for bringing her name into it when she knew 'that we never lived together or anything of the kind'.

She didn't see Lawrence again before he went to Palestine with Winston Churchill, so that was that. She did see Hilton. He drove her to the Austen Chamberlains one Sunday. 'Oh dear! Oh *dear*!!' she wrote in her diary. After her death Hilton, clearly remembering the day perfectly, added, in his left-handed half-uncial: 'Oh dear! Oh *dear*!!'

She went to meet his parents, Sir George and Lady Young. Sir George talked about shells with Peter, and Alice told Kathleen how much she adored Hilton. 'It's no use expressing what pleasure this sunny day gave me,' Kathleen wrote. 'Suffice to say that Pete and I travelled back to Salisbury like a couple of radiant drunkards. If this is nothing then life is nothing.'

Peter was now twelve, and about to start at public school. Barrie was dead against Eton, despite the fact that four of his Llewellyn Davies boys had been there. Shaw said, 'why send him to school at all? He can read and write, can't he?' Oundle was decided upon, because of the science. Peter had inherited his uncle Rosslyn's taste for animals. (Kathleen had it too – she had kept newts in her office at the Ministry of Pensions.) He liked fish and reptiles and birds – he had to deposit the tortoises and the other boating companions at London Zoo when he went to school. He had a baby goat which had joined their social life, going for walks in the park and on to tea parties. He gave talks at school about pterodactyls and deep-sea fish. London Zoo and the Natural History Museum were his second homes, and he spent much of the summer of 1921 deep-sea dredging at Plymouth.

Kathleen was there with him, sketching, being shown around submarines ('an occupation I only half enjoy') and thinking about Hilton Young. During this period Peter became clingy; partly no doubt because grown-up school beckoned but partly also because he sensed that something was up. He would check on her at night, said she was distant, and had 'some foreboding that something terrific is going to happen to me', Kathleen observed. She said herself, 'what violence I have to do to myself to restrain from letting him or anyone else know the turmoil that is going on in me. How I laugh at this blind adoration, and how little laughing does to lessen it . . . Damn this young man is too good to be true.' For a woman bent on happiness, she fought it and fought it. Her fear was still bigger than her desire.

And for once, she didn't know whether the man wanted her. His letters to her were charming, funny, and completely impersonal. She told no one how she felt, until she confided, without names, in Stephen Gwynn.

'I didn't mean to tell you, indeed I'm trying not to tell you, because I haven't told Geoff and Jan [Colonel Stirling] and I'll have to tell them first and I don't want to tell them and of course nothing may happen but I haven't had such an extraordinarily acute attack for twelve years – indeed it is like nothing that ever happened before (crossed out) since. Everybody always says that but you will own I haven't said it before . . . No I won't go on telling you . . .' and she does, for several more pages.

> You see he has never made love to me and I am sure that as soon as he does it will burst my bubble and so I am so careful that he doesn't . . . It's trying because I haven't the least notion whether he likes me or not . . . I am delirious with admiration . . . He takes no initiative. If I ask him to do something he always does it and seems to like it, but I can count on the fingers of one hand (without the thumb) the number of times he's made any suggestion for an outing – Oh damn! I wonder what would happen if I wrote what I think!! I expect he'd fly for his life . . .

'Is it perhaps a crime for the female of the species to love where it has not been told to?' she wondered in her diary.

But there were clues. She told him he was a prig; he replied: 'Quite all right about priggishness. But I claim that it is a disguise, and a jolly good one, that saves infinite trouble . . . If I spoke and acted according to my natural impulses I should get slung out . . . I have no manners at all, only a good heart, a powerful brain, and a rugged exterior.'

Meanwhile his behaviour with Peter really could have given her an idea. Once he stood on his head and retrieved his pipe between his teeth, just to please him. And his letters to Peter were a certain clue. One, in the style of their birdwatching correspondence, alerted the twelve-year-old to a new species, Memberius Communis. 'This species, like the Red Grouse with which it is frequently found in company during the latter part of the year, is exclusively British. Large numbers have been observed at times on the Thames at Westminster. It is abundant in Pall Mall . . . the nest can be easily detected by the amount of waste paper that accumulates in the neighbourhood. The note most frequently heard is a loud quacking noise, often continued long after dark, but it also imitates the song of other birds, and especially that of *Pressus Harmsworthii* . . .' and so on. Perhaps Peter would have got the jokes; certainly his mother would have. Another would, if addressed directly to Kathleen, have been a love letter worth the keeping:

> It's better to think more of all the great times to come. Where shall they be? We'll climb the steep hillside up to Styhead Pass, with the mist hiding all but the grey stones and cushions of stag's horn moss at our feet, and hear the ravens barking unseen overhead. We'll stand on a shiny rock in the Bay of Salamis in Greece, and take a header into the water as blue and transparent as the sky, and swim deep down to visit the sponges and the corals at the bottom . . . We'll walk up in a golden sunset to a ruined castle in 'a gash of wind-grieved Appenine', somewhere among white olive groves, where the towers of Urbino or San Gimignano stand black against the sky . . . We'll wander amongst the oak-woods of the Albanian mountains, and see the lanky Albanian hill-men in their white wrappers slouching and lurking through the shadows, with their guns and daggers bristling round them . . . We'll ride on an elephant under burning sun, to see the red sandstone palaces of the dead city of Foothepore, and the plover with the stalky legs that stands in the ruined tank, and calls 'Why do you *do* it?' At Madras you shall go out in a boat like an admiral's hat to trawl for fishes that are like a nosegay of flowers, each of them, waving with fronds and streamers, and shining pink and green and blue . . . To Burma to see the golden pagodas sticking out of the green jungle, and the golden people dressed in topaz and amethyst silk, and to hear the tuck-too lizard barking like a dog from the wainscotting in the dead of night . . .

To Kathleen he wrote about the Trade Facilities Bill, and whether or not the Goat (Lloyd George) wanted him to go to Washington. But he did take the trouble to mention to her that he had written Peter a letter 'all about what we will do some day'.

'I am building a great stone wall around me,' she wrote to Stephen

Gwynn. Hilton wrote of 'the shell of concealment and repulse that I have grown'.

She thought he was insincere, self-conscious, unnatural, reticent, a detrimentalist, terrified, unapproachable, unresponsive, contradictory and not very good company, so she invited him to France, where 'Me and Pete, Mrs A Chamberlain and Jo, Convers [the chauffeur], Alice [the nurse] and the baby, the baby hedgepig Pico della Mirandola the rabbit and the bicycle and the pram and more impedimenta – all in the Cadillac' were going for a summer holiday. He wasn't sure if he would be able to join them, which kept her on hot coals for weeks.

The house in France was called Solitude, on the island of Noirmoutiers, approached over a low-tide road, and surrounded by ilex and pines. There were lizards and swimming and sailing and figs, bathing by moonlight, eating and sleeping out. 'Entirely dull and happy,' she said. Peter sent Hilton Young a poem about how beautiful it was. After a month he arrived, and watched the sunsets beyond the ilex grove. Kathleen feared he would be bored or 'dislike us', but he wasn't and he didn't.

On the last night she wrote: 'It is wonderful that suppression of a suggested gesture can create more upheaval than the whole gamut of words or embraces . . . Even now I don't believe it. It was probably some mistake.' The suppressed gesture was a reaching out to touch her foot, in the moonlight, by the sea. It wasn't a mistake, but it didn't finalize anything.

Back in London Hilton worked very hard. Kathleen fretted. She had to pack up Shingle End, the cottage at Sandwich that she had found for Con all those years before, and which he had never seen. The Admiralty wanted it back, and she was grateful for the company of her neighbour there, Nancy Astor, to cheer her up ('She is part saint, part harlot, part fool, part glorious artist'). She lost patience with her round of friends, she worked, she worried. Peter clung, checking on her, expecting something terrible. She lived from note to note from Hilton and told herself off for doing so. At Christmas she, Hilton and Pete set off for Tunisia together. At times Hilton's mood reminded her of Con's black blight; she had a cold which made her 'feel like an amoeba and look like a turnip'. Hilton thought her volcanic. Peter was jealous, though Hilton paid him such attention that

Kathleen thought it was 'him he loves, not me'. Peter looked under stones for reptiles; Hilton looked up in the air for insect warblers and kingfishers. Kathleen looked at ruins and museums. On camels, in trains, in tents, on deck between Tunis and Marseilles, gradually, gradually the ground between them was broken and they came together.

'January 18 1922: At 10 H came and now we are going to marry each other. How absurd.'

Colonel Stirling sent flowers; Geoff Dearmer was 'sort of stunned'; Shaw was 'not in the least surprised'; Lady Young cried 'Hurrah'; the Scotts said they had been expecting it; Austen Chamberlain was very pleased. Asquith wondered whether Hilton was up to 'our standard', which was, he reminded her, very high. Stephen Gwynn said Hilton reminded him of Con. The Bishop of St Albans (who in his time had felt 'fluttery' about her, and felt that perhaps bishops shouldn't flutter) said he'd marry them anywhere, any time. And to Kathleen's amazement and dismay the press became very excited and sent reporters who hung around all day. She had to go out by the back door, and stay out.

They were married on 3 March in the crypt of the House of Commons, by the fluttery Bishop. She was forty-three. Austen Chamberlain gave her away; Pete stood at her side. She dropped Hilton off at his flat afterwards to change, and when she arrived home alone afterwards the reporters were aghast: 'Beg your pardon m'lady, but did the bridegroom not turn up?'

Then they went to his 'wretched little cot', in Wiltshire; a tranquil, low-key, green-surrounded thatched house where 'great rest and peace were upon us'.

MARRYING HILTON was a good idea, and not only because they were in love. It kept the distracting and demanding admirers one pace away, allowing her to accept their admiration with no question of any sexual demands. Hilton had not on the whole met the admirers before, and apart from a slight resentment that initially some seemed more at home in their house (he had moved in with Kathleen at Buckingham Palace Road) than he, meeting them went well. The mixing of their friends was fraught ground, though, for two people who had both been so long single. Kathleen was quite perturbed when Hilton preferred Wells to Shaw, and was not at all inclined to like his 'decadent' friends the Monds. Hilton didn't like Sybil Colefax, with whom Kathleen had been friends for years. Kathleen was alarmed by 'a bevy of Arnold Forsters, most of whom seem to have had a love affair of some sort or another' with Hilton. She didn't like the sexual habits of the Bloomsbury people, their promiscuity rather than their homosexuality. (She had no adverse reaction to faithful homosexuals such as Ricketts and Shannon – in fact in her more contrary moments she would express surprise that all interesting men weren't homo-sexual, for what could an interesting man see in a boring old female when there were so many attractive men around?) She called the Bloomsburies 'the depraved artistic' and deplored their talking at concerts. E. M. Forster was all right because he recited poetry, and so was G. M. Trevelyan. But then there was a whole new set of in-laws to get on with. It seemed best to maintain open minds.

And marrying Hilton gave Peter a father, and a good one. Kathleen was a very rewarding and very demanding mother. Peter was a very rewarding boy: he sang solos, won races, boxed, hatched out moths, danced, talked fluent French and regularly supplied London Zoo with creatures (trap-door spiders, scorpions, axolotls, three hundred baby praying mantises which had hatched from the one they had brought back from Carthage 'in H's buttonhole'). She was very very proud of him, and frequently took off to his schools, where she knew all the masters and had definite opinions on how they treated him. When he was beaten for climbing on to the roof she was furious: 'Bless him. The roof via fire escapes at night is to a 13-year-old what the South Pole via tempests is to the 30-year-old. Perhaps he went for the sake of astronomy.' Peter's childhood friend Rachel Malise Graham, Sydney Holland's daughter, had clear memories of the relationship between son and mother:

> Absolute trust . . . she treated you [Peter] with almost respectful equality, and what a fine straight look you had when you talked to her. And she was so heavenly – childishly happy with you . . . You were always with her, or nearly always, usually lying on your tummy drawing endlessly under her grand piano . . . you will remember the delightful free happy way you lived. I never remember her saying you were naughty, just 'Don't be a *stupid* a–ss, Pete'. She never left you just to sit and look at grown-ups as they talked . . . You were not constantly being told not to do this and that, and *not watched*. Such a fearless, magnificent, broad-minded, fair mother. Her energy at her work – her joy in life – and you – but I know she never spoilt you. I shall never see a son, like you were, to your mother – nor a mother, like she was to you. Everyone knew it.

(Kathleen's second son Wayland recalls her as always being on their side, no matter what, and though occasionally bad-tempered never hostile.)

Where Kathleen and Peter were too close, Hilton diluted the atmosphere. Where her compulsion that Peter be brilliant became too strong, Hilton reminded her gently not to push him; to let him play with children as well as with Sir Ray Lankester and Julian Huxley, to let him like silly childish things, to remember that most twelve-year-olds don't correspond with the US ambassador. And Peter gave Hilton a new name: he was to be Bill, and Bill he remained.

The marriage gave her some financial security, and in the end made her rich – though between her earnings, the pensions and her canny investments she had been admirably competent and independent in her finances since Con died. Bill didn't initially earn a great deal from his journalism, politics and public service work, though later he put his financial skills to work for his family too. However, money didn't matter to Kathleen. 'I am not, never have been and never intend to be [short of money],' she wrote to Bill in 1921. 'To the likes of me so few indispensable things to happiness are purchasable with money and it seems equally easy, or difficult, (as temperament dictates) to live within your income be it £50 a year or £50,000.' She would on occasion go to Fortuny and 'spend in five minutes what I used to live on for six months, and what other folk are still living on', but it did not thrill her. She thought that bequeathing more than a minimum to get children on their feet just encouraged laziness.

The marriage also gave her constant access to the politics she found so fascinating. The official duties of an MP's wife she did not take to happily: she had to open a building in Norwich and 'made a complete ass of my fatuous self'; it reminded her of the Antarctic Expedition meetings, 'the unnatural relationships with one's fellows'. The debates, the intrigues and the talk she loved. Since Asquith she had not had a political confidant of her own to support and be trusted by. (House didn't quite qualify because his politics were purely international; Austen Chamberlain was good but not exclusive enough.) Now she walked Bill to the Treasury in the morning, picked him up or was joined by him in the evening, and followed with him every detail of his political life. In 1922 he was delegate at the Hague Conference with Russia on finance; she went with him, and before they left she sat on the lawn at the Lacket writing synopses of papers for him. She felt herself primarily a listener, though perhaps she was rather more than that. 'April 23: At dinner at the House Austen was silent and cross and then flashed at me "This is awful. I've to speak at ten, and I haven't a notion what to say. You've heard the debate. What would you say?" I gabbled what I should say, and I'll be blowed if he didn't say it, only glorifying it.'

The question can't help arising – what side was she on? Her husband worked cheek by jowl with Lloyd George, 'the snake in Goat's clothing' of 1916 who had brought down Asquith. She and the Goat got on well enough now; she and Bill dined with him and his wife, and went to stay with them. The Lloyd Georges were moving house and asked her help with flowering shrubs (not that she'd be much help with that; she had once had occasion to scold Asquith for writing to her about something as dull as Lady Ottoline Morrell's garden). Kathleen was impressed by Lloyd George's intention to give the proceeds of his book on the war to charity. Still, she thought most of his talk, such as cancelling all foreign debt every fifty years, 'beautiful eloquent nonsense'. She agreed with Austen Chamberlain that the risk in the Liberals and the Conservatives combining permanently (which was a possibility at the time) was that then Labour would be the only alternative. Simply, she believed in her own sometimes eccentric principles rather than in party political policies, and she believed in loyalty to friends, and she often didn't care if her friends agreed with her or not. Her opinion of Nancy Astor was a case in point: 'In public life I abhor her, in private I mostly adore her.'

Bill always worked long hours. In some ways this was nice for Kathleen – she could carry on her furious social life, joining him for meals and sometimes luring him away to join her at dances. In other ways it was not so good. After the Hague trip came the school holidays. She wondered if she should ever work again, or just be a wife and mother. At the Hague she had a crisis of wifedom: 'I am unutterably depressed. Standing by is not what I was meant for. I'm a parasite here on suffrance. I'm a woman. Damn! I make myself frocks. I wash frocks. I read novels. I am apathetic. I shall presently become hysterical.' (Later, during a quiet moment at the Lacket, she wrote: 'I want time to sit and review the situation. I can't recognize myself. This is none of I! and I'd better make haste to discover who it is, and whether this I is like to be the permanent one, or whether reversion is to be expected.')

She visited the Rijksmuseum at Amsterdam to cheer herself up: 'I looked long at Rembrandt's Night Watch and was not as much impressed as I should have been. The longer I live the more I think that skill dexterity and technique without beauty of line or of meaning or of expression mean not much to me.' Her favourite that day was a Peter de Hooch of a smiling mother giving a drink to a child. As the conference broke up in acrimony she took the French representative's young sons to a Charlie Chaplin film.

In October 1922 the Liberal/Conservative coalition collapsed, Lloyd
George resigned, and there was a swift general election. Kathleen
dashed between her studio in London and meetings in Norwich,
where she consistently disguised her immense and physical dislike of
the rough and tumble of electioneering. Bands of rowdy Labour
supporters sang 'The Red Flag' and booed Bill; she 'shouted hymns';
addressed meetings of women, drank tea with mayors, made speeches;
acted 'this laborious part'. Worse than the pressure on her, she felt
the pressure on him. Sneaking off to a crèche and helping to repair a
stone figure in the cathedral were her releases.

> *November 15*: At 8am we set off in the Cadillac covered with blue
> and white stickers saying what fine fellers we are, and returned at
> 6pm. We smiled without ceasing and waved to everyone from the
> crossing sweeper to the dean, and were cheered wildly, and called dirty
> dogs, and at last put our feet on the mantelpiece and said 'let them
> do their worst'.

Bill won. 'We had hatpins stuck through our tyres and everything
hooliganish you could think of, but what matter now?'

Bonar Law's Conservatives were now the government. Bill was
invited to join the new government in his old position at the Treasury,
but turned it down – he became instead Chief Whip of Lloyd George's
National Liberals. (Shaw suggested that Bill should become a Bolsh-
evik: 'It is the only reputable party left in Europe, and as it isn't in
office here (unhappily) he could be in bed every night by ten.')
Kathleen felt that the best thing for her to do was to work to bring
the National Liberals and the Asquithian Liberals closer together.
Lloyd George impressed her by saying that it was 'a terrible pity'
that he and Asquith were estranged, and speaking of how well they
could have worked together – particularly, he said, if Asquith had
always been drunk, because he was so likeable when he was drunk: 'I
could supply some things that he has not, and God knows he could
supply plenty that I have not.' He blamed, among others, McKenna
and 'fools like Margot' [Asquith] for perpetuating the divide. When
Lady Mond invited the Asquiths to dinner with the Lloyd Georges,
Margot sent a 'curt, offensive reply in pencil'. 'But what *did* she
expect?' Kathleen wrote. Her own method was to 'look round for

hands to which I might hold out mine', and reached for Violet
Bonham Carter and Sir John Simon. Unfortunately everyone hated
Simon, and Violet, who was president of the Women's National
Liberal Federation, was not in favour.

Kathleen enjoyed the duties of a political hostess: tea at the House
of Commons with 'the Chancellor, Herbert Fisher, some Americans
and seven Burmese'; a luncheon for the National Liberal ladies. 'God
what a gang! The party was designed to arrange for the ladies to give
parties for the party. It was huge fun seeing Lady Mond desiring to
make the parties social aristocratic and gaudy and Mrs Ll G wishing
to make them democratic suburban and provincial.'

And she worked. She made a war memorial for Huntingdon; and
accepted commissions for portraits (a wax model of a little girl earnt
her £70). She began a large male nude, first without a model ('how
Rodin would have disapproved!') and then using as model Colonel
Lawrence's brother Arnold, who was twenty-two, told her all his
secrets and amused her by behaving as if he were 'the only person
who had ever lived and emotioned'. This statue, an exuberant figure
flinging his arms wide to the sky, now stands outside the Scott
Polar Research Institute in Cambridge. In later years young Lawrence
became Professor of Archaeology at Cambridge, and frequently cycled
past his naked youthful self.

She did a portrait of Lloyd George, and gave him a piece of clay
to model to keep him still. 'He made an absurd head of Megan [his
daughter] and was delighted with it.' She started to work out of
doors; 'out of doors and at top speed, that's the way to work.' She
had two pieces in the Royal Academy in 1922 and in 1923, and
several small exhibitions. Varnishing Day and the Private View at the
Academy became annual dates for her. There was an amount of press
interest too, which, because it was for a good reason, she did not
reject. With the recognition came responsibilities: unfortunately one
of the first was 'a dinner about women sculptors – I don't believe in
them, I don't consider them helpable or worth helping, but I didn't
think it would sound nice to say so so I held my peace. What help
did I have or need – less than none.'

In 1922 a shadow emerged: Cherry-Garrard's book *The Worst Journey
in the World*. Read now it is a very good and interesting book, but

Kathleen, too close, found some of its criticisms of Con 'very offensive'.
Worse were reviewers who 'accentuated and exaggerated' the criticisms. Barrie cheered her up by wanting to write something in reply
(in the end they decided that would only give the book publicity)
and by thinking it very funny that Cherry should accuse Con of being
humourless, 'knowing them both'. Later this took another twist when
Kathleen learned that Cherry had shown his original manuscript to
Shaw, and that Shaw had encouraged him to take a more critical view
of Scott, saying it would make a fuller and more objective book.
Whether she ever knew that Shaw in fact had drafted and rewritten
parts of the book himself, we don't know. 'It would be fatal to
make any suggestion of collaboration on my part,' Shaw wrote to
Cherry. 'The book would be reviewed on the assumption that I had
written all the striking parts of it, and that they were "not
serious".'

In the spring of 1923 Shaw wrote Kathleen two long thoughtful
letters giving a careful analysis of Con (whom he never met) and of
Cherry's attitude and of the expedition itself.

'He seems unconsciously determined to make me angry and resent-
ful agin Cherry,' she wrote in her diary, 'a thing I do not want to be
at all. I have never admired Cherry but I am fond of him and don't
want to have to cease to be . . . his rendering of Con's character is so
ludicrous it should not even make one cross, only Shaw seems determined I should be cross!'

'Shaw's . . . evaluation of Cherry-Garrard was distorted by his need
to see him as a superman,' wrote Michael Holroyd in his biography
of Shaw. 'In his imagination the appalling conditions of the Antarctic
became a metaphor for the moral climate of Britain between the
wars, and Cherry-Garrard's survival a triumph of human will over
social adversity.'

In admiring Amundsen as a great explorer (which he undoubtedly
was) Shaw made the mistake of falling into the trap of competitive-
ness: if Amundsen was great, Scott must have been a louse. (Shaw
also habitually promoted foreigners over the British at this stage.)
Two generations later it is possible to look back and agree that they
were both great, in different ways. Shaw, however, wrote to Bill after
Kathleen's death that Con's 'best right to his celebrity is that he
induced her to marry him'; and said too, 'How to do justice to

Kathleen without debunking Scott is the problem' when writing about her. Scott had originally been very bunked, over-bunked; much later he was ridiculously over-debunked; the truth as ever is more subtle and somewhere in between. Pre any debunking, Shaw wrote to Bill: 'There is only one way of sparing him, to leave him out of her story altogether, which is possible, as he had almost no part in it.'

But Shaw, though understanding in many ways, was absurdly wrong about this. Con was crucial to her story, and she to his. It is in the same letter that Shaw says, 'Kathleen never played the grief-stricken widow' and that 'she did not seem to me to feel her loss at all.' Shaw didn't know that Kathleen kept a diary, and nobody in her lifetime saw her expressions of grief therein. Bill replied courteously: 'If she did not seem to feel her loss, that is only a seeming. Joy was her principle, and she would not let what she felt be seen and make her friends less joyful.'

The greatest thing her marriage gave her was a chance to have another baby. At the end of the year she found that her 'hopes were far from groundless', as the doctor put it. It was a risky proposition, as she was now forty-three, and she took the risk seriously. The following letter to Peter was found among her papers:

Little Sweetheart: I want the person who tells you I am dead to give you this letter. I am writing it before I die, because I am afraid I may. I want you to take it very sensibly [this phrase is almost word for word what Con wrote to her in his last letter] – don't be too miserable – I've had a lovely life, but I am getting fairly old and it is very nice (since one must die sometime) to do so before one gets ill and blind and deaf and bored and tiresome. So let's all be quite cheerful about it. And remember if I can see you in any way after I'm dead (and tho' I don't think one can one can't be too sure) if I can see you I want to see you gay and merry and funny, working hard and playing and keeping Bill happy. No tears for me dearies! only hurray that your gay little mother stayed happy till she died. I'm not going to give you lots of advice – only this 'Keep fit!' and I've taught you how to do that. I wouldn't learn to drink or smoke if I were you but if you do, be moderate. Add to that 'Be always kind' and with those two precepts you should be happy. If you feel sadly about me now, know that it will pass surprisingly soon. I shall not be unhappy, so you must not be. If you feel inclined to howl, go out and run violently, and know that I am shouting 'bravo' to you. Bless you ever.

She cancelled dinner with the McKennas, lunch with Asquith, lunch with the Victor Cazalets, a dance at the Welbys and supper with the Monds, and stayed in bed for two days. The main challenge to her getting rest, however, was that she and Bill were getting on so well, discovering and revealing each other's secrets and revelling in each other's company, that they kept staying up till two in the morning. 'The love that is engendered by such confidences is terrifying,' she wrote. She allowed herself to sleep during the day; to breakfast at noon; to spend quiet days where she saw no one and didn't even comment on the fact. Bill was 'divine', he read to her (the Gospels; essays by his great friend G. M. Trevelyan; letters from an Eton boy of 1479, about 'grub and his gal'), cosseted her, built her 'a parlour on the lawn' at the Lacket with chair, table, cushions and rugs, and put lavender bags under her pillow. It was a hot summer, and she wasn't always well, but her pregnancy didn't stop her working.

'The pain of childbirth is so different from operation pain,' she wrote. 'There is an element of adventure and useful struggle.' In August 1923, at the age of forty-four, she gave birth to her second son Wayland. She was in labour for four days, feared a Caesarian, thanked god for chloroform, and though scarily weak afterwards didn't die. There was a wild hot summer thunderstorm on one of the nights; her bed was as always across the open window and the lightning and rain played in and out. 'It made the pain seem more fun,' she said.

She was put in an ambulance and taken to the Lacket, where she lay on the lawn with Wayland while Bill read aloud and Pete collected and drew wild flowers. In a month they had two visitors. 'Never in the past twenty years have I past a month so uneventful,' she wrote. Wayland, meanwhile, was 'radiant, divine and very beautiful'.

And then it was back to the round: Bill went to Poland for two months on a financial mission, she had a show at the Grosvenor Gallery; the new cook and chauffeur turned out to drink so they had to go. Peter wrote from school that his housemaster beat his wife. The League of Nations claimed her attention: at a meeting Salisbury said 'Some folk think that the League is just ideals, and therefore not practical; let me tell you that ideals are the only practical thing in the world.' Colonel House had asked her to try to persuade Lloyd George to go to the United States to reinspire them there to ratify the League; she quietly arranged dinners, dropped suggestions, brought people together. She hated to be publicly connected with things. Health issues and city pollution bothered her, and she was irritated with the National Liberal Women for being more concerned with extending the female franchise. She determined to bring about a smoke-free London by the time Wayland was Peter's age, but to do it 'without showing at all'. There was 'a very good luncheon party with Shaw and Wells; Wells is always at his best with Shaw and conversation was fast and good.' Wells had taken Shaw to her exhibition. One bronze nude, *I Want*, Shaw thought 'a most surprising affair' and wanted to know about it. Bill had modelled for it, and it was supposed to represent his disposition, so Kathleen told Shaw that Bill had made it, and left it at that.

On Armistice Day 1923 her war memorial, a large seated soldier, was unveiled at Huntingdon.

A glorious cold sunny morning ... it was all done with beautiful solemnity. Last Post, Lord Lieutenant in scarlet, apple-faced boys singing in the open 'Oh God our Help' etc; church bells ringing, two minutes silence, little grey women weeping, and my brooding soldier looking down beneficently over all. It was terribly moving. I never dared to hope my soldier would look so fine or have such a beautiful birth. Curiously enough I had no qualms at all. I never feel any nerves where my work is concerned. It is because I implicate no one else.

A local poet, Kenneth E. Knowles, was inspired to write a poem, 'A Rhyme of the Thinking Soldier of Huntingdon'. It is not very good. It starts:

One night in November when passing the square
Folk saw what seemed was a spirit there,
A strange apparition in khaki clad
Like the homing wraith of some soldier lad,
Where the gray shadows crept from the churchyard trees
Whose boughs creaked and shuddered and groaned in the breeze ...

and goes on for fifteen pages.

After the birth of her second son, happy with her second husband, Kathleen settled down, in a fashion. In 1927 the family moved to Leinster Corner, the house on Bayswater Road looking over Kensington Gardens where Wayland and some of his children and grandchildren still live. Barrie had lived there before with Mary, and it was the model for the Darlings' house in *Peter Pan*, which Barrie had written in the coach-house behind it. Kathleen now took the coach-house over and converted it into a two-storey-high studio. (Among the house's other attractions was the proximity of the ice-skating rink in Queensway, where she regularly spent hours.) After a visit to Stockholm in 1927 where she visited the sculptor Carl Milles she followed his example and took to sculpting and keeping her statues in the garden.

Throughout the artistic revolutions of the early twentieth century, Kathleen was a traditional sculptor. Modernism, post-impressionism, abstraction, cubism passed her by. The 'desire to break with nature and infuse the resulting work of art with profound spiritual content' (Whitney Chadwick) would have seemed to her a nonsense. 'My allegiance is given in sculpture to those exquisite elongated ladies of Chartres, and to their lovely archaic ancestors, the maidens of the Acropolis; and in life . . . to the springing grace of the stripling, and the majesty of thought-worn faces,' she wrote. She sculpted a great deal at this time, clambering up her immense scaffoldings and shifting clay and statues on a little railway built for the purpose. She was a working sculptor: she made portraits and monuments to order, plus her saleable statuettes of mothers and children and life-size figures of naked young men. In 1925 she had three figures on show at an exhibition at Wembley, including a twelve-foot plaster of Con. It took sixteen men to put it up, and the King opened the exhibition.

Her work was not only for her own satisfaction. Con, as a naval officer, had been expected to be of independent means; the same expectation was made of Members of Parliament only more so: Bill was not paid at all except for expenses. As a backbencher he earned from writing articles and broadcasting; he had four years' naval pay from the war, none of which he had spent at the time, and he had some savings from his journalistic career before the war. In 1928 he went to East Africa, heading a government commission (the Closer Union Commission) into the possibility of a federation of East African states. (Kathleen's 'untutored sympathies', she wrote, were 'for the black'.) Again, this was unpaid but for the expenses. People kept asking her why she was not with him in Africa, and she would have loved to have been. His letters report from up the Nile and down the Zambesi, of meeting Masai and stalking elephants. (He also pointed out in a message to Peter from Northern Rhodesia that: 'There are few beasts left in this part of Africa. The north east is the Zoo, and stupid people are fast exterminating the great beasts there, in the name of sport.' Perhaps this contributed to Peter's later development as a conservationist.)

'I could not tell them,' she wrote, that 'I was staying to make our living while Bill serves his country.' She was working on a figure of Edwin Montagu (Venetia Stanley's husband): 'I had engaged a man to help but he was idle slow and clumsy, so I dispensed with him and I am getting on like anything alone. I have already put up a ton and a half of clay. If only I could leave it nude. If this thrill lasts I should have it finished in a fortnight . . . I work like a fury till dark. God how I love big work. I push the great eight-foot thing out into the garden and back like a great juggernaut into its cage at night. The weather is glorious and I am so happy.' Later she made a statuette of the juggernaut: 'It is nasty niggly work but I stick to it because it seems I can sell half a dozen or so at £45 or so. I don't want the money . . . but even so I would like to make my garden pretty and mount my statues well. I shall have had a turnover of £2,700 this year. Pays for the studio all right!'

Kathleen was never cowardly about the physical side of her work, though she was not particularly strong. A journalist writing about her in 1926 watched 'the small figure of a woman climb on a scaffold, carrying a bucket of plaster and some rough knives' to finish off the twelve-foot replica of the Waterloo Place bronze of Scott shown at Wembley; and describes also the casting of her head of Baldwin: 'A thrilling sight it was, to see the molten bronze at white heat in a large cauldron, held with long tongs by half a dozen half-stripped men, their anxious faces aglow with the furnace heat; to see them gradually lift the crucible, and pour the stream of molten metal into the rough-looking plaster mould, which contained, securely hidden, the finished features of the Prime Minister.'

Alongside her work, Bill's political life was central to her existence. He gradually became her hero, as Con had been before (several times she absentmindedly refers to him as Con in her diaries) and as Peter was growing up to become, in a different way. In 1923 Bill lost the election at Norwich which was a horrible blow; a year later, however, he regained it and held it till 1929. Kathleen continued to loathe elections: this time the hecklers shouted 'go and get an arm' to Bill.

In 1926 Bill joined the Conservative party, after a period as an Independent. Kathleen didn't like the idea of not being a Liberal any more, but conceded that in practice the move was right for him. His career was a constant source of worry to him. In 1931 to his great joy and Kathleen's apprehension he became Minister of Health, which at this time included housing, planning and social security (and a salary, which was a relief to him, as he had never liked having to rely on Kathleen to help support the household). It was a big job. 'I saw visions of Leinster Corner surrounded by angry mobs whose dole Bill had cut; of Bill worked to death and of greatly reduced income, but . . . this after all is the climax and meaning of Bill's life and training, and if he can't do this dangerous and difficult work then who can? I rejoiced. He will be so glad!'

And so was she, when it came to it. 'It is fun knowing all the cabinet doings again after about fifteen years.' The angry mobs weren't entirely a figment: a 'poor old man who they say is mad and had been cheated about his pension' did throw a stone through their window.

Bill's particular baby was housing. One bill he was responsible for gave local authorities the power to allow or refuse development along-side main roads, the point being to prevent too much ribbon develop-ment and keep towns instead pleasantly round and sociable. This was the first town-planning bill in this country. His other significant legislation was on slum clearance. The country's cities were still full of seventeenth- and eighteenth-century housing, more or less unfit to live in, occupied by whole families to single rooms, without water, baths or sewers. The replacement of these slums with the balcony-and-courtyard estates which are so familiar was a big, expensive, emotive and delicate work, made more so by the Depression, and one which Bill took very much to heart.

Kathleen's diaries are packed with political detail and gossip throughout the twenties and thirties. She never lost her taste for prime ministers and ex-prime ministers. In 1928 her old and best prime minister died.

> *February 15.* Asquith died early this morning. It's odd I've had two weeks to prepare, I knew on Feb 1 that he wouldn't live, and yet now he's actually dead I feel all upheaved. He certainly was for some years a very large thing in my life. Probably it was more the excitement of discretion that was so thrilling, more than his actual love. It was a marvellous acrobatic stunt knowing everything that the Prime Minister knew during the War and yet not only not talking, but not letting anyone know I knew. Even Violet who I saw constantly I know had no notion that I was seeing him almost daily for several years. I can't write to anybody to say I'm sorry. Indeed I'm not, I have wanted him to die for ten years. It's rather a bore I can't write to him. To him of 12 years ago.

'Great tenderness, no regret, ripe for the sickle,' she noted after the funeral, and wrote to Baldwin about some 'high explosive' letters from Asquith to her that she had returned to him at his request when he was writing his memoirs. 'They are not love letters, but never the less unrestrained,' she said. As with Nansen's letters, she was concerned that a man she had cared for should not be compromised by things he had addressed to her in private.

The time had come when friends from her old life started dying. Isadora died in 1927 in the famously terrible accident where her long scarf was trapped in the wheel of her car. 'There was something akin in us but she drank and I didn't,' Kathleen wrote to Bill.

> And then I was fastidious. But we were both soaring artists subject to terrifying elations. She tells {in her autobiography, *My Life*} of some 20 or so of her lovers and then apologises to the countless ones she had no room to mention . . . every word was true, starkly terribly true. She describes childbirth (I was holding her hands) and she admits her drunkenness and yet there was a great generous creature and an unsurpassed artist. But she ended ugly – do you wonder at my horror at drink?

The friend of her youth had become for her an image of what could have gone wrong with her own independence. She wrote to Bill in 1929, 'How easily I might have been like Isadora, without a penny to buy my next meal, and longing to share a bottle of champagne with a roguish young chauffeur – I guess she wouldn't have changed with me though. Darling beloved Bill you are a very good warder.'

In 1929 her sister Podge died. 'My reflections on funerals are not fit for writing,' Kathleen noted. 'A savage relic of barbarism, an ugly superstition that makes intelligent men and women crawl snivelling after a corpse in a coffin . . . it disgusted me to have all that dreary ugliness connected to my jolly robust loving Podge.' She considered herself lucky that Con had had such a clean burial, and resolved to be cremated. Then in 1930 Sidney Russell Cooke shot himself, and saddest of all for Kathleen, Nansen also died: 'That stirred me more than anything has done for long and long,' she wrote.

Though Asquith was gone, prime ministers went on. Lloyd George remained a friend despite Bill's defection from the Liberal party. Kathleen agreed to teach him to dance as long as he promised not to do it in public (he was 'beside himself with joy' dancing to a Chaliapin record). More seriously he told her that until he read Colonel House's book (*The Intimate Papers of Colonel House*) he had not known of an offer of mediation made in 1916 by President Wilson. 'Grey, or more probably Asquith, had suppressed it and never told him.' Lloyd George and House agreed that 'it would probably have shortened the war by a year. How strangely awful it would seem if the misjudgment of one or two old men could have made such a difference to such countless lives.'

Stanley Baldwin was a regular visitor, often for breakfast. She sculpted him (and hated the result: 'it is very bad and very unlike him. I almost wish I had suppressed it.') In November 1924 he came round to talk to Bill about Russia; he was so early that Bill was in the bath so Kathleen received him in a dress over her nightdress. They talked about Sydney Webb's smooth tongue and 'bloody goatee'; about the 'hysterical letters' that Austen Chamberlain wrote Baldwin and Baldwin took no notice of, and about confidence: 'Ah, well, I've got the people's mandate and that makes one very independent,' he said. 'He strode up and down the room jumping the fat round stool every time. I couldn't decide whether to move it and give him a clear run, but feared I'd put him out of his stride. He sat on the side of the sofa swinging his legs, he seems happy as a schoolboy.' On another occasion he told her that what with Birkenhead winning diving competitions in Madeira, Leo Amery leaping like a chamois over the Swiss snows on skis and Sam Hoare flying to and over India, his cabinet made him 'feel like a keeper of performing fleas'.

The bad side of politics was the effect on Bill's health. When home, and when the House was sitting, he worked often from eight in the morning to one at night. On his return from East Africa in 1928 he suffered his second attack of acute neurasthenia. (The first had been in 1908/9.) He couldn't sleep, jumped at every noise, fell silent for hours on end. 'I took him to Sir Somebody Something in Wimpole Street who charged five guineas for telling us what we all knew, that he wanted a rest.' She wanted him to drink less and stop smoking cigars. He spent some weeks in a nursing home and, typically, tried to keep from her the extent of his suffering.

Unfortunately this coincided with Peter going through a baddish patch. After Oundle he went (in 1927) to Trinity College, Cambridge, where he read first natural sciences and then history of art. What he really liked was being outside, on water, with birds. At this stage he liked to shoot them, and he did so with remarkable success. Second to that, he liked drawing them. Neither of these were strictly academic pastimes, and Kathleen worried a good deal about what was to become of him. He was not doing well academically and seemed to be turning into something of a dilettante. She was relieved when his drawings and paintings turned out to be extremely marketable, so that he could at least pay for his sport and for the large collection of wildfowl that he was building up for himself, and later for his adventures to Hungary and Iran where he went in search of rare birds.

When he announced the day they were due to go *en famille* to St Moritz that he would much rather go to the Solway Firth to see wildfowl driven down by unexpected harsh weather, she said fine, do it. 'It was so like *me*. Just what I used to do before I was encumbered . . . Why do what you don't want to do just because you've arranged to?' She did realize that something born of such

passion as he had for wildfowl was bound to be of some good in the
end, but she had no idea what, and felt that 'at nineteen one should
be beginning to realize there's more to do than shoot and paint'. At
that stage no one could have known that the young man who loved
to paint and to shoot wild birds would evolve after the Second War
into the grand old man of wildlife conservation, the founder of the
Wildfowl and Wetlands Trust and co-founder of the World Wildlife
Fund.

That year Peter's first girlfriend appeared, a Canadian three years
his senior, called Elizabeth Osborne. This might have been a problem,
had Kathleen's protectiveness turned to possessiveness, but it seems
not to have. They took her to the Lacket, and 'I think it is very good
for him,' Kathleen wrote. 'If she's a nice lass, and I think she is, it
will be a tonic. I love love.' It didn't last. 'He has about one a month,'
she reported in 1929. 'Like Byron, his heart always alights on the
nearest perch.' She had to write to a mother who wrote supposing
that Peter 'would not be in a position to marry for some time'. 'Leave
them alone,' she said, 'and they'll come and bring their tails behind
them.' She was more worried about his health: 'He is always wet, and
neglects himself terribly . . . often eats nothing all day.'

She wanted to keep Peter up to scratch; to give Wayland the
attention he needed (he kept getting 'snorting colds' and terrible
coughs, which proved to be asthma brought on by a severe allergy to
horses); to make Bill 'human and cheerful', and had 'at my back and
always here, work – sculpture – weeping at the neglect, moaning that
it gets nothing but the leavings, the spare moments, when most of
my energy has been spent – then – well, then I seem to fail. Whereat
damn and damn.'

'1928 was her worst year,' Bill wrote. 'I broke down completely,
Peter was having a short eclipse as [is] usual at his age, and Wayland's
health needed care. Against all these disgraces she reacted violently.'
Disgraces? Yes, to her. She saw her duty to be to make things right
and keep people – particularly her family – happy and good. They
were not; therefore she had failed.

Working took her mind off it. When Bill went to a nursing home,
Peter to Scotland to shoot and Wayland got a new nanny who didn't
suffer from tempestuous PMT as the previous one had, she was able

to write: 'really life is very pleasant. I work all day long after taking W to the swimming baths . . . How I love my family and how I love being left alone.'

'It is hard to be a sculptor when there are cooks and nurses and political parties in the world,' she wrote. 'One imagines one might have been a really fine artist if one had been just selfish and slovenly.' Male sculptors, she observed, often had wives.

She was now having regular exhibitions and parties for private views and the unveiling of portraits; most parties she liked, but these ones filled her with terror. She was elected to the Royal Society of British Sculptors in 1928, which didn't particularly impress her: 'It seems to me of no conceivable import, but it was in all the papers and dozens of people wrote congratulating me.' The admiration of artists she respected, such as Charles Sergeant Jagger and William Reid Dick, was more important.

'I ought to know more of my colleagues,' she decided, so she went to Derwent Wood's memorial service, agreed to judge paintings and sculpture at St Martin's School of Art and gave a class there. 'Horribly shy', she reports. Art was all very well; artists and the art world were more problematic. In 1928 she made a speech at a meeting of the Artists' Benevolent Society: 'never have I been in a bluer funk. I thought I might faint.' (She was however determined to be better about speeches in order to help Bill in his constituency work. She could never tell if her speeches were good or not, and felt sure that if audiences laughed at her jokes it was because they were well brought up. And she was aware of her proper mode of expression; admiring Bill's letters to her she wished that she could sculpt him a letter, or dance him a letter, or even knit him a letter.)

Ricketts and Shannon were still the artists she liked best as companions. (Shannon had a manservant who, after showing out Bernard Shaw, inquired, 'Excuse me, sir, is that the gentleman who wrote Shakespeare?'). Sir Charles Wheeler also became a friend, as did Glyn Philpot, and Wallace Wood. She couldn't stand John Tweed: after a dinner at his house she sent him the cost of the meal so that she could continue to dislike him honourably. Pretention about art annoyed her. Two Tennant boys, David and Stephen, 'gave a lamentable exhibition of affectation. The most jejune and illogical foolery, then they sneered at Rodin, and finally after a volley of preposterous and flowery phrases meaning nothing they asked me what I thought of art! I said "Damned hard work." '

Her opinions of the work of others were, as ever, strong. Rodin and Augustus John were wonderful, others less so.

> A comic lady Miss Marion Scott (a composer) came to ask my opinion on women as artists. I told her it was absolutely negative, there were no constructive women in any branch of art or music so far as I knew, that I hated women in arts, and indeed in anything but the reproduction of the species. I told her that the only time women made any success of anything was when they had some man prompting them, etc etc. Poor little woman she went away quiet and quelled.

Kathleen must have been in a particularly contrary and mischievous mood that day so happily to write off her sex and her sex's, even her own, achievements. Or perhaps it was that she was irritated by the separating off of 'women artists' from artists in general, and decided to tease. She never liked to see women playing on their gender.

She admired Eric Gill. After a show of his in 1928 she wrote to Bill: 'it was very queer and beautiful, very sincere. He, like Blake, does, I am sure, queer things because he must, not because he wants to attract attention.' The work of Epstein, on the other hand, she described as 'foul eruptions. It is creative however – creative of great ugliness and vicious unpleasantness.' Of his contribution to the Hudson Memorial she said: 'I think one of the reasons it angers me so is that it is very nearly good and yet so silly and hideous. I went to the unveiling. Baldwin spoke. The curtain was lowered, and not a sound from the breathless shocked crowd. An intake of breath which finally exhaled with an horrified "Oh God". Epstein was there with a model dressed as an Egyptian princess but alas with a cockney accent.'

Baldwin told her afterwards that he felt like bringing up his breakfast, and that it looked like something conceived under drugs and executed in a brothel, to which Balfour, also present, replied, 'Aren't you being a little hard on drugs?' Shaw's opinion of Epstein was that he 'really supposed Epstein couldn't help it' – Kathleen felt that he *could*, and that was the problem. She felt it fair, in art as in life, to look for the good in people. 'Why not be content to look for what is good, for strength, mirth, kindness and vitality?' In 1935, when the King sat for Kathleen, he offered her £100 'to break up' an Epstein that he particularly disliked. ' "You'd be arrested, but you'd be let off at once – you'd be fined £25 – and you'd be £75 to the good, what do you say. Will you do it?" I said, God forgive me, that I would. He said "he's an outrage, and lives with a woman who isn't his wife." ' She didn't do it.

She had some sympathy. 'Poor sculptors! Is it to be wondered at that as a last resort in order to get people to look at their work they sometimes break out into stuff that is so fantastic and extravagant that people cannot help noticing it?'

In this sea of disapproval only Colonel Lawrence liked Epstein. Kathleen was surprised that he didn't seem to mind that a child (in *Morning*, at the London Transport HQ in Petty France) had been cut in half. He pointed out to her that the pattern was good, and she granted that, and agreed that *Night* was 'rather lovely'. She was truly shocked though to learn that Mrs Epstein had written to Charlotte Shaw asking for subscriptions to buy *The Study* (The Enceinte Hag, Kathleen called it) for the Tate Gallery. 'Now I know how it's done, and now that I know I do not propose to do it!'

This made her joy all the sweeter when a few weeks later (July 1926) 'Sir Joseph Duveen came and professed simply to adore my work, used most extravagant adjectives, and finally said he wanted to buy *These had most to Give* (this was the life-size naked figure modelled for by Arnold Lawrence, or my unfinished *Vision Splendid* for the Tate Gallery . . . oh dear I mustn't count my chickens, especially such a sudden chicken, but it would be very nice to be represented in the Tate, and me a woman and alive and all . . .' In the end neither of those works went to the Tate, but in 1929 Duveen gave the gallery her bust of Asquith. That same year she was in competition with Dick, Goscombe John, Jagger and Tweed to do a bust of Lord Northcliffe for St Dunstan's, Fleet Street. 'I haven't the ghost of a chance,' she wrote, but she won.

She went for dinner with Reid Dick, 'fearing the worst', and with reason; at one dinner Dick spent most of the evening 'telling me what good portraits he did and what bad ones I did. "Oh yes I know your heads, hard harsh cuts and shadows." I asked if he had ever seen my wax childrens' heads. No he hadn't.' At another she found herself next to Goscombe John, whose bust of Lloyd George had been accepted for the Academy when hers hadn't been. But mingling with artists and visiting their studios showed her that 'gifts are very different' and comparisons not useful. In 1930 she visited the studio of 'a boy, Bacon, who was making appalling paintings with a certain flash horror. He was about 20, and rather a sweet kid. He came back here to see my work which I expect he liked as little as I liked his.' This was Francis Bacon. Modern taste she did not have.

At a private view of Max Beerbohm's caricatures she met again Kennard, who as a young man had lounged beneath her window at Cheyne Walk, and taken her to an opium den; that same night she sat at dinner next to Graham White the flyer, with whom she had flown in 1910. 'Oh, I was young!' Beerbohm still made her laugh: 'Talking of Asquith's meticulous choice of words, Max said whenever he was listening to him and Squiff hesitated he always wanted to say, "Don't worry sir, the word you want is 'the'." '

In 1925 she had been to India with Bill, where she saw more impressive sculpture than she had seen for years. At Elephanta 'The vast quantity of most impressive sculpture is a stupendous show. The Trimurti, a vast three-faced bust of Brahma (or Siva as Brahma, Rudra and Vishnu) is one of the most splendid works of art in the wide world.' Murray's guide book amused her. ' "This was thought to be the birth of the War King; it has later been discovered to be Parvati in a temper". And so on.' The Buddhas at Ajanta delighted her:

> There are looming figures of Buddha half hidden in recesses and gloom that seemed to me most awe-inspiring, and on either side are strange realistic standing figures that give you a start of terror when you see them after your attention, long rivetted to the Buddha, is released. There is a gigantic lying figure in stone of Buddha in Nirvana. It tries by bigness in size to get the majestic idea of supreme conscious nothingness and I think it succeeds – all these great stone carvings were originally covered with a thin layer of white plaster (?) and coloured – one can't help thinking they are more impressive as they are. Time is the greater artist.

And she went to Jaganath's garden temple: 'a fantastic barbarous place. It may be – is – decadent, and may be unlovely – but it is moving and real. A dark temple containing a single solemn shadowy idol. It was Kali, who demands human sacrifice and what's more gets it – as little as three months ago a priest demanded a rich man to sacrifice his only son to Kali. The priest then inherits.' She also loved the native bearers, whose 'sinewy necks and twisted muscles are unspeakable joy to a sculptor', and was 'ashamed of her race' because of their manners to the Indians.

Whenever she went away with Bill – to India, to Geneva for the League of Nations – she took the opportunity to get in a little vagabonding and a few days' solitude. And she still suffered the old division of loyalties between her boys and her man.

Sept 3 1926. Very sadly left the Lacket leaving behind me my two little sons. As they both stood by the little gate in the sun to see me off I had to work very hard not to weep at the sheer beauty of them with their sun-bleached hair and their russet skin, my big one and my little one, each looking healthier than the other . . . It's so insane but I never leave either of them without thinking 'There, I shall probably never see them again'. These feelings are disgustingly morbid.

Bill, she thought, would probably go mad if anything were to happen to Wayland. Like Peter, Wayland was introduced early to the great and the good. He 'confidingly put his whole fist into Lloyd George's mouth', sat in the crook of Shaw's arm (sending Kathleen into paroxysms: clever old man and gorgeous baby, her favourite) and learnt from Rudyard Kipling how to put out a candle by saying 'boiled pork' to it. Kathleen was worried that with Bill away so much Wayland might not remember him; on the contrary on their return from the trip to India Wayland greeted Bill with 'Hello Bill my daddy. Who's that?'

IN 1929 KATHLEEN turned fifty. There was a general election: Labour won but Bill was easily returned in his new constituency, Sevenoaks. She held her second one-man show, at the Greatorex Galleries in Grafton Street.

> Hundreds and hundreds of people came. I hated it. Silly asses. I had some lovely things there and they say such silly things. I had a lovely pair of arms stretched up [out of a pool of water], with [a fountain of] water coming between them, and a lovely boy blindfolded. Did I mean this? Did I mean that? I could bear the frank jesters better, who said I should call the arms SOS etc. The press said I had a tremendous success because all fashionable London was there – I wanted to take all their stupid heads and bang them together. But I didn't, I just cackled like the rest of them. One is supposed to create and then put one's babies naked for anyone to palaver over, and to be quite insensitive impervious and polite. Well I was, as far as anyone in the world saw.

The man from *The Times*, noting that portraits included Sir John Simon, the Marquess of Reading, Sir John Reith, Stephen Gwynn, the conductor Antony Bernard, Robert Lynd and Gustav Hamel, admired her 'excellent modelling from life'; the 'music of form and movement'; the 'direct sculptural appeal' and command of character (by which he seemed to mean faces), but he questioned her command of form (by which he seemed to mean angles, planes, and the shape of the head). 'It would do Lady Scott [K. Scott was her professional name] no harm to model some heads of very stupid people for practice,' because (he supposes) they have less character, and she was so carried away by character that other aspects lost out. But he had a point: her attitude to work, her own or other people's, was emotional and pragmatic, not intellectual at all.

'I have never so far had to do a portrait of a man of whose personality I knew nothing,' she wrote. 'I think it would be very difficult, for in portraiture it matters, perhaps, to study the measurements of a nose and the angle of a chin, but it matters so much more to discover what the man stands for, what he is after . . .' What she wanted was to provoke feelings. The comment she most liked was from the painter Sir John Lavery, who said, 'I really want to thank you. I feel refreshed with the beauty.'

Whatever the man from *The Times* thought, Kathleen did not lose her taste for clever people. 'Rather a nice weekend with John Buchan, he is really very amusing company. He was consistently nice about everyone but Barrie, he laughs at him unmercifully and takes off his accent.' One lunch she is learning about astronomy from Sir James Jeans; another she is finding Kipling 'a dear; his language is like a boy in prep school – "My Aunt!" etc'. Arthur Ransome 'whose books are Wayland's delight' came to tea and was 'extraordinarily good company'. Somerset Maugham she thought was 'a bad man I expect but fatally attractive'. André Maurois was 'sharp-faced elegant middle-aged thin . . . English good, French entrancing. Writing a history of England.'

Noël Coward visited: 'I feel rather like the young lady of Riga,' Kathleen wrote.

One never knows that he isn't going to talk of you afterwards as he talks of other folk to you. He said the most witty devastatingly scourging things about Victor Cazalet, Evelyn Waugh etc . . . About Victor that he had said one day 'tell me about your life' and Victor had – for two hours! I allowed myself to seem like a homely prating sunday-school teacher on showing forth that Victor had a few merits and some worth. About Evelyn Waugh becoming an RC he said he had said to him 'How magnificently monkmaking' and Waugh had professed hurtdom. Then he told a lovely story about Nancy Astor – when her sister Norah eloped with Flint they went off to the Riviera and one evening when they were walking home up the hill hand in hand, suddenly from behind a bush dashed Nancy who flew at his face scratching and tearing at his clothes and shouting 'Lust! Lust!

Lust!' . . . Thinking it over I don't think I'd like to entrust my life's adventures to Noel. Still he *is* fun.'

The woman she became now was the woman who is remembered by those of her friends who survive – and there are some, for she always liked young people. She slowed down a bit: a bout of bad health in 1932 ('I have got an appendix, or cancer, or colitis or nothing at all,' she wrote as she set off for the nursing home where Bill had recovered from his neurasthenia) had her feeling old and ugly: 'maybe it would be best to settle down and be both'. (It is typical that she didn't tell Peter about this ailment, a spastic colon possibly connected to her typhoid fever years ago in Macedonia, until some years later, though it bothered her regularly.) A trip to the Paris Salon earlier that year made her think that there was quite enough sculpture in the world, and perhaps after thirty years of it she might pension herself off. Perhaps it was this brush with physical frailty which led her to eat her earlier unsympathetic words and become a member of the council of the Artists' General Benevolent Institution, a relief charity founded in 1814 by and for professional artists. In 1936/7 she arranged through Sir John Reith, whom she had sculpted in 1929, for a wireless appeal on behalf of the Institution, by Dame Laura Knight, and in 1942 she was elected a vice president.

Despite the Depression, which she observed with sympathy touching the lives of friends and people in all walks of life, with Bill's cabinet job they were financially secure. The Lacket remained their personal haven; they would go for long walks over the Downs, preferably by moonlight, and the boys would frolic in the garden. Pete built a tank for amphibians, sending his mother detailed plans by every post from school. Kathleen still slept out when she could. But the Lacket wasn't big enough for guests, and apart from the Kennet, where they would often bathe, there was no water nearby, which, as Pete grew more involved in wildfowl and sailing, became more important. They rented larger houses for the summers. At Horsey Hall in Norfolk all eleven beds were occupied for six weeks in the summer of 1933; in 1934 at Greatwood near Falmouth they had twenty-eight guests (including E. M. Forster) who each stayed about a week.

They would often go with the Chamberlains to Menabilly in Cornwall, the original for Daphne du Maurier's Manderley. Then there was Kneesworth with the Knutsfords; Cranmore with the Pagets (before they had to sell it because of the Depression); Hatfield with the Salisburys; Dane End with Herbert and Dolly Gladstone, Churt with the Lloyd Georges, Cliveden with the Astors, Chequers with the Baldwins (before Ramsay MacDonald came in). Each year Kathleen would go away for a few weeks alone with Peter, usually to Switzerland where they would skate. She and Bill would also go away: walking in the Tyrol or the Lake District. In April 1933 she and Bill rowed three miles up a lake to find Hugh Walpole. 'He gave us tea and showed us his possessions. He had *lovely* things. A first edition of "Endymion", a lovely missal, a Carl Milles bronze figure, some Sickerts and Duncan Grants, an Egyptian incision and many more.' On Coniston Water in 1934 they visited Arthur Ransome, who had a barn stacked with books and who played the concertina to them. He took Wayland sailing in the *Swallow*, and they explored a 'lovely island'.

When Bill was occupied she went travelling, as ever, with companionable young men. There was no hanky panky:

March 26 1930: I think the way you pay for even falling in love with someone other than your mate is that it lessens and weakens the pleasure you take in your mate, and therefore maybe my natural self protection of my hedonism would prevent [my] succumbing to the ephemeral attractions of beautiful young creatures who encircle one with flattery and cajolery.

Bill didn't mind: after a trip of hers to Italy with Geoffrey Eley in 1930 he said, 'I don't doubt your chastity but I do doubt your practicality', and during it he wrote: 'How you have earned your spree, darling dear . . . kick up your heels unto the Lord and make a joyful hopping to the God of Jacob.' The stony face which Bill sometimes presented to the world, which James Lees-Milne complained of ('I do resent [his] superciliousness. He is so morose too') was not the whole of the man. He loved Mickey Mouse. (Kathleen liked Katharine Hepburn, Veronica Lake and Fred Astaire.)

On 5 June 1935 Bill hurried to the House of Commons for the

final division on the India Bill, and 'was sent for by Baldwin and told he was to relinquish the Ministry of Health and go forthwith to the House of Lords.'

Why? There were many reasons. Bill believed that he had been promised Chancellor of the Exchequer; when this post was not forthcoming a bad feeling remained. He was overstrained by disagreements (mainly over India) with his constituency party, which as Minister of Health he did not have time or energy to wrangle over, and he had told Baldwin that he did not want to fight another election. The government as a whole had been getting some vicious press, and changes had to be made. Perhaps most significantly, when it was suggested that slum landlords should be compensated for property that was being cleared, Bill had dug his heels in and said that a public health inspector does not compensate a butcher for confiscated flyblown meat. Simply, this was an unConservative attitude to property. And thus he was kicked upstairs, taking the title Lord Kennet, from the river that flowed near the Lacket.

He was very upset about it. He had wanted time to finish off his housing schemes and make them foolproof; now they were overnight no longer his. After having been in the cabinet his political career was now all downhill. Kathleen was philosophical.

> For the work it is clearly a pity, on the other hand it is equally clearly impossible to change each minister at the moment most convenient to their work. To my thinking it is quite time Bill has a rest [he had been ill that year, with phlebitis in his leg and more pain in his stump], taken now he will shortly regain his ardour; taken a little later and I would not be surprised had he permanently lost all resilience. It is a large break in life to give up the H of C but it is not death!

They had a holiday in Italy planned anyway for the next week, and they took it. They had no letters, so Bill had nothing new to worry about, and there were gentians and lilies of the valley and woodpeckers and fireflies, one of which 'was so kind as to walk on my arm'. Then the letters arrived: 'many just conventional congratulations, some ecstatic jubilations, some furious indignation at the waste of Bill, some half pitying. One from Neville Chamberlain as nice and enthusiastically appreciative as could be, one from the Archbishop of Canterbury full of the highest praise. It really is a rummy business and Baldwin is a *fool*, but nevertheless I am glad, we may now save Bill's health, soul and sanity and they are worth saving.' He did not want his political career to end like this – for this was, effectively, the end. He spoke only twice in the House of Lords, and instead went into the City. He was at different times chairman of the Hudson's Bay Company, Commercial Union Insurance, timber importers Denny Mott and Dixon, and the Union Discount Company, among others.

Kathleen was not particularly bothered about becoming a peeress. Rosslyn thought it funny that she should change her name yet again: she had been Miss Bruce, Mrs Scott, Lady Scott and Mrs Hilton-Young, and now she was Lady Kennet. He wrote a poem about it:

> When an artist has once made a name
> He is properly proud of his fame;
> But when one can contrive
> To have not one but five,
> She is clearly quite good at the game.

In fact Rosslyn missed one out: she had also been Lady Hilton-Young when Bill was Sir Edward.

Rosslyn was now rector of Herstmonceux in Sussex. Sir Paul Latham, MP for Scarborough, visited him there, fell in love with the castle and bought it. He restored the castle and lived there in some magnificence until the war and scandal took it from him. Latham was a friend of Kathleen's too and bought a blindfold nude, *The Kingdom is Within*, to stand among yew bushes at the head of the swimming pool. It was at Herstmonceux that Kathleen met Cecil Beaton, and was disappointed to find that he was not wearing make-up. Despite his marriage and baby, Latham was involved later in a homosexual scandal and went to prison; Kathleen received a message that he felt she was the right person to explain it all to his young son Richard, which filled her with trepidation.

Bill's going into the City made the family richer, but Kathleen as ever didn't care about that. 'Il faut souffrir pour être homme de commerce, et pire encore pour être sa femme (You must suffer to be a businessman, and suffer still more to be his wife),' she wrote, after having to host a party where people ate caviare: 'that one person should swallow 2/- in a mouthful – enough to feed a growing lad for two days!' And she carried on working. The Duke of York; the new King; Queen Mary on a plaque for the eponymous liner (she found it hard to stop it looking like a half crown); Neville Chamberlain; the Australian poet Adam Lindsay Gordon for Poets' Corner in Westminster Abbey; Sabu the young film star, better known as the Elephant Boy; and many more large and small nudes.

'Why does one work so hard?' she wondered in 1935.

> Why does it matter what one has in the foolish RA? Of course it doesn't and yet, and yet, one goes on until one's limbs ache and one's eyes are dim. I am not ambitious – I want nothing – certainly not money, nor honours – I suppose I must want admiration – yes I expect that must be it, for it can't be just the urge to produce for if merely that I wouldn't care about RAs and such. The *Illustrated London News* had a whole page of my bust of the King – and I am pleased. How silly to be pleased, it does not make me a good sculptor because the *ILN* reproduces my work.

Another press report on her work, in the April 1926 edition of *Home* magazine, sweetly headlined 'Wife, Mother and Genius', had given Kathleen's status as Scott's widow in both the first paragraph and the main picture caption. This was typical. Throughout these years the legend of Scott never let her be, privately or publicly. Her fame was inextricably linked with his. Every now and then, regularly if not too often, something would come up which required to her to be Scott's Widow, and each time private grief and public pride – pride in him and pride in not letting him down – recurred. In 1925 a monument to Scott was unveiled at Devonport:

> We stood among the crowd. Later we were discovered and cinemaed during the saying of prayers. Rather awful. Etty Ellison McCartney made poor Pete stick a wreath on – he did it all right, but it was very uncomfy for him. How I loathe that kind of conventional tribute. How absurd! One might as well give God a buttonhook. I simply clenched my teeth and hardened my heart and viewed quizzically the sobbing relatives around – I shouted the hymns and thought all the while of bobbitty bumble bees and peppermint creams, but that night in bed I wept most foolishlike, and many other nights I have. How idiotic after 13 years.

In 1926 the Scott Polar Research Institute in Cambridge came into theoretical being. Frank Debenham came and 'was delighted with the things I can give him for the Scott Institute. I shall *give* nothing, they shall all be "deposited" by Pete and retrieved when he likes. Heaps of *Discovery* papers and journals, 4 sledges, maps, pictures etc.' (Debenham wrote a feeling appreciation of her in *The Polar Record* after her death, mentioning her and Bill's assistance in raising money for the Institute, and her personal help for the expedition and for its members after their return.) She sculpted a head of Scott to go in a niche above the entrance. At the opening Baldwin unveiled the statue of Arnold Lawrence in the grounds.

She was more generous with Scott mementoes than with their private feelings. A young man came from Toronto in 1928 and she happily gave him 'a pipe, a pouch, a Wilson painting and a bar of medal ribbons'. She was not so happy when in 1930 Stephen Gwynn's biography of Con was published. This was an approved biography, published partly to counteract the perceived bad effects of Cherry-Garrard's book, and Kathleen read the proofs. Even so:

> I don't know how I'm going to bear having that published. I'm told he is not my property, he is public property, that I have no right to withhold anything that throws light on his character, that I must subject my own susceptibilities to what is best to sustain his name at the loftiest. All this may be, nay is, so, and yet when I come to see letters that have made me weep and will make me weep every time I think of them till I die, when I come to see these letters laid bare for my chauffeur, my grocer, small boys at my son's school etc to read I confess that my skin shrinks round me tight and hard. Shall I be able to bear it when the book actually comes out? My god how I shrink. 15 or 20 years ago and it seems to me as present as today. How would it be to stop the whole thing? Cowardly? Bill says it should be published. Bill's judgement is right and seemly generally and yet . . . Con, what would he say . . . Con might like it. It only shows his fine calibre. But me – Pooh!! Despicable self pity . . . So long as no one ever speaks to me about Con's letters. What would I give for a heart of stone and a tough unprickable skin.

Also that year a play about Scott and Amundsen was put on in Berlin. Kathleen went to see it, taking Geoffrey Dearmer, and her reaction was better than she had feared it would be. She didn't particularly mind Lady Scott being portrayed 'as much unlike me as it would be possible to make a woman' or Pete being portrayed as 'a nice stripling about 13' rather than a toddler. But then Con 'emits a sob, and altogether puts up a poor show', and there is a 'long, unhistoric and intensely melodramatic scene of the failing of Oates, where they all howl and shriek like demented Latins – a sorry affair', and 'they all sit about outside as though enjoying a sunny picnic, then they rant and shriek and finally die.' The psychology behind the play, she suspected, might be 'the desire in the German to prove that defeat may be more noble than success'. This was not a view she shared: what made Con's 'failure' good to her was the manner of it and the successes that went along with it, and those she felt were not brought out in the play. The British press was keen to hear her opinion; she did not give it. It is probably as well that Kathleen did not live to see the 1947 film of Con's expedition, with John Mills's matinee heroism and Diana Churchill's rather smug little wife in a clean overall, though she would have loved the scenery.

In 1932 Levick (the senior surgeon on the *Terra Nova*) came to lunch, bearing tales of Mrs Oates's unhappiness that Bernacchi (who had been a physicist on the *Discovery* expedition) was writing a book of Oates's life. In 1938 the *Discovery* was presented to the Boy Scouts; Kathleen went to the ceremony and renewed her old acquaintance with Lord Baden Powell. (She and Peter went for a weekend with him and his wife; he gave her a splendid example of how a person should be at eighty: 'he leapt upstairs two stairs at a time, draws awfully well, sculpts, paints, writes and speaks . . . stepping forth like a youngster.')

The calls of the legend were not all so official. In 1941 Kathleen received a strange illiterate letter from a woman in New York, saying she was dying and claiming to have borne Con a daughter when she was fifteen. A note on the envelope said 'the lady is now dead'. Kathleen thought it was some sort of half-cocked blackmail attempt. The story was 'palpably untrue, it doesn't hang together at all', and she tore the letter up. No more was heard.

In 1936 the Kennets 'lent/let' the Lacket to Colonel Lawrence's

mother, and took Fritton Hithe, a low thatched house on Fritton Lake
in Norfolk, as their country house. There is a visible air of enchantment to these days of the late thirties. With Bill working in the City
Kathleen divided her time between Leinster Corner and Fritton,
sculpting, gardening, walking, punting on the lake, looking after her
boys and watching them sail. Diary entries and letters are full of
nectarines, daffodils, sunny afternoons, ski-ing in the winter and
sailing in the summer. Kathleen got hold of a cine-camera and they
made films of each other, falling over sand-dunes in their swimming
things, Kathleen as heroine (of course), Peter as the hero, Bill as the
villain and Wayland as the 'Angel Child' in complicated stories.
Peter's and Wayland's friends (including one James Mason, 'quiet,
romantic-looking, going to be an actor' and Peregrine Worsthorne,
aged about twelve, 'a little Bolshi') and theirs would overlap. 'Like
flocks of gulls they fly about screaming between sea, broad and lake,
upsetting and having to be dried, eating enormously and mostly
winning their races.' In 1937 Peter won the Prince of Wales Cup:
'47 entries, 15 miles open sea in 14-ft international dinghies, he won
by 16 seconds, John Winter 2nd and Stewart Morris 3rd. Nice boys
but not a well-bred one among them and absolutely no topic of
conversation but sailing.'

Forster came regularly; Arthur Ransome came; George and Janet
Trevelyan; and Duncan Grant: 'A sweet attractive terribly nervous
little creature. His eyes are very blue, his nose very red, his clothes
deplorable, but there is something there that is infinitely endearing.
I mended his coat for him!! I can scarcely believe it.'

Even fretting takes on an idyllic tinge: young George Trevelyan,
son of Bill's great friend Sir George, came to Fritton in a flurry of
wondering what to do with his life. He told Kathleen that 'he got
up at 2am and took a boat across the lake and walked and walked
through the woods and got as far as Ashly church, found it open,
went in, lit the altar candles and played on the organ. Then wandered
to the Somerleytons' [neighbours] summerhouse . . . and waited for
the birds to begin to sing.' He thought he should be a schoolmaster,
Kathleen thought he should study to be a land agent so he could run
his father's estate properly when he inherited.

Another young friend, Keith Miller Jones, described Kathleen as the most sympathetic woman he had ever known. She was in a better position than ever to play the green stick, and liked to use her experience and position to help: with introductions, trips, money sometimes, encouragement. Publishers would be introduced to young writers, conductors invited for young musicians, and exhibitions arranged for young artists, not least Peter himself who had his first exhibition at Ackermann's in Bond Street in 1933. The organist of King's College, Boris Orde, was a friend and would come and talk music and play with Wayland, who in 1937 recorded two of his own compositions in a shop in Bond Street for Bill's Christmas present. As well as a piano (and sometimes two) they had a pianola, and a curious little instrument called a dulcitone: it had a keyboard but instead of strings it had tuning forks.

Kathleen did have high standards, and she liked to help people to achieve them. This can be unpleasant for the receiver, but she often got away with it. The conductor Antony Bernard dashed off the podium after a concert in March 1928 to say to her, 'I love you I love you I love you, do you understand?' to which 'I replied very gently that I hoped that was jolly for him and that I wanted to tell him lots of mistakes he makes in conducting . . .' It didn't put him off her. And in many cases her help was welcome.

Rosslyn's daughter Verily, a student at the Royal College of Music, recalls walking across Kensington Gardens to join in the ever-social household at Leinster Corner, and being rung up and told to wash her hair and put on a frock, because Kathleen was giving a party and Sir Malcolm Sargent would be there. Sargent was good value at parties: 'We had the loveliest fun,' Kathleen wrote after one. 'They all played and sang and Mimi [Rambert] danced divinely, but perhaps the star was Malcolm who was the most graceful and witty clown – they stayed till 1 am, turning cartwheels all over the place, and all on lemonade.' Sargent invited her to rehearsals ('It was fun to hear him say, with an orchestra of 100, "someone gave me a D sharp there" ') and introduced her to Ravel: 'a thin dapper little man with white hair, quite nice and civilized'. Wayland often went to concerts with her, and sat rapt from an early age. After one concert she went with Sargent 'to see the gramophone record being made, in an electrified motor lorry'. Shaw was good value with musicians; he suggested to the cellist Suggia that she might find a nice little fiddle less cumbrous.

Another helpee was the writer and art historian James Lees-Milne. 'She was frightfully good to me. She took me to Switzerland [in the winter of 1936/7]. I adored her. She was never in awe.' (Indeed she wasn't. She told the Queen of Norway she was 'adorable', and laughed like anything when Peter as a toddler grabbed Queen Alexandra's bustle and made her play trains, chuff chuff chuff, pushing her around the garden. She did however constrain her urge to call the Queen – now the Queen Mother – darling.)

'And Kathleen was wonderfully blunt,' Lees-Milne continues. 'She'd look at you, and say nothing, and then estimate you. She was so like a man it was like having another man friend. We were so inhibited then with women, but with Kathleen all that went by the board. I thought she was wonderful. She was affectionate in a rather proprietary way, as one might be with a nice young dog. She didn't want it to be hangdog or scruffy when she took it to dance at the Savoy. One had to make an effort.'

She was not, however, easy, and even those who loved her best admitted it. 'She was better with boys than with girls,' says Lees-Milne, and she had strong opinions and occasionally a sharp tongue, which she may not have confined to her diary.

On Winston Churchill: 'He may be a genius but he disguises it very well.' On a nameless art dealer: 'A cross-eyed shark of the very worst type.' On a performance of *Rheingold*: 'Brünnhilde's "Mountain Song" sounded like a very bad Channel crossing.' On Lord Birkenhead: 'I suppose the world does not hold a more repugnant individual. How does he get away with it? He should die. I have always known he is a drunkard and a libertine, but I did not know he had such an evil tongue.'

Sybil Colefax told James Lees-Milne that Kathleen was 'a snob who tried to vamp every distinguished man'. ('The pot calling the kettle black,' wrote Lees-Milne: Lady Colefax's house was known as the Lions' Corner House.) Kathleen happily admitted to being an intellectual and aesthetic snob; she loved intelligence and beauty, and probably would have dismissed Sybil's comment as detrimentalizing. But she was never a social snob. 'She didn't care tuppence for society ladies and Mayfair,' as Lees-Milne put it. Sybil Colefax also said that Kathleen dramatized her widowhood, seeking publicity at every turn, which goes exactly against what Shaw observed, and is equally wrong.

'She expected adulation, and she got it,' Lees-Milne says. 'She fascinated men. Scott was a very great hero in those days, and she was in her own right a great sculptress, and everywhere she went people were agog.' This she didn't like. She hated people not trusting their own instincts to like her or not, and then being charming when they realized who she was. She would rather have been ignored – or preferably adulated – on her own merits.

John Winter, a close friend and sailing companion of Pete's, remembers his stays at Fritton fondly, with Kathleen 'always on the go' and not in the least frightening. If, however, there were a flaw in a guest's self-confidence, they could feel excluded. Lees-Milne felt it on occasion, and records with some passion in his published diaries Kathleen blowing her sons' trumpets so loudly that everyone was deafened. Now he says: 'Peter was good at everything, which was irritating of him, and Wayland was very clever, and Kathleen was infuriatingly proud of them.'

Peter *was* good at everything: a dinghy-racing champion, a champion-class skater, an Olympic yachtsman (he won a bronze in Berlin in 1936), an acclaimed painter, a famous wildfowler, a published journalist and author. In five weeks in the summer of 1936, between Olympic trials, he painted forty-eight pictures, a dozen of which sold before his exhibition opened, at prices from £18 to £135. (Kathleen thought Peter's drawings were better than those of Augustus John, which they weren't, and anyway so different as to be incomparable, but maternal pride was ever blind.)

Kathleen, however, worried about the point and purpose of Peter's talents. He was living now in a lighthouse on the Wash, with a cockle collector called Charlie living in the cellar, and surrounded by pens of wildfowl that he had collected. He came back from Hungary in 1935 with fifteen live geese in crates. Kathleen put them in her car and then her garden, and all 'was merry as a wedding'. On another occasion she kept a seal in the bath for him.

In November 1934 she went out with him into his element:

Pete woke me at 4 am bringing thigh rubber boots and three pairs of socks. Then we tip-toed down to a meal laid the night before: bread, butter, ham and ginger beer (said to be warming!) and then we started forth in dark and rain, first ten miles by car, then in pitchiness along a grass bank, then for a mile or two over the salting, stumbling and tumbling into all kind of crevasses. Pete was tenderly mindful of me. At last we got to a big creek full of water. Along this we waded – me in imminent danger of sticking in the mud, Pete's boots being so big and heavy. Once Pete had to pull me out. At last we sat down on a mack, in the mud in the creek with our feet in water, by now quite close to the geese which we heard honking and bustling. Presently just before dawn groups of five or six began to fly over us and then suddenly with a grand flurry and honking over they all flew about 1500 of them. As grand a sight as I could hope to see . . . It was fun being out with him. He calls all the birds and they fly over him. He knows exactly where to find them. Countless curlews, greenshanks etc. He is so completely in his element. A grand fellow. It must be right not to interfere too much with what *appears* to be a 'waste of time'. It's not work, it's true; it does no good to anybody, it makes no money but – at any rate it does no harm to anybody and I think some good to yourself. Anyway I felt those nights I wouldn't have him be any other sort of boy at all! *So there.*

Kathleen's work was more in demand than ever in the five years before the Second World War: a bronze head of Montague Norman, a great naked figure originally called *The Strength Within*, later retitled *England*, which Glyn Philpot thought the best thing she had ever done; a bronze bust of the Bishop of Liverpool, and one of Shaw, now eighty-one, and one of the Duke of York (with whom she had a merry relationship: he would give her news of the Princess Elizabeth's budgerigars, which had recently had babies), and one of the King; a small portrait of a baby, Deirdre Bacon; an immense Lord Delamere for Nairobi – an eight-foot bronze on a ten-foot base, price £2000. 'I hope it won't kill me,' she wrote cheerfully in her diary.

Between 1920 and 1940 there was only one year when she did not have at least one piece in the Royal Academy; she also had pieces in the Paris Salon, of which she several times received the Diploma. She exhibited at the International Society and the Society of Portrait Painters. In 1938 a quarto volume, *Homage*, was published by Bles, illustrating her work. 'She is particularly good in expressing the hard clear dynamic features of statesmen and men of action,' wrote the reviewer in the *Times Literary Supplement*, commenting also that her 'symbolic nudes', 'if occasionally lacking the freshness of originality . . . are always well poised, graceful, well-conceived and competently carried out.'

She took on some of the responsibilities of success too; in addition to her involvement with the Artists' General Benevolent Institution she was elected in 1937 to the council of the Royal Society of British Sculptors, the first woman to be so. One of her duties was to find speakers for their dinners: she got J. B. Priestley and Malcolm Sargent.

She appeared on television too, probably through Sir John Reith. 'I am to televize!' she wrote with glee and trepidation in March 1937. Television had only just started and audiences were not big: the BBC's inauguration had taken place in November 1936, to about 400 viewers, and television sets cost about £100, the same as a small car. The coronation procession in May was watched by between 10,000 and 50,000 people – calculation of viewing statistics was not very advanced either. It was all live.

Kathleen was advertised in the *Radio Times* (her programme was one of a series called *The World of Women*, and appeared between the British Movietone News and an interview with Professor Walter Gropius). She went to the studio at Alexandra Palace

in a dither of nerves. A huge studio with 1000 blaring hot lights streaming down, a vast machine on wheels propelled by men in white coats with earphones to their ears comes rolling to within a foot of your face. Wire, steel and pipes surround you and there is a dead and grim silence. The scene seems set for a gigantic surgical operation on some gargantuan god of the future. In the centre of this burning glare cowered the poor trembling jelly 'Lady Kennet the world-famous sculptor', whose heart beat so loud she felt sure it must upset the radio vibrations. For 17 minutes in a kind of trance I said my piece, I put up a clay figure and Maxton's head, I showed 15 pieces, I made dreamy generalizations about sculpture, I carried on as tho' I were an accomplished self-possessed matter-of-fact person, instead of a lacerated quivering crumb of exposed sensitiveness.

In September 1938 trenches were being dug in Kensington

Gardens; there were guns at Marble Arch and 'every soul had taken home his gas mask'. Peter, in the United States, wired to know should he come home. Kathleen told him there wasn't going to be a war, and then wondered to herself whether she lived in a fool's paradise. 'Well I would rather be a fool in my paradise than one of the trembling jellies that represent the wise. It's like hell – I don't believe in hell, nor any future life so I am happy. What a gall if I am wrong about the war and wrong about hell. Well, in the meantime I am more carefree, and allow my sons so to be too.'

On a trip to Cambridge to see the Trevelyans she learnt that seventy babies had been evacuated from London to Newnham during the 'war scare'; the next day seventy-one had been sent back, all in the wrong clothes and to the wrong parents.

In March she ran into Neville Chamberlain. 'You're looking awfully well,' she said to him. 'Some people might say better than I've any right to look,' he replied. She reminded him that he had once told her he was never worried or rattled. 'Well, I try not to be,' he replied, 'but that man [Hitler] – grrrrr.' 'You just feel grrr about him now?' she asked. 'Grrrr and grrrrr. To think that thousands and thousands of people are being kept in a state of fear and uncertainty, dreading and not able to make decisions . . . I truly heartily wish someone would stab him.' Kathleen said that if she had tuberculosis she would take on the commission, after all an American woman had got close enough to kiss him. Neville wondered if it was his duty to get her infected with the disease.

Kathleen's willpower couldn't hold off the war when it came, but it could continue the idyll with a vengeance until the last minute. First there was a Greek cruise: the Parthenon looked 'so aerial and light it seemed like gossamer floating and swimming in the breeze', and a policeman accosted her to tell her that her cousin Mme Nasos would like to meet her for lunch – she had got the Chief of Foreign Visitors Police to locate her. Kathleen went back to find the house that she had helped Isadora and her troupe to build; everyone told her it had been demolished, and new houses were creeping up very near but 'there were the actual stones I had put in their places . . . there was the artesian well we had dug for and that every few days the man said had sprung water so everyone stopped work and had drinks and then going back found there was no water. There was grass in the inner courtyard but the big room was all right though inhabited by a pigeon.' She remembered the one revolver between them, and how they would bang on petrol tins during the night if they heard anything suspicious, and she remembered the beautiful shepherd who had thought she was a ghost. 'It all came back, it all came back. How young I was and how brave.'

She spent much of her time with Hugh Walpole, who told her that he had 'had spiritual communication with Henry James through a medium'. James had commented on Walpole moving some of his books, and told him to dare to be himself. Walpole was as ever very confiding: he told her that Ned Lawrence had told him in 1921 that he had never had full satisfaction from any sexual relationship; and he told her about his own relationship with his chauffeur/companion Harold: he 'sometimes liked people who weren't at all of his habits and how it was so awkward'. Kathleen had met Harold before in the Lake District and met him again later in 1938 when he drove her and Walpole to the opera: 'Hugh is obsequiously engaging to him, he surly and rude to Hugh. It's horrid until you understand, and so far I don't understand.'

Then there was a tour of the cathedrals of France with Bill, Wayland and Sir Sydney Cockerell, admiring the restoration work that had been done on damage from the last war. Then, in June 1939, Kathleen took Peter to Venice to stay with her old friend Prince George Chavchavadze, the pianist, who had married an immensely rich American wife and moved into a fifteenth-century palazzo. 'I always before thought I did not care for Venice,' Kathleen observed, 'but it is very different staying in a lovely palazzo with a private gondola, with gondoliers called Emilio and Julio and a butler called Pepino and a pretty maid called Rosina. It was all like a Verdi opera, and George leading on a chain a ridiculous little white lap dog with blue ribbons in its hair and a bell round its neck.' The company was international: two Russians, two Italians, one Luxembourgeois, two Sudeten Germans, two French, one Greek and the two English (Kathleen and Peter). 'If ever I said anything about the war the attitude was 'War? What war? Oh yes of course you're English, the English are always bothering about the war.'

In July she went with James Lees-Milne and about twenty others on a National Trust tour of the châteaux of Belgium. They drove about in a charabanc seeing two or three châteaux a day and being given tea by Belgian aristocrats, and were greeted by King Leopold. In August Kathleen, Bill and Wayland were at Fritton, sailing, walking and entertaining as they did every summer. J. B. Priestley came to stay with his wife and various daughters. It never stopped raining, so they played games. 'A silly turn but so irresistible was him on all fours going round to each person in the circle looking up pathetic-like, and each person was to stroke his head and say "poor pussy" without laughing. I like an idiot resisted from laughing, whereat he got up and said it wasn't a funny game after all. I wake up nights kicking myself for not bursting my guts with laughter.' 'Priestley is queerly half-educated,' she wrote. 'He is brilliant, he is sensitive, he was at the university, his manners are faultless, he is a great dear, he is not, however, at all a gentleman. Now why? Is it his slight Yorkshire accent, or his build, or what? I liked him immensely. He wrote chapter 9 of his new book with us.'

That was the last occasion on which they could be jolly without having to admit, if only to themselves, that they were maintaining jolliness consciously. As Bill wrote to her in 1941, 'It was very pleasant that destiny allowed us to have those years . . . before it cut all the threads.'

NINETEEN

+

The Second War and the End

+

1939–1947

AUGUST 1939: 'Rumours, rumours, clearly inevitable and yet still a hope . . . It seems very clear there is no good going on fooling oneself,' she wrote.

War was declared on the morning of 3 September. They heard it on the radio at Fritton. Wayland and some young friends were racing small boats on the lake, Kathleen said to carry on and they carried on. Pete was restless and fidgety and went to his lighthouse because he had to go somewhere. Bill was steady and calming. Kathleen went to the station at half an hour's notice to fetch 'eight dirty little objects from Dagenham', evacuee children aged between five and twelve, who had been travelling three days, walked two hours to get to the boat, been seasick and had nothing to eat but bread and cheese.

That night there was an air-raid warning. The next day the pump broke down and there was no water. There were 24 people in the household: 72 meals a day. One of the sailing boys got a sore throat and a temperature of 102°. All but one of the evacuees were wetting the bed. 'But hey!' wrote Kathleen. 'What does it all matter? If George has diphtheria or anything we'll be in the soup . . .'

'It really was a marvellous work,' she observed two weeks later as she packed the eight off to their more permanent billets, Wayland back to school, his friends back to their schools or families and herself to London. 'There is a young green woodpecker within six yards of me. It is hard to believe there is anything amiss.'

Three weeks later she was back at Fritton with Bill, and the mood had finally and irretrievably changed. 'October 13: It rained and rained and the garden was covered with leaves. We walked determinedly round the lake and tried to remember how lucky we were – and by Jove we *are*.'

This war was different for Kathleen. She had seen the last one. She had her own boys to lose now: Wayland had shaved for the first time that summer, and Pete was 'pawing the ground . . . [he] cannot leave well alone but must needs use all his and our influence to get himself killed as quick as maybe.' Rosslyn's son Errol had recently been gassed in a submarine. Pete joined the Royal Naval Volunteer Reserve, and in October off he went. 'At an hour's notice off and away no one knows where. [In fact it was to HMS *King Alfred* for shore training, and thence to the destroyer HMS *Broke*.] He looked more like Con than ever. Now maybe it will all end. But there! Maybe it won't.'

She signed up to do work for facial plastic surgeons as she had done in the last war, but there was none. Bill, she felt, was 'eating his heart out' that he could not go too. She was simply pleased that he was not strong enough. She occupied herself 'thanking whatever gods there be . . . that I am not, and Pete is not dead, and that I have not and Pete has not to see bloody and terrible sights, and that I and Pete can still look into the sky and watch the high winds chasing the clouds and chasing the autumn leaves. Each day is so much happy relief gained.' She arranged jollities for Pete's periods of leave, thinking that each time he came might be the last: dancing, skating, cheerful dinners with singing and playing and games afterwards. George Chavchavadze came to stay, filling the house with piano music, including compositions of Wayland's. The dinghy-racing youths of Fritton were now young naval officers; the introductions and helping began to centre around admirals.

But she could not work. 'It seems too irrelevant.' In addition her health was making it difficult for her. She had suffered intermittently from a fluttering pattering heart which had caused her some trouble while working on the big figure of Lord Delamere, and now she had 'a tiresome constriction across my chest'. The doctor said it was old age and cold, and told her not to skate or dance or bathe or run or catch a bus. She thought that nonsense; it was just digestion and 'a d—d nuisance'. Out in Kensington Gardens one day, watching the autumn leaves dancing, she found herself saying, 'Oh god *don't* let me die yet, I do enjoy it all so much more than most people, I

mustn't be stopped in the middle of my delight and appreciation.'
But the illness went on, and she was almost surprised by it. 'I move
like an old woman, which I am, but I never felt like one before.'
Then she developed lumbago: 'How humiliating.'

So she was old, and the action moved away from her. Where she
had lived so actively, she now actively observed and commented on
the lives of the young, most notably of course her sons. Wayland was
at school, music and sailing were his joys, and her biggest concern
with him was how far ahead of his age she should allow his precocity
to lead him, and whether the war would end before he had to serve.
He was taught the facts of life. Schoolmaster: 'Young, do you know
what stags do in autumn?' Young: 'Yes sir.' Schoolmaster: 'I thought
you would.' Another master asked Wayland's advice on what to say
to the boys about homosexual activity at school. 'Tell them it's bad
for their nerves and their health,' he recommended. (Earlier he had
founded an Anti-God League, and given its members badges made
by Kathleen.)

Peter was altogether more vulnerable in his mother's eyes, and not
just to the dangers of war. She didn't like the way she perceived
modern young girls to behave. She thought it wrong of them to 'hang
around these boys' necks and then say they *must* marry them'. She
felt they made themselves easy very quickly and then expected to be
proposed to. Peter, she felt, expected to be killed any time, and of
course wanted to marry and procreate; equally he felt it improper to
do so for just the same reason. The combination made her nervous
for him.

Peter was committing acts of extraordinary bravery. As if his official
naval duties weren't enough, in 1941 he volunteered to go on bombing
missions over Cologne, ostensibly to foster good relations between
the navy and the air force but more personally because he wanted to.
He was made MBE, for his work designing and painting camouflage
for ships ('and slightly for being in HMS *Broke* so long,' he said); he
was mentioned in dispatches twice. Kathleen was publicly proud and
privately terrified.

'The boys are going thick and fast now,' she wrote in May 1940.
'The Falmouths' eldest, Davina's husband, Gerald and countless
others. It seems like just a matter of days before it is Pete's turn and

one just sits by impotent . . . The lists of dead and missing are coming thick and fast and one dare scarcely ask how anyone is.' Before the war each had been 'just another hungry untidy boy to look after'; as soon as people had schooled themselves to see these boys as defenders of the nation they started to be killed. Kathleen's optimism was sorely challenged.

'Well, we've got everything to fear now,' she wrote as France capitulated. Churchill gave her no comfort. She'd never liked him and she didn't like him now. 'This evening he broadcast in a husky, hesitating voice that an invasion probably was inevitable. He could not have been more sinister. He as good as told us we'd all be in our graves tomorrow but there wouldn't be any time to put us there, but that we ought all to be very pleased and proud about it.' Arranging an exhibition for Pete was a comfort simply because it was so irrelevant. George Chavchavadze was going to America: would Kathleen come too? For Wayland's sake she almost considered it, but 'it would be rather difficult to be a quitter'. 'I'm getting duller and weaker and uglier,' she observed. 'The only thing I still am is cheerful.' She did not believe there would be an invasion, 'but I am always wrong, I didn't think there was going to be a war. Yes I am always wrong but I don't believe we're going to be beaten.' And she quotes again Stevenson's lines: 'I will not falter more or less/ In my great task of happiness.'

Peter was '*very* deeply engrossed in his destroyer and its activities', in his mother's words. She referred to the *Broke* as 'his latest love, he really does love her.' He kept Kathleen in as constant touch with what was happening to him as security allowed. In June 1940, after the Germans had taken Paris, the *Broke* was ordered to Brest to take off any troops they could find and destroy installations. Brest was in a topsy-turvy state, no one knew what was going on. Pete went ashore six times in thirty hours. He wrote to Kathleen:

June 1940
Back again from another tremendous adventure. This time we have done a real service in the war effort, having saved and brought back with us some very valuable units of the French Fleet as well as about 250-odd refugees, BEF, Poles etc: I had the most terrific time – made

five separate landings on my own – acted as embarkation officer at the port – we were bombed four times, once heavily . . . Chief adventures were driving wildly through the streets of the town in lorries we found lying about and subsequently destroyed – collecting and saving all equipment in the form of guns and small arms ammunition – blocking roads and quays with useless lorries. Setting fire to oil tanks and blowing up cranes, power houses, etc: this was mostly done by special demolition parties but I was sent to destroy a 150-ton crane. We went in a motorboat notoriously difficult to start when warm. We lit the fuses (at pistol point from French sentries who queried our orders) and had kept the motor running. We had ten minutes to get half a mile away for the biggest explosion of the evening. It was about 11 pm and the Germans were supposed to have entered the town at 7 pm, actually they hadn't but were just outside. We jumped in the motorboat and put the clutch in and the motor stalled . . . [Well, they got away; and they] set out along the cliffs . . . Gorse and broom – hayfields – maize – a Dartford warbler flitted across the path. Dawn broke. Enormous clouds of oil smoke from the fires we had started filled the Southern sky.

Kathleen wrote back: 'My sweet, what an adventure, it's breathtaking. I rush around with you, I demolish, I ignite, I embark, I signal, and most of all I stride out, dead tired along the gorse-covered cliff. What a life, what marvellous service, how grateful we are to you.' Bravery is nothing but the overcoming of fear. As with Con, she would not let her fear contaminate her hero's bravery. For the volunteer bombing raids she was less enthusiastic.

9.9.41:
Very Dear Pete I've just had a lovely letter from you. How thrilling your Cologne bombing must have been, and your description of the sunsetting and the apprehension and the comradeship made one's heart glow, and I thoroughly and completely sympathise with your delight – never the less I think you should now refrain from that delight. I was thinking that if you had been lost on that last adventure I should have been very angry.

In his uniform he looked very like Con, and echoes of Con ran through and through her mind. She wished she could send him

Pete's letters. Above all she wanted Pete to come back alive, and to be happy.

Kathleen had been both mother and father to Peter for the first thirteen years of his life. She did not want to be the cause of any defect in his character that might let his father down. She was fully aware of the public scrutiny under which Pete lived – she had had enough of it herself. She was aware that the public expected heroism from the Son of the Antarctic, as Mimi Rambert called him. War gives opportunity. She was aware that he was also aware of this. It frightened her.

More personally, Pete was all she had left of Con and the early years. Colonel Stirling, many years before, had joked that the umbilical cord between her and Pete had never been severed; he had a point, and she knew it. Their letters, from prep school through to the navy, are not duty letters, they are letters between close friends with common interests, a long shared past, the same sense of humour and a deep trusting love. When Kathleen accepted Bill as her husband, his capacity to be a good stepfather was one of his main qualifications. She wrote to Bill in 1921 of the difficulty she found in expressing the 'warm comforting enveloping support that your love of Pete gives me', and she would not have married him had she not had faith in that.

The line between pressure and support was ever thin. She was aware of that too, and bore it in mind. In the same letter to Bill:

I have builded him with such effort. I invented him when I was very young, and withstood until I had found the all-glorious father for him. He is no accident, is Pete. And so, and so. Dear, you know I'm a fool about this infant – but you know, Con is a rather remarkable creature, and I wouldn't like it to be my fault that his son didn't come out as seemly as may be ... please don't laugh at me too much for taking my one only little tiny responsibility so seriously.

In 1925, she puts it even more clearly in her diary: 'He is so terribly like Con – hatching and planning [an expedition] and looking so like him too – oh dear oh dear I hope he'll be as good and with a happier temperament as well ... Con was happy when he was with me. Maybe if Pete marries a decent human being he will avoid unhappiness.'

Well, Pete had had girlfriends and dancing partners and skating partners, and he had broken a few hearts, but not until 1941 did he fall in love. Her name was Elizabeth Jane Howard. Now she is a distinguished novelist; then she was a shy seventeen-year-old actress who wrote plays, had been bullied at school, played the piano and was very much in love with a man almost twice her age and very close to his mother. Her mother rang Kathleen 'to ask "whether it's all right". How the hell am I to judge?'

Her judgment was the less confident for being without Bill, on whose calm good sense she very much relied, and for whose cheerfulness she felt personally responsible. Kathleen and Bill had decided that when things got 'ugly' (i.e. bad air raids and/or invasion) they should remain apart, so that there was a better chance of Wayland coming through the war with at least one parent left. Fritton was impossible; it would be right in the line of the imminent invasion. They had gone to close the house up and the roads there from London were semi-blocked all the way. 'The hedgerows were ablaze with roses, which seems to make it seem sillier still, but perhaps the war makes one value all this loveliness even more.'

So Bill stayed in London, working. Leinster Corner was closed up. All its windows were blown out in September 1940, and the furniture had to be removed. It seemed to Kathleen like 'shutting the door forever on one's friends and music and theatres and the old London life. I wonder even if we shall ever go back.' Bill took a flat in Sloane Street. When that was made temporarily uninhabitable by an unexploded bomb he went to stay with the chauffeur in Hounslow. He was now sixty-one, he continued to work, and like most of London he got very little sleep. The stump of his arm gave him trouble again.

Kathleen, meanwhile, took her ill-health to the Lacket for the summer of 1940. She lived there with Mrs Lawrence, Colonel Lawrence's mother, who was 'like a figure in the Old Testament' and would tear Kathleen's bed apart if she had the nerve, as an invalid, to make it herself. Whenever the national anthem came on the radio Mrs Lawrence would stand to attention and Kathleen, in bed, would lie to attention to keep her company. Bill came at weekends and nursed her. Kathleen felt 'like a lump of lead, only not so useful'. In the autumn she went to Rockley Manor, near Marlborough, to stay

with Lady Wakehurst, probably because she could not either continue
to crowd Mrs Lawrence or throw her out. 'It is very tense living in
close proximity with people not of your own choosing,' she wrote
restrainedly.

There were moments of jollity amidst the gloom. Wayland, just
seventeen, won an exhibition to Trinity, and in November 1940
Kathleen and Bill went to Cambridge 'to hold George Trevelyan's
hand while he became Master of Trinity. It seems he goes to the
Trinity Gate and the Elders peep through the keyhole and George
says "Peep-bo" or some such and then he's allowed in. Then a few
highly selected ones sneak off to the chapel and have secret words
there, then they all go and have an awfully good lunch and lo and
behold George is Master of Trinity.' Then the next day she had a
letter from Pete saying he couldn't get used to handling corpses,
specially if he had to try to revive them.

When the threat of immediate invasion receded they were able to
go back to Fritton. The Christmas holiday of 1940 was almost like
old times: Boris Orde came, plus two friends of Wayland from Stowe,
and E. M. Forster. He and Wayland played Beethoven sonatas together,
Wayland playing the right hand and Forster the left. He also read
aloud 'with very little persuasion. He reads in a queer little argumentative voice. I think he is the most difficult person to talk to, he seems
so sure (in spite of his modest manner) that he is a superior being. I
suppose it is really only that he is not at all interested in me and
that is rather an unusual experience for me. Salutary but not a
bit congenial.

'Why do I go on asking him?' she wondered. 'Snobbery, quite
clearly snobbery.' Also she thought him a very good writer, and she
pitied him. 'He is terribly tied by his mother, she hates him going
away even for a night. The poor man lives in this rented (by him)
house at Abinger with four old women – there are just five chairs
but none is comfortable. They have no bath and no electric light, one
servant. Poor Morgan, for he greatly likes comfort.'

More importantly Bill and he were still deep and challenging
friends. In November 1939 Forster wrote a review (of Jan Struther's
Mrs Miniver) which mocked the idea of national character. Bill considered this untimely and unpatriotic, and wrote to Forster saying so,

and that he was 'against criticism. In our race and society and time it is the besetting sin.' Forster replied mentioning Kylsant, a shipping magnate imprisoned for publishing a fraudulent company prospectus:

> You do believe that a society which encourages money-making is good, and that good men should try to make money in it, and you have faith (which I don't share) that the Youngs rather than the Kylsants will come out on top. Your other motives I follow pretty well, and some of them I even imitate: I too want to be comfortable when I'm old, and to keep up my little family tradition – though I don't believe that the present fabric of society is going to survive. I love my books as dearly as you can love yours, but it is typical of us that when you should stick in armorial bookplates I should only write in mine 'E. M. Forster at West Hackhurst'. I don't feel *of* anywhere. I wish I did. It is not that I am deracinated. It is that the soil is being washed away.
>   ... I cling to criticism, much as you cling to that still mistier abstraction, justice ... Why should you think that just *now* dumb obedience is best? It might be if we were sure it wasn't the Kylsants who were giving the orders.

On the way to Fritton Forster took Bill to Howard's End, 'a holy pilgrimage to him', Bill wrote. Forster also told Bill of his homosexuality. 'I should not have known that he was positively homosexual if he had not told me so himself,' Bill wrote. 'I should doubt whether he was ever in bed with man or boy.' Forster told them too about *Maurice*, the homosexual novel he had written but could not publish while his mother was alive. 'I imagine that his refining fire could make it palatable to the coming generation,' Kathleen wrote. She found him shy-making, though Bill wrote that he was attached to her.

Sadly, the friendship ultimately declined through a lack of trust. Bill detected a coolness after Forster settled at King's, Cambridge. 'I heard he had refused a knighthood,' he wrote in April 1958. 'I asked him – had he? – He said yes; and said anything *before* one's name changed it too much. But not *after*? I asked; and he agreed. Soon after, in company with the King's librarian, another old friend, Morshead, he (Morshead) asked me who should have the next OM, about which he was the advisor. I said Morgan. He took other counsel, and told me Morgan hadn't written enough.' The story got around, and

'Morgan repeated it to another friend of mine in the form, after the usual changes of "Russian Scandal", that Hilton had advised the King that he Morgan hadn't written enough. Now I am going to try and see him again when I go up in a month's time; forgetting anything amiss.'

IN JANUARY 1941 Yarmouth was bombed and machine-gunned while Kathleen and Bill 'were in the car in the market place idly contemplating Coomber [the chauffeur] who with £1 in his hand had gone to buy two chickens. The plane flew very low and noisily over our heads dropping one bomb and machine-gunning furiously.' Twelve people were killed and eighteen wounded. 'I remember in the last war I used to enjoy raids. I didn't think I would now, but I did. It's queer, perverse, rather shocking but *a fact*. But not when I learnt twelve dead.' She referred to the bombs as 'Hitler's droppings'.

Then came a different kind of bombshell. Peter wrote to his sailing friend Stewart Morris in June: 'I nearly decided to marry a girl called Jane, of 18, which is quite ridiculous at my time of life . . . She has the priceless gift of sincerity, which burns with a bright flame. She has unbounded energy, and if she can't do a thing she says "let's try it again". She's quite without fear and takes a boat out knowing it will capsize for certain. With all that she's very young and human . . . She's very excited about being in love for the first time, more with that than with me, I think.' And he let slip in a letter to Wayland in August: '. . . Do any of you mind much if I marry Jane. I really think she's quite nice.'

This, in Peter's words, 'dropped a feline among the columbidae'. 'Dearest Mummy,' he wrote. 'A fleeting word as we go. I've written to W. Open it if he has gone. It's only to say that my remark was quite casual and very far from a settled plan or course of action, yet. I must post this at once. Jane is a good and sweet girl I think but agree with all the complications of her extreme youth . . . heaps of love darling sweet sympathetic mummy.'

Kathleen wished they could find 'a Jane of 25'. She wanted Peter to find someone 'binding'. She thought that Jane seemed impractical, and she knew that Peter could be, and felt that in an ideal world a wife should 'know how to prevent your first born from getting pneumonia, or who to go to if you were wrongfully arrested'. She was afraid she had spoiled Peter, and that he would not be able to take care of himself. Part of her wanted to hand him over to a woman who would tax his car and organize his exhibitions and sort out his career and fetch his geese as she had all these years. She was cross too to be told by gossips that people were saying that Jane was saying that she and Peter were to be married. (Jane says she didn't say that – but that never stopped gossip.)

Most of all, she wasn't sure that Peter really loved her, and 'it's difficult enough to be married if you are in love'. In February 1942 Jane was staying at Fritton:

> Peter has got up at four a.m. each day to be on the right marsh before dawn. There he lies in ecstasy under a white sheet in the snow, then perhaps creeps on his tummy for half a mile or so, then perhaps shoots a duck or two . . . he went to bed about 9 each evening. The rest of the day he painted. He didn't take much notice of poor little Jane, who poured out her woes to me after he had gone to bed. She has a lot to put up with. If Peter is in love with her he has a very quaint way of showing it . . . I am getting really quite fond of little Jane. It's not an easy situation for one so young.

Bill was more optimistic about the match: 'She is young, but not too young. It may enrich and illuminate these dark days to have each other. Indeed, has she (or hasn't she?) more promise of the right sort of character and intelligence than most girls?'

Kathleen told Peter she would not advise him. 'If I say yes and it's a failure I'd feel bad and if I say no and the perfect one doesn't turn up it would be my fault. Anyway a man of 31 should not be interfered with even at his own request.'

Peter rang his mother early in 1942 to tell her he had decided yes. Kathleen was swamped by conflicting feelings.

'I have wanted him to do some such for so long . . . I have been dining with E. M. Forster and they are still downstairs smoking cigars. Peter says he is coming in to see me before going to bed. I shall have to be happy and excited. If she ever hurts him I shall kill her . . .' The next day her feelings clarified and her policy emerged. 'As I get used to the idea and I know I must, I get to like it quite well enough not to act overmuch. I wrote Jane an adorable letter. I don't believe I'll have to kill her at all. She will be good.' She thought that Bill thought she needed consolation, and decided that she didn't: 'it's nicer than I thought it would be.' 'Thank you for having such good taste in girls,' she wrote to Peter. 'I am loving her whole-heartedly.'

She ironed over potential situations and brought good humour to the fore: 'Brenda [an old flame of Peter's and a family friend] spends tonight here,' she wrote in her diary, 'and I shall be much surprised if we can't make that as hoitsy toitsy as can be by loving laughter . . . A startling interruption of a large body of armed and helmeted soldiers. Says I "are you the invasion?" "No we're on a *scheme*." Finally we agreed they'd all come and have a fishing holiday here when the war is over.'

And she wrote to Peter: 'My heart is overflowing with love for you and your pretty . . . The spring and love blots Hitler out of the picture a bit doesn't it?'

'I suppose in Germany the boys and girls are loving and the spring is bursting,' she wrote in her diary. 'The Spring Offensive. My god what a thing for humans to do with spring!'

On 28 April 1942 Jane and Peter were married at Christchurch, Lancaster Gate, near to Leinster Corner. The party was at Claridges, and Kathleen recorded that they drank beer, though Jane is certain now that they couldn't have. Kathleen had wanted to pay for the party, the Howards had insisted on going 50/50; Kathleen had not wanted to seem either extravagant (in the 'spirit of the times') or stingy, or to embarrass the Howards by letting on that she knew they were not very rich. 'We weren't enormously rich,' says Jane now, 'but we weren't badly off at all.' She gave Jane a turquoise and diamond ring belonging to her Greek great-grandmother, and forty clothing coupons on condition she at least tried to cut down her smoking.

Kathleen wrote to Peter: 'You may have guessed that I want, I suppose, no single thing more than that you should have an abundance of enduring happiness. I have written to the dear atom telling her I love her, which indeed I have done since the first moment I saw her.' And: 'Oh darling I do rejoice in your happiness – a merry happiness is much easier with a young thing and that's so lovely . . . I felt chucklingly pleased with Jane at that party, so lovely, such poise, like a sainted queen in a fairy book.'

Peter replied: 'Darling . . . Jane cried with joy when she read it, just to know that you didn't think she'd been a disappointment at the wedding.'

And he wrote to Kathleen on 29 April from the Lacket where they went on honeymoon, of the heavenly bluebells and primroses and high winds and sun and Jane looking like a fairy princess and saying to him 'I can't think how anybody ever gets married not to you.' 'Every ten minutes Jane says something which makes me jump for joy,' he wrote.

But it was not all jolly. There is an echo in these letters between Peter and Kathleen and those between Con and Kathleen in 1909, reassuring each other that Kathleen and Hannah Scott really did like each other a great deal. Also, Jane rather shared James Lees-Milne's feelings about Fritton: about the exclusivity of the family and their unmitigated talentedness. She had composed a song about Nelson which she didn't dare to sing at Fritton; on a previous occasion when Jane had done her performing bit at the Kennets', Joyce Grenfell had rather stolen the show, so perhaps it is not surprising.

Kathleen patronized her, she made her put her shoes back on at a party ('oh dear, am I a prig?') and lectured her about giving up smoking. Jane, looking back, feels that simply Kathleen loved Peter too much to let anyone else love him; that their relationship was so close that no other human being could get in, and that that was why Peter ended up getting on so much better with birds. Kathleen's problem, according to Jane and with hindsight, was that she terribly wanted grandchildren, and therefore had to accept a daughter-in-law, which otherwise she would not have wanted. Also, as she got older Kathleen was becoming more impatient with women generally, and Jane suffered under that. Jane recalls Kathleen opening her letters (both Peter and Jane had previously shown her each other's letters, and as we have seen the family was in the habit of sometimes opening letters before sending them on, but that is not really an excuse); and looking in on them when they were in bed. What excuse can there be for that? That Peter was always her child, and that she saw Jane as a child?

So, beneath all the cheerfulness we have a possessive, patronizing though well-meaning mother-in-law; a devoted child-bride who did not like being patronized and did not really know what she had let herself in for, and an optimistic young man with a war to fight as well as a marriage to live, who was almost as much in love with birds and with his mother as he was with his wife.

He wrote to Kathleen in June: 'At this rate you will be a grand-mother in no time (March to be more precise).' Kathleen was delighted. She believed Jane to be too. So did Peter. Jane knitted matinee jackets 'so he can go to *Blithe Spirit*' and hoped that Peter, with his experience of breeding caterpillars, wouldn't want to put him on a leaf.

In May Peter wrote to Kathleen: 'Being away from Jane for a day or two . . . is a bore but *c'est la guerre*.' It was indeed. The summer before he had written, 'I wish that my ambitions didn't hold so much sway', but they did. Between the war and his ambitions he was not in a position to give the marriage everything that a marriage needs. Kathleen frequently comments on his ability to concentrate absolutely on the matter in hand; it boded ill for the next matter down the list, and at this time marriage had to be second to war.

In her recent quartet, *The Cazalet Chronicles*, set during these years, Jane Howard paints a fictionalized picture of these times. This exact period is covered in the third book, *Confusion*, in which Louise (Jane) is utterly miserable; Michael (Peter) is so busy and absent as to be almost characterless and Lady Zinnia (Kathleen) is absolutely terrify-ing. Jane describes vividly Louise feeling excluded, suffering post-natal depression after a difficult labour during an air raid, alone in London in a horrible nursing home with vicious nurses, missing her husband who was away fighting the war, fearful for him yet not capable of appreciating the fear and stress he was suffering; lost among his close and clever family, and frightened of her powerful and possessive mother-in-law.

In the book, Lady Zinnia takes the young bride into the woods and tells her that if she ever made the son unhappy she would stab her to death, and enjoy doing it. She is not the only mother to feel something like this, though the enjoyment factor *is* unusual. Most don't say it. Kathleen did feel something like that as we know from her diary, and Jane remembers her saying it, with pain. Taking an educated guess, Kathleen would be mortified to know it. 'Mothers with cubs are fierce creatures,' she once wrote to Bill, and deep down, that *was* part of it. In the diary, late at night, it sounds heartfelt. The next day she is making merry of it: 'I don't think I shall have to kill her at all.' Jane did not think it a joke, but it probably was. Jane's little brother Colin once asked his mother to kill him because he didn't want to go back to school. And Wayland says: 'It was a very light word in Kathleen's vocabulary. She was always threatening to kill me.'

'You will like Falcon if she's Nicola, won't you?' Peter wrote to his mother. She was and she did. She sent £100 and 100 snowdrops to 'the entrancing Nicola' on her birth, because 'I like women to have a little independence'. After all 'Jane is a girl and so was I and Pete loves us a bit.' Jane was upset, though, because Peter chose to spend the last two days of his week's leave at the time of the birth at Fritton.

As Kathleen became accustomed to the demands of war: the constant fear for Peter, the poor food, lack of petrol and the fact that she had to shear the lawn by hand because they couldn't use the motor mower – she became able to enjoy Fritton again.

Wayland spent four terms at Cambridge studying music and history, and in July 1942 was called up. His first duty was sweeping dormitories. Kathleen was mortified at 'the waste of his brilliance', but thought it might be good for his character. And at least it wasn't dangerous. Soon afterwards it became so: he spent the first three months of 1943 in motor gunboats, which went out at night to protect coastal shipping from German E boats. Throughout 1942 and 1943 he was frequently ill, which was a mixed blessing as it meant he could come home. The pre-war gaggles of boys returned as sailors on leave, sometimes sick or wounded, and Kathleen did her best to make it nice for them. The fruit from Fritton's garden was a major attraction – when there were no boys to eat it Kathleen would take it to the hospital at Yarmouth, or up to London, where bunches of grapes went down very well.

A favourite boy was Charles Newton, who refused to leave: he jumped out of the window and lay on the lawn, saying 'Déesse, je ne te quitte jamais (Goddess, I shall never leave you).' He was killed in

June 1944, leading a death-or-glory bayonet charge at Anzio. 'How often have I seen the wild child brandishing a stick and charging down the lawn, showing me how he'd do it when he got the chance. I like to think he had his moment of exultation,' Kathleen wrote. Another favourite was Alfred de Pass. Once when he was staying a respectable old lady came to tea; Alfie, stark naked after a swim, ran up to the drawing-room window crying, 'Has she gone yet?' She had. He too was killed. Another young fellow came on his new motorbike, and was 'so surprised that it had delivered him here instead of into a ditch' that he felt he should not risk getting on it again, so stayed. One Freddie Warner (later ambassador to Japan) recited Blake to Kathleen's sunflowers: Morgan Forster 'leaned against the privet hedge enchanted; he said later that he nearly cried for pleasure'. Kathleen was constantly amazed that the weather and the flowers could be so beautiful in such dark times. Sometimes she slept in a punt on the lake.

She read a lot: *Cold Comfort Farm* 'with great amusement'; Barrie's published letters: 'There are about twelve pages of ones to me . . . I think on the whole he comes out a kind man,' and she mentions for the first and only time that he promised Con £1000 for the expedition and only gave £500. 'He seems to have been so careless about money that he probably hadn't the foggiest recollection . . . and probably wouldn't have the least realized that Con had absolutely been banking on it.' She read Hesketh Pearson's life of Shaw: 'a moderately able compilation of Shaw's estimates of himself, some rather vulgar and some I think fallacious. We are told in great and ugly detail about his affairs with women and it's my belief he never had any.' Shaw had once told her of a trip to Richmond with Mrs Patrick Campbell, and how she had lain down on the grass and pulled Shaw down beside her, and how he had been *terrified*. Also Kathleen had known some of the women: Florence Farr, 'A hard-faced common creature, a bad actress' and Edith Nisbet, 'a buxom mother of quantities of nice children, one of whom (a girl) was a friend of mine at the Slade', and she just couldn't see it. And she read Graham Greene, whom she found shockingly unpleasant and modern. 'I felt inclined to write to him and ask for my money back.'

In May 1943 they were given three weeks' notice to quit Fritton.

'What does it matter? It has been nice to have a lovely garden for a few years but there are other joys, and I shall find them altho' I am so old.' She arranged everything, and then they didn't have to leave at all. Instead the lake was to be 'requisitioned' for amphibious tanks to practise in. Soldiers 'flowed through the garden in trickles and surges', come to see about barbed wire and passes. She gave them beer and cherries and wondered if she would be able to endure it. The lake was to be encircled with barbed wire twice, and the house was between the two circles. They could not go out or come back without passes, and no one was allowed to visit them. Wayland's twenty-first birthday was celebrated in a ditch outside the barricade. 'I feel like Brünnhilde,' she wrote.

That summer Wayland got a job at the Admiralty, much to his parents' relief, and in September they opened up Leinster Corner again after three years. Bill wouldn't let Kathleen help with the furniture and unpacking: he took her 'wobbly heart' extremely seriously, and washed all the pots and crockery and cutlery single-handedly – literally.

That month too Peter was awarded the DSC, for 'skill and gallantry in action with enemy forces'. 'He has now two medals and two mentions,' wrote Kathleen, 'and he deserves them.' He was overdue for leave but declined to take it, feeling he didn't need it. 'He has always been thus absolutely engrossed and single tracked for whatever it is at the moment that has gripped him. I understand why he is so good an officer.'

But he was not a good husband in the immediate sense. Nicola was now four months old. As reality encroached on the good intentions and the primroses, Kathleen's original fears for Peter's marriage were justified. The problems that Jane describes fictionally in *Confusion* took their toll, and the marriage succumbed to the stresses of wartime. Jane had been living in seaside hotels while her husband was away, maybe being killed; having to share him with his mother (who shared his interest in ships and naval activities where Jane did not) during his leaves; coping with the child that with hindsight she knew she had been too young to have; trying to work out what her own adult life would be; beginning to write. Towards the end of 1942 she was unfaithful. Peter forgave her and offered to back out if that was her real love. Jane was torn. Peter wanted the marriage to work. Kathleen now believed that it couldn't, and told Peter so. Peter did not agree. Kathleen was convinced; Peter was adamant. It was the nearest thing to a rift that there had ever been between them. Peter said that if it came to it his loyalties would be with Jane. They all hated it.

An uneasy stalemate was reached: Peter was as ever away a lot, coming home on leave to Jane who was living in their house in London (Kathleen had lent them the money to buy it) where young people came and went in the nomadic way of war, Kathleen waited for the worst, and the war dragged on with its cargo of fear and resolute cheerfulness. There were bright moments for Kathleen during the boys' leaves: concerts at the National Gallery, going to see *Fantasia*, which she thought quite wonderful, and defended fiercely when her musical friends sneered at it. She went dancing with Peter, Thora Hird and James Mason. She argued with James Lees-Milne over a letter she had written to *The Times* saying she would gladly sacrifice Rome for the lives of her two sons. 'So likely she will be given the choice!' said Lees-Milne. She said he was subversive, and 'a coolness ensued'. Then they made it up. Lees-Milne's friend Nancy Mitford and her cronies had a passion for the Antarctic stories, such a passion that they called their chilly upstairs lavatory the Beardmore after the glacier. Lees-Milne arranged for Nancy to meet Kathleen, and Nancy wrote to her sister Diana Mosley about it:

4.12.44
Fancy, I met Scott's widow. I said I am keen on Captain Scott she said So am I and we talked for an hour. She was fascinated at me knowing so much. I asked her if she thinks there might be another expedition and she says certainly after the War, and a woman might go as far as the HUT but not on a serious journey. *Oh dear.* She was dressed (Ritz) from head to foot in pale blue hand woven but I thought her heaven. She said Marie Stopes very nearly went on the THE journey and Scott had to use all his willpower to stop her!

(This last is something of an exaggeration, but certainly as a biologist Stopes was interested in the scientific potential of the expedition.)

Lunch at the Ritz was not an everyday occurrence at this stage. Bill's brother and his wife were bombed out and came to stay at Leinster Corner. Kensington Gardens was heavily bombed: it seemed on fire, a sheet of white flame as they watched from their windows. There were doodlebugs, to destroy sleep and much else besides. And there were funerals and memorial services, mostly for the young men but not only. Charlotte Shaw died; GBS, aged eighty-seven now, came by tube and told Kathleen how it had happened.

She got all shrunk up in the chest 'like an old witch'. She had illusions, one of which was that the flat was full of people. She would say to him 'You must get up the manager. We pay for the flat and it's very expensive, we have a right to have it to ourselves.' He thought out the idea to explain to her that she was clairvoyant, that all these people existed but that they were in Australia or Oxford or anywhere and that if he got up the manager he would not be able to see them. That comforted her. Then a few days before she died he was helping her to the dining room . . . and he looked at her and saw all the deep hard furrows on her brow had gone and her face looked young and happy. He felt a great lightness of relief, although he felt it must mean she was going to die. This rejuvenating process went on progressively and she talked like a happy child, but he couldn't understand a word she said, though she understood him. Then she got to look as when he first saw her, and then again younger. There was a night nurse who 'was trained to be always cheerful'. So one morning she came into his room and said very gaily, 'Your wife died at 2 am last night, I didn't wake you.' 'So,' said Shaw, 'she had been dead six hours before I knew. She looked so young I had to keep going back all day to talk to her.' Then he said he felt much better since she was dead. So free. 'For the burden of someone, even though you love them, ill and dependent is a burden, and one feels lighter without it.'

Kathleen records deaths, funerals and illnesses with some detail now, more than she used to. It is not done in a lugubrious way but an observant one, as if she is looking for examples of how to be old, how to be ill, and perhaps how to die. A pretty old lady of ninety-three with white hair and black velvet clothes impressed her, and so did Max Beerbohm: 'Exactly like I could have hoped he would be as an old man: white hair and moustaches, bald, but neatly dressed in light grey and looking like a surprised and slightly shocked baby with wide blue eyes.'

Then in the summer of 1944 came the invasion of France – a week after Charles Newton was killed. Kathleen didn't know whether Peter was in it or not. 'He has been living in a tunnel at Fareham for two or three months preparing it, but whether he goes with it I know not. Wayland has been silent too for a long time. Probably their mail is held up. He is at Portland.' In August Leinster Corner was bombed, then a week later burgled. The debris was 'woeful, woeful'. She and Bill were staying here, there and everywhere – at Bill's parents' house Formosa, with friends, in the Charing Cross Hotel, at Fritton, near their sons when they could.

By the end of August she knew that Peter had been in France, getting 'the first impact of the kisses (as it was hot it was a bit smelly) and of the flowers. They strewed welcome patterns of flowers on the roads ahead of them. Roses roses all the way, and hydrangeas.' Wayland was with HMS *Attack*, sleeping one night in two and getting very thin. 'The navy has given him nothing to do except issue rum.' He had written a novel, which Morgan Forster was nice about, as was Desmond MacCarthy, so she sent it to Roger Senhouse at Secker, but he turned it down. In the spring of 1945 Wayland was released from the navy on health grounds (a primary tubercular lesion), which had Kathleen 'walking on air'. The declaration of peace in May seemed almost secondary.

WITH PEACE came rebuilding. Kathleen reclaimed Fritton from the barbed wire and the passes, and entertained among others Owen Morshead, the King's librarian from Windsor, who told her how he had had a man up from Garrards to cut the Koh i Noor and Cullinan diamonds out of the crown so they could be safely kept in a Bath Oliver tin. 'How nice it must be to be you,' he wrote in his thank-you letter, 'and give happiness away with both hands.' Leinster Corner was replastered and reglazed, and Peter and Jane were living across the park at Edwardes Square; Peter birding and painting, Jane straining at the leash.

Largely because other people thought it would be a good idea,

Peter stood as a Conservative candidate in the immediate post-war election: he lost narrowly and didn't mind a bit. More important to him was his first post-war exhibition, at the rebuilt Ackermann's in November. The Queen (now the Queen Mother) came: Kathleen made Jane give her three dozen roses, and some for Princess Margaret who had just had her appendix out. A letter of thanks from Buckingham Palace said 'how proud you must be of your gallant and versatile son'.

The war had had a definite and identifiable effect on both Peter and Wayland. Peter gave up shooting birds and began his life's work of studying and preserving them. 'He is starting a new wild goose sanctuary and is employing a great deal of labour [twenty German prisoners of war at £12 a day] and spending a great deal of money.' This became the New Grounds at Slimbridge in Gloucestershire, then the World Wildfowl Trust, now the Wildfowl and Wetlands Trust. Wayland went back to Trinity: before the war he had read music, now he read history, and took the Foreign Office entrance exams, and passed. He relegated his beloved music to the territory of his own pleasure, and started instead towards a life of writing and, in the end, politics.

For Kathleen, at her stage of life, there was no such change to be made, though outside changes affected her, as when she was amused to find the whole household rearranging their plans to fit in with the cook, who wanted to go to a party. She continued to entertain, to hear people's life stories and sympathize over their broken marriages, to go to the theatre (she fell wildly for Laurence Olivier) and to concerts. She sat on her sofa with an orange rug over her knees, writing monumental numbers of letters with a fat tortoiseshell pen. Names from the past and the future wandered through her days: Sybil Thorndike, Rebecca West again, Ludovic Kennedy (the 'best to look at' of a group of young men), Geoffrey Dearmer, and Claus Bulow, 'an amusing international lad', without the von in those days. She took him to see *The Importance of Being Earnest*, and he remembers her saying, 'This is a very important play; so-and-so says this about it, what do you think?' and feeling, as others had, that he must come up to scratch with an intelligent response. Many years later he was Bill's lodger for a while. His quietness inspired this poem by Bill:

> The most agreeable of people to have about the haus
> Was dear Claus
> It would have been more than permissible
> That he should not have been so invissible.

In 1946 Bill, now chairman of the British Bank of the Middle East, was called upon to go to Persia again, for two months: he was going on a troopship through the Bay of Biscay and Kathleen very much wanted to go with him but he wouldn't let her. Young King Faisal of Iraq came to visit before Bill left: 'a nice bright child with a good hearty laugh'. They took him to lunch on board the *King George V* and 'gave him a very good time. Shut him up in a gun turret and twirled it round; put him down a manhole. He is a merry lad. Rather like a monkey but definitely a nice monkey. That boy, what will he become?'

'Well, now here's my chance,' she wrote on 26 September 1946, as Bill left,

> and it is up to me to take it. I have perfect freedom, I have a good household, I have several commissions. Wayland is well and in a job, Pete is 35! Well now really if I can't get down to good work it will prove pretty conclusively that I am getting too old for my job. I have to carry the Ritchie plaque through, I have to do a bust of Eckersley, I have to do the West Downs memorial, and I can do the Victory medal. I have to arrange a show for the Royal Society of British Sculptors, and I have to organise some television shows for them. I have two months in which to do all this. Formerly I would have done it on my head; I wonder whether I still can. Fun to try. If nothing crashes to make me nervous, I believe I can. Larks!

What she failed to mention in describing her situation was her health. Between her digestion and her heart she had not been strong for some years. Though she didn't know it she had angina. In October she called on Bernard Shaw, now ninety, and sat and gossiped with him for some time. His memory for times past put hers to shame. He told her that Charlotte had wanted her ashes scattered over some particular hills in Ireland and he had said no, that's too much trouble, how about mixing them with his and scattering them any old where, and she had agreed. 'He was sitting up in a dressing gown and looking really very frail . . . Oh dear he is the oddest maddest mixture. He told me yet again how so many women wanted to marry him, knowing they would only have to look after him for a year or two and then have his fortune . . . he was a little sentimental finally. Waning is a sad sad thing.'

Despite her active and happy intentions, she too began to wane. With the turn of the year she became iller, and as ever ignored it as far as she could. In December 1946 she spent a weekend with Peter 'at his wild goose resort . . . We sat in hides behind the sea wall for hours. *Really* hours, but the movement of the geese was enthralling – or at least Pete makes it seem so – at least to me. How I adore that creature. And then the evenings back at the Inn, very snug with big wood fire, then up early in the frost and back to the marsh. I felt enjoyably guilty too because I had left Bill alone in London with Wayland.' They came back to London to a lecture at the Royal Geographical Society, where she introduced Pete to Mountbatten.

It is a typical diary entry, and her last. What happened now was not the kind of thing on which she cared to dwell. Soon after Christmas, she took to her bed at Leinster Corner, and through the first months of 1947 her health declined. She was diagnosed as having leukaemia. It was, as Wayland described it, 'quite long, very unpleasant, with not a lot of pain but growing weakness and all the futile attempts to get the red corpuscles going again.' She left her bed only to go into St Mary's Hospital, Paddington.

After thirty-five years of constantly recording her adventures and observations, she stopped writing, because she was weak, and because she found nothing to say. No more now than when Con died would she waste paper and effort on recording pain, negativity, and unhappiness which even she could not avoid.

Wayland wrote to James Lees-Milne on 23 July 1947: 'I am writing to tell you that my mother's state has got rapidly worse in the last few days, and is now very grave. She is not well enough to understand that I have written to you, but if she were, I think she would be glad that you should know.'

The next day Kathleen died. Leave-takings with Wayland and Peter were unilateral, and Bill was with her when she died. Afterwards he told her sons that she had regained consciousness and spoken words of love and peace, but Wayland didn't think he believed him.

The family was quite bereft by the loss of their powerhouse, but the habits she had encouraged in them came through: accentuate the positive, remember the happy times, don't squander your energy in grief. She was cremated, and Bill, Peter and Wayland scattered her ashes over the sea at Sandwich. The wind was blowing onshore and the ashes blew back over them.

Bill sorted all her letters and bound them in leather with gold lettering; he read her diaries and selected some for publication along with her autobiographical fragment; he catalogued her sculptures. A memorial exhibition was arranged for May 1948, and George Trevelyan opened it. 'Trevelyan said that K was a woman whose life was devoted, primarily, to the arts – which is true – that she hated fraud, sentiment and lack of courage; that she loved beauty and the young; and that it is not true she was among the dead,' Lees-Milne wrote. In fact Trevelyan said:

> We are met to recall to our memories (how easily that is done) a personality so vital that we may say of her 'so strong a spirit is not of the dead' . . . She had what is sometimes called a masculine spirit; open-eyed courage to realise and accept calamity and sorrow; a dislike of all forms of sentimentality, falsity and feebleness. Her strongest feminine characteristic was the maternal instinct, which . . . made her specially able and ready to help folk in trouble. Though she had very many friends . . . she was far from being 'a woman of society'. She was essentially an artist, a wife and a mother.

How is she remembered? Fragments of stories still exist of a dreadful Kathleen: the woman who made the toddler Peter Scott run around with next to no clothes on; the harpy who forced Captain Scott to the Pole and slept with his mentor; the woman who hated women; the one who thought everyone was in love with her; the one who vamped clever old men. A review in 1993 of Elspeth Huxley's biography of Peter dredged up these negative views of her, saying that she was promiscuous, and an 'unscrupulous egomaniac', and that Peter had 'a Freudian case of mother fixation'. These are detrimentalist views, as she would have put it, of an adventurous and determined woman in a world where these qualities in women were not, and in some ways still are not, really approved. Friendships with men must equal promiscuity; determination must equal unscrupulous egomania; a widowed mother of strong character can only produce a son with a fixation. Time can surely allow now that it's not *so* bad to leave a child unbundled up; to support a husband in the way that is best for the two people involved in the marriage; to despise female stereotypes; to enjoy admiration and the company of the clever; to love people, be tough, and look out for your child.

Other, more positive stories outweigh the negative: of the loyal friend, of the woman who made beautiful figures of young boys and of mothers with children, and fine portraits of great men; who bred the father of modern wildlife conservation; who tended Isadora Duncan in her hour of need; who responded with such dignity to her husband's tragedy; who would set off for the ends of the earth with nothing but a comb with three teeth in it; who was loved by Scott and Nansen, Asquith and Barrie, Bernard Shaw and Max Beerbohm, Gilbert Cannan and Bill and her sons and the countless young men whom she cheered up during the many hard times of the first half of this century. The testimonies of these friends speak for themselves.

Kathleen was born nothing special: one of thousands of Victorian girls from large middle-class families. But she took hold of her life with rare glee, and raced through it without shame, without fear and with scarcely a backward look.

She had told Bill what she wanted on her *'tiny'* gravestone: 'Kathleen. No happier woman ever lived.' In the end her victory medal was adapted, and put as a memorial in the church nearest to the Lacket. Shaw, at ninety, wrote to Peter: 'The news from Leinster Corner reached me on my birthday, and for a moment struck it all of a heap. But I cannot feel otherwise than gladly about her, nor imagine her old. She was a very special friend.'

A letter from Bill to James Lees-Milne expresses how her surviving family had taken her lesson of determined happiness to heart: 'Dear Jimmy, Thank you for thinking of and sharing so deeply with us: and thank you for much happiness your friendship gave K. For the rest, she would hate to be the cause of sorrow: so we'll try and think only of her lovely joyful life: and not about the loss – as much as we can.'

POSTSCRIPT

The summer Kathleen died Jane finally left Peter, taking her half-written novel and leaving her daughter. Peter moved to his goose resort and later married Philippa Talbot Ponsonby. They had two children, Dafila and Falcon. Peter was later knighted, and died in 1989. Wayland married Elizabeth Adams in 1948 and they moved into the studio at Bayswater Road, eventually swapping with Bill (who had remained in the main house – they called the exchange Operation Lear) as they started to produce their six children: Easter, Emily, Mopsa, Thoby, Zoe and me. Bill died in 1960, still missing her.

Biographical Details

Nancy, Lady Astor, 1879–1964. American wife of William Waldorf Astor. Unionist MP returned at Plymouth in 1919, where she took over her husband's seat. She was the first woman to appear in the House of Commons.

Herbert Henry Asquith, Earl of Oxford and Asquith, 1852–1928. Liberal Prime Minister 1908–1915, of coalition government to 1916, ousted by Lloyd George. Secretary for War, March–August 1914. Resigned leadership of Liberals 1926. Created earl 1925.

Margot Asquith, Countess of Oxford and Asquith, 1864–1945. Née Tennant. Married Asquith 1894. 'To her politics meant men, not measures', and she 'could never bring herself to believe that truth could wound', which between them made her something of a liability as a prime minister's wife. Benjamin Jowett called her 'the best educated ill-educated woman I ever met'; she wrote a novel, *Octavia; Lay Sermons;* an autobiography and some volumes of reminiscences. She was one of the Souls, before which group's existence members of different political parties didn't talk to each other.

Stanley Baldwin, Earl Baldwin of Bewdley, 1867–1947. Son of Shropshire yeomen; MP from 1908 (he took over his father's seat in Worcestershire) to 1937 when he was elevated to the Lords. Three times prime minister, in 1923, 1924–9, and 1935–7. First cousin of Rudyard Kipling. Believed that the salvation of the country lay in faith, hope, love and work. Very attached to pigs. A bust of him by Kathleen is in Bewdley Town Hall.

Harley Granville-Barker, 1877–1946. Actor, producer, dramatist, playwright and critic. Friend of Shaw till 1918, through Fabian connections and the

Stage Society. In 1904 drew up a scheme for a national theatre, which might well have come about for Shakespeare's tercentenary in 1916 had it not been for the war. Married first to the actress Lillah McCarthy; then to Helen Gates, novelist and poet, who insisted on severance from the theatre largely and Shaw specifically. Died in Paris. 'He was, perhaps, too far in advance of his time' *DNB*. A bronze of him by Kathleen is in Stratford, and a statuette at the Garrick.

Sir J. M. Barrie, 1860–1937. Astonishingly prolific Scots novelist and playwright whose accomplishments (*Dear Brutus* and *The Admirable Crichton* are perhaps exceptions) are now almost entirely obscured by his invention of Peter Pan.

Sir Henry Maximilian (Max) Beerbohm, 1872–1956. Author and caricaturist. Wrote *Zuleika Dobson.*

Andrew Bonar Law, 1858–1923. Leader of Unionist party, 1911–21 and 1922–3; Colonial Secretary, 1915; Chancellor of the Exchequer, 1916–19; Lord Privy Seal, 1919–21, Conservative Prime Minister, 1922–3. His ashes were buried in Westminster Abbey and Asquith said, 'It is fitting that we should have buried the Unknown Prime Minister by the side of the Unknown Soldier.'

Henry Noel Brailsford, 1873–1958. Journalist. In 1897 he volunteered to fight in the Greek war of independence; became Manchester Guardian correspondent in the Balkans. Organized relief work there in 1903, and served on commission of inquiry into Balkan atrocities on his return. Non-communist socialist. He believed war to be the result of economic rivalry between the great powers, and was one of the first western journalists to visit Soviet Russia. Met Lenin. Stood unsuccessfully for Labour in 1918. Wrote for the *Nation* 1907–23; *New Statesman* until 1946, and was editor of the *New Leader*, the organ of the Independent Labour party, 1922–6, where he commissioned Shaw, E. M. Forster and H. G. Wells to write.

Austen Chamberlain, 1863–1937. Statesman, son of Joseph, half-brother of Neville. Liberal Unionist MP from 1892; Financial Secretary to the Treasury, 1900; Chancellor under Balfour, 1905; Secretary of State for India, 1915–17;

member of war cabinet, 1918; Chancellor of Exchequer under Lloyd George, 1919; leader of Conservatives in House of Commons, 1921–2; Lord Privy Seal, 1921; Foreign Secretary under Baldwin, 1924; First Lord of the Admiralty, 1931. Birkenhead said of him that he 'always played the game and always lost it'.

Neville (Arthur) Chamberlain, 1869–1940. Statesman, son of Joseph, half-brother of Austen. Director of National Service, 1917; Postmaster General, 1922; Paymaster General, 1923; Minister of Health, 1923, 1924 and 1931; Chancellor of the Exchequer, 1923 and 1931; Prime Minister, 1937–40; Lord President of Council, 1940. Lloyd George called him a pin-head.

Aleister Crowley, 1875–1947. Occult magician, born in Leamington Spa to a wealthy brewing family of Plymouth Brethren. His mother was the first to call him The Beast 666. Liked chess, rock-climbing and writing pornographic poetry. What he called 'The Law of Thelema' – 'do what thou wilt is the whole of the law' – was revealed to him in a vision. Founded the Abbey of Thelema in Sicily in 1920, where he, his mistresses and devotees took drugs, had sex and practised ritual magic. One, Raoul Loveday, died, but it was probably food poisoning. Retired to Hastings and died there.

Joseph Duveen, Baron Duveen of Millbank, 1869–1939. Art dealer, patron and trustee. Gave the Tate Gallery several new galleries including five for modern sculpture.

Sir Jacob Epstein, 1880–1959. Sculptor, born in New York, came to Europe in 1902 and London in 1905. Rejected by Royal Society of British Sculptors in 1910 and by the Royal Academy. Attacked by Roger Fry and a passing policeman who thought his more-than-life-sized nudes on the BMA building on the Strand 'rude'; defended by Augustus John and Apsley Cherry-Garrard, who bought his first Christ in bronze. Public taste caught up with him by the 1950s.

E. R. G. R. Evans, Baron Mountevans, 1880–1957. Ran away from home as a boy. After serving under Scott went on to become commander of the *Broke*; promoted captain and appointed DSO after ramming a German G42 in 1917. Distinguished naval career. When he left the Australian squadron he took 2000 ratings and their wives to the cinema. Became Admiral, 1936, and Baron, 1945. Returned South in 1934 on the *Milford*, but had to turn back because bad weather depleted coal stores.

Eric Gill, 1882–1940. Stone-carver, engraver, typographer and author. Encouraged by Roger Fry and Augustus John. Started out as letterer – stone inscriptions, painted signs. First exhibition, 1911 in Chelsea. Designed typefaces (Gill sans serif, 1927) and sculpted mainly bas-reliefs, very pure, precise and beautiful.

Sir Sydney Holland, Viscount Knutsford, 1833–1931. Hospital administrator and reformer. Known as the Prince of Beggars; raised £5 million for the London Hospital, of which he was chairman 1896–1931. His obituary in *The Times* called him the 'founder of modern hospital efficiency'.

Colonel Edward Mandell House, 1858–1938. Texan democrat, friend and representative of US President Woodrow Wilson particularly in Europe before, during and immediately after the First World War. Architect of the 14-point peace plan; US representative at inter-allied peace conferences and at the formation of the League of Nations (drafted tentative covenant for League of Nations). 'No American of his time was on such close terms with so many men of international eminence.' Generally regarded as discreet to point of taciturnity.

Sir James Hopwood Jeans, 1877–1946. Mathematician, theoretical physicist, astronomer and popular expositor of physical science and astronomy. Could tell the time at three, Fellow of the Royal Society at twenty-eight. Honorary Secretary of the Royal Society; President of the Royal Astronomical Society, lecturer at Cambridge and Princeton. Concluded that God was a pure mathematician.

Philip Henry Kerr, 11th Marquess of Lothian, 1882–1940. Journalist, statesman, Christian Scientist and crony of Nancy Astor. Private secretary to Lloyd George, 1916; Liberal representative in Ramsay MacDonald's all-party cabinet, 1931; ambassador to US, 1939. Owner of Blickling Hall, Norfolk, which he bequeathed to the National Trust.

Sir Edwin (Ray) Lankester, 1847–1929. Zoologist. Jodrell chair at University College London, 1874–91; Director of the Natural History Museum and Keeper of Zoology from 1898; KCB, 1907.

Sir Edwin Landseer Lutyens, 1869–1944. Architect. Consulting architect on Hampstead Garden Suburb, master of Edwardian social architecture and planning. Built Gertrude Jekyll's house, Munstead Wood, the Cenotaph and much of New Delhi.

Reginald McKenna, 1863–1943. Liberal statesman. Home Secretary, 1911; Chancellor of the Exchequer, 1915, under Asquith. Baldwin offered him the Exchequer in 1923 but he failed to find a constituency and remained chairman of a bank.

Frederick Maugham, Viscount Maugham, 1866–1958. Judge (Lord of Appeal in Ordinary) and Lord Chancellor, 1938–9. Born in Paris, elder brother of W. Somerset Maugham. Remembered fleeing Paris during the Franco-Prussian War.

Edwin Montagu, 1879–1924. Chancellor of the Duchy of Lancaster, 1916; Minister of Munitions, 1916; Secretary for India, 1917–22. Married Venetia Stanley, to whom Asquith wrote letters.

Fridtjof Nansen, 1861–1930. Norwegian explorer, scientist and humanitarian; professor of oceanography at Oslo university (1908–30). Walked across Greenland on skis, 1888. In 1895 he set the specially designed ship the Fram to drift across the Arctic pack ice from the New Siberian Islands in the east, then walked to Franz Josef Land. The Fram crossed the Arctic and arrived at Spitsbergen in 1897. First Norwegian ambassador to Great Britain, 1905. After the First World War he worked for the repatriation of prisoners, for famine relief and for the League of Nations, where he was responsible for the Nansen Passports which meant the opportunity for new lives for refugees. Won the Nobel peace Prize (1922).

Sir Matthew Nathan, 1862–1939. Soldier and civil servant. Governor of the Gold Coast, 1900; Governor of Natal till 1909, Secretary of the Post Office, Chairman of the Board of the Inland Revenue, Under-secretary for Ireland,

1914; Secretary to the Ministry of Pensions to 1919; Governor of Queensland, 1920–25.

Henry Woodd Nevinson, 1856–1941. Essayist, philanthropist, journalist, war correspondent. Wounded at the Dardanelles. Organized relief in Macedonia, 1903; Albania, 1911; Flanders 1914. Influenced by Ruskin, evangelical turned agnostic. Nicknamed 'the grand duke'.

Noel Edward Noel-Buxton, first Baron Noel-Buxton, 1869–1948. Politician and philanthropist. Liberal MP from 1910. He was a social idealist. Travelled widely in the Balkans (founded the Balkan Committee, 1903) and was shot by a Turk in Bucharest in 1914: he wore a beard to cover the scar. Joined Labour in 1919, MP for Northleach from 1922, Minister of Agriculture, 1924 and 1929. Was active in the Anti-Slavery Society, and President of the Save the Children Fund from 1930–48.

Montagu Norman, Baron Norman, 1871–1950. Governor of the Bank of England 1920–1944. Married Priscilla Worsthorne, thus stepfather of Sir Peregrine. His bronze by Kathleen is the property of the Bank of England.

Sir Nigel Playfair, 1874–1934. Actor manager with 'a very individual gift for dry but good-humoured comedy, as pungent in private life as on the stage' (*DNB*). Resurrected the Lyric Theatre, Hammersmith, in 1919, with Arnold Bennett.

Charles H. Shannon, 1863–1937. Lithographer and painter. Spent his life 'pursuing the plastic arts in almost every form with single-minded ardent intensity' (*DNB*) alongside his life's companion Charles Ricketts, 1866–1931, painter, printer, stage designer, writer and collector. They met when apprenticed to the same wood engraver, and jointly illustrated Oscar Wilde's *House of Pomegranates* (1891), and founded and edited *The Dial*, radical arts magazine, 1889–1897. Ricketts designed productions for Shaw, and Wilde's *Salome* (1906) which was boycotted by the press. He once bought a medallion by Masaccio for 35/- (£1.75) in Queensway. Shannon fell off a ladder while hanging a picture in 1929 and never recognized anyone again. He died in 1937. Though they made only £1000 a year at their most prosperous, they left a collection worth more than £40,000, not counting the Persian miniature Ricketts sold to pay for Shannon's care.

Sir John Simon, 1873–1954. Statesman. Attorney General, 1913, Home Secretary, 1915, under Asquith; Foreign Secretary, 1931, Home Secretary, 1935, under Ramsay MacDonald; Chancellor of the Exchequer, 1937, under Chamberlain; Lord Chancellor, 1940–45. Lloyd George said of him that he 'has sat on the fence so long that the iron has entered into his soul'.

F. E. Smith, Earl of Birkenhead, 1874–1930. Solicitor General, 1915; Attorney General, 1915; Lord Chancellor, 1919; Secretary for India, 1924. Lord Beaverbrook called him 'the cleverest man in the kingdom'.

Sir Edgar Speyer, 1862–1932. Financier, philanthropist, patron of music. Born New York, naturalized British 1892. A wealthy banker, well-considered and socially lavish. Debussy and Strauss conducted their own work at his house in Grosvenor Street. President of Poplar Hospital; Director of the White-chapel Art Gallery, Privy Councillor from 1909. Returned to New York during WW1 because of anti-German feeling, despite Asquith's full support. He was accused, absurdly, of signalling to German submarines from his home in Norfolk.

Edward Steichen, 1879–1973. Photographer. Chief photographer at Condé Nast, 1923–38; director of photography department of the New York Museum of Modern Art, 1947–62; exhibited there, at the Whitney, the Metropolitan (NYC), et al. Awards too many to mention. Served in both wars and was decorated. Honorary President of the American Delphinium Society. Married Clara Smith in 1903; then Dana Glover, 1923.

Lytton Strachey, 1880–1932. Writer, backbone of the Bloomsbury group. Wrote *Eminent Victorians*, et al.

Sir Hugh Walpole, 1884–1941. Novelist and man of letters. Born New Zealand. Popular and successful author of forty-two novels including the Herries Saga, *The Dark Forest; Mr Perrin and Mr Traill; The Secret City.* First chairman of the Book Society.

Bibliography

The main unpublished source I used was the Kennet Papers in the University Library, Cambridge, which include Kathleen Kennet's diaries, a volume of reminiscences from Macedonia, her partial autobiography, a childhood recollection by her sister Podge, collections of letters from Max Beerbohm, H. H. Asquith, Colonel House, Colonel T. E. Lawrence, Fridtjof Nansen, George Bernard Shaw, Gilbert Cannan, Sir James Barrie, Captain R. F. Scott and Lord Kennet; letters from Kathleen to Lord Kennet, and between her and her sons; letters from Clive Bell and E. M. Forster to Lord Kennet. Further family letters are in the possession of Lord Kennet and Lady Scott. James Lees-Milne's letters from Kathleen are in his possession; letters from Rosslyn Bruce are in the possession of Verily Anderson.

Published sources include:

Roald Amundsen, *My Life as an Explorer*, William Heinemann, 1927.
Verily Anderson, *The Last of the Eccentrics*, Hodder and Stoughton, 1972.
Andrew Birkin, *J. M. Barrie and the Lost Boys*, Constable, 1979.
H. J. Bruce, *Silken Dalliance*, Constable, 1946.
Apsley Cherry-Garrard, *The Worst Journey in the World*, Picador, 1994.
Aleister Crowley, *Confessions*, Routledge, 1979.
Geoffrey Dearmer, *A Pilgrim's Song*, John Murray, 1993.
Isadora Duncan, *My Life*, Gollancz, 1966.
Diana Farr, *Gilbert Cannan: A Georgian Prodigy*, Chatto and Windus, 1978.
P. N. Furbank, *E.M. Forster, A Life*, Secker & Warburg, 1977.
Sir Harold Gillies, *Plastic Surgery of the Face*, Henry Frowde, 1920.

Sir Harold Gillies and G. Millard, *Principles and Art of Plastic Surgery*, Butterworth, 1957.

Jean Goodman, *The Mond Legacy*, Weidenfeld and Nicolson, 1982.

Stephen Gwynn, *Captain Scott*, John Lane, 1929.

Michael Holroyd, *Shaw*, Chatto & Windus, 1988/9.

Elspeth Huxley, *Scott of the Antarctic*, Pan, 1979.

Roy Jenkins, *Asquith*, Collins, 1964.

Ruth Kelton, *Edward Steichen*, Aperture, 1978.

Lady Kennet (Lady Scott), *Self Portrait of an Artist*, John Murray, 1949.

James Lees-Milne, *Ancestral Voices* and *Prophesying Peace*, Chatto and Windus, 1975.

Dennis Longwell, *Steichen: The Masterprints, 1895–1914, The Symbolist Period*, Thames and Hudson, 1978.

Charlotte Mosely (ed.), *Love from Nancy*, Hodder, 1993.

Henry Nevinson, *Fire of Life*, Victor Gollancz, 1935.

Nigel Playfair, *Hammersmith Hoy*, Faber and Faber, 1930.

Reginald Pound, *Scott of the Antarctic*, Cassell, 1966.

Peter Scott, *The Eye of the Wind*, Hodder and Stoughton, 1961.

Capt R. F. Scott, *Scott's Last Expedition*, Smith, 1913.

Francis Steegmuller, *Your Isadora*, Macmillan, 1974.

Edward J. Steichen, *A Life in Photography*, W. H. Allen, 1963.

John Symonds, *The Great Beast*, MacDonald, 1971.

Sir Charles Wheeler, *High Relief*, Country Life, 1968.

E. Hilton Young, *By Sea and Land*, Jack, 1920.

Wayland Young, 'The debunking of Captain Scott', *Encounter*, May 1980, vol. 54.

Wayland Young, 'Scott and Amundsen: an exchange with Roland Huntford', *Encounter*, November 1980, vol. 55.

Index